A STUDY IN CHRISTOLOGY

THE PROBLEM OF THE RELATION OF THE TWO NATURES IN THE PERSON OF CHRIST

By HERBERT M. RELTON, D.D.

WITH PREFACE BY

ARTHUR C. HEADLAM, D.D.

Professor of Dogmatic Theology in King's College, London

THESIS APPROVED FOR THE DEGREE
OF DOCTOR OF DIVINITY IN THE
UNIVERSITY OF LONDON

SOCIETY FOR PROMOTING
CHRISTIAN KNOWLEDGE
LONDON: 68 HAYMARKET, S.W.
1917

TO MY FATHER

PREFACE

WHEN my old pupil, Dr. Relton, asked me to write a preface to his thesis on the Enhypostasia, I was glad to be able to do so. I have known his work for some years; I was one of the examiners appointed by the University of London to adjudicate on the thesis; and I had a high opinion of the industry and ability that he had displayed in working out the problems connected with the Person of Christ. I felt, further, that I might be of some service to him, not indeed in adding to the strength or the profundity of his argument, for that I did not feel that I could do; but in interpreting and perhaps putting in somewhat simpler language the result of his investigations.

The fundamental problem that he has before him, of course, is this: What do I think of Christ? A problem which, as much to-day as ever, demands the attention of a thoughtful person. Every one interested in religion who allows his intellect to play upon the problems connected with it cannot avoid considering the many difficult questions that are raised; and Dr. Relton's dissertation, dealing though it does with some of the most intricate problems of technical theology, yet is very close to the most vital and, we may add, the most widely considered questions of the day.

What do I think of Christ? The Christian consciousness from the beginning has seen two things clearly. No reader of the Gospels can doubt that he is reading the life of one who was in every essential feature man; not indeed an ordinary man by any means, but emphatically a man; one who was born of a human mother, lived a natural human life, talked and taught in the language, phraseology, and ideas of a particular time and place; died as a man too. And as a man He has aroused always the admiration and love of mankind.

But the religious consciousness of mankind has never been able to stop there. We turn to the record again, and we find that, while it is always that of a man, it is always that of one more than a man. And this conception is clinched by the Resurrection. He dies as man, but He rises again as other than man. And the testimony of the record has been added to by the testimony of experience. Christ in religious thought has been associated both in intellectual conception and in religious experience as in a unique way the source of human redemption and atonement —a redemption which would not be possible unless He were God. So the religious consciousness has equally held that Christ is God.

It was these two problems that first occupied the attention of the Church when it began to think about things, and the issues entailed were the two first on which it formally pronounced its opinion. It laid down definitely at the Council of Nicæa that Christ was truly God. It laid down definitely at the Second General Council, that of Constantinople, that Christ was truly and completely man. In these two decisions it recorded what was the fundamental experience of all Christians.

But then a series of questions arose as to how

and in what way He was truly God and truly man. There were two different points of view, either of which a religious man might incline to. Some dwelt on the absolute reality of all that was human in Christ. They wrote of Him as a baby, as a boy growing in wisdom and stature. He clearly lived as a child, and grew up and reached manhood just as other men do. He probably worked in His father's shop. At any rate there was nothing outwardly to distinguish Him from the ordinary Galilæan of His time. And they felt — a writer, for example, like Chrysostom, who was continuously studying and interpreting the New Testament, felt—that this man, with all His natural virtues, presented a beautiful model of what man should be. And then they raised the further question : Can I really call an infant in arms—can I really call a young child—God ? And so they conceived of Him as growing up to manhood as a man, and in some way united with God ; perhaps it might be put : ' In Him the fulness of the Godhead dwelt.' Prophets were divinely inspired persons. At any rate these men seemed to talk as if they thought that in some way God had come and taken up His abode in a human being. And so they were held to imply that there were two Persons, Jesus and the Christ.

Then there was another point of view. The Egyptian monk or devotee who gave up everything for Christ, and lived in the desert an ascetic life, hoping more and more to gain some union with God, had his mind overborne by the fact that in Christ Jesus he saw the Godhead on earth ; that God thus incarnate in man had taken frail human nature capable of sin and had glorified it by union with

Himself, and made it divine ; and he| lived always
with the vision that, just in the same way, his own
weak and imperfect and frail nature might be made
divine. He could not see how the glory of the
divine nature could really bear being injured by any
thing so weak as human nature being permanently
connected with it ; so he felt that this human nature
had been dissolved in the divine, as it were a drop
of water in the ocean. His life demanded that by
conquering his flesh he might attain, perhaps here,
at any rate hereafter, true union with God. And
the example of Christ in the world meant nothing
for a man who had fled from the world and did not
wish or care to live in the world.

So in these two ways arose the heresies which
were known by the names of Nestorianism and
Eutychianism ; and the controversy between these
two points of view put before the Church great
problems. There were the one side who laid such
stress on the human nature of our Lord that they
talked of a divine Logos dwelling in the man Jesus
Christ ; they seemed to speak of two persons and
two natures. And then there were the others, who
were so impressed with the fulness of the divine that
they felt that only the divine nature really existed
in the Incarnate God.

It is of course well known that these two heresies,
as they were called, were condemned : Nestorianism
at the Council of Ephesus in 431, Eutychianism or
Monophysitism at Chalcedon in 451. At the last
Council was drawn up the Definition of Faith of
Chalcedon, which is formally looked upon as the
orthodox presentation of the nature of Christ ; and
it said that there were two natures, the human and

divine, both perfect and complete, but only one Person, that of Jesus Christ, the eternal Word.

This definition is formally the teaching of the Catholic Church, and would be accepted very widely as the basis of all thought about our Lord; but it never succeeded in being accepted by a portion of the Eastern Church, and in modern times it has been exposed to considerable criticism from more than one point of view.

Let us take some illustrations of this. Professor Harnack, embodying what has always been a tradition of the Lutheran Church, criticises it at considerable length and with considerable severity. Here are some of the things that he says :

In the ' coming together ' each nature continues to exist in its own mode of being ; the divinity has not absorbed the humanity nor has the humanity been exalted to the height of the divinity, but the human and divine natures are simply united in the *person* of the Redeemer, and therefore only mediately and in an individual. No pious Greek who had had Athanasius and Cyril for his teachers could acknowledge that to be ' the right mean.' [1]

And again :

Nor is it of any use to point to the fact that the Council merely gave the mystery a definite standing and thereby furthered the interests of the Greek Church and the Greek theology. *The true mystery, on the contrary, was contained in the substantial union of the two natures themselves.* It was seriously damaged by being banished from its place here, and when in place of it the *conception* of the union, a conception which was supposed at the same time to involve a state of separation, was raised to the position of the secret of faith. The real mystery was thus shoved aside by a pseudo-mystery which in truth no longer permitted theology to advance to the thought of the actual and perfect union.[2]

[1] Harnack, *History of Dogma* (E.T.), iv. p. 222.   [2] *Op. cit.*, p. 223.

PREFACE

Professor Harnack's point is that no real union was attained ; that the human and divine natures were each left as separate entities, not really united. The Council failed in fact to give the one Christ which Eastern and Alexandrian theologians had always demanded.

Curiously enough, Dr. Loofs approaches the subject from just the opposite point of view. He would hold that Nestorius had followed the more ancient tradition, and that what this contended for, the true human personality of Christ, was gone.

The same is to be said [he writes] about the doctrine of the incarnation. Cyril thought he had treated the idea of incarnation in a serious manner. He, too, however, did not assume that the *Logos* was confined by the body of Jesus during his earthly life ; the *Logos* remained, according to him, pervading the world, and this by his Godhead alone. As regards the time after the ascension, the same must be assumed. Then also in Cyril something heterogeneous is added to the Trinity by the manhood of Christ and, what is still more noticeable, the idea of *incarnation* appears as not sharply distinguished from that of *inspiration*. Mythological and popular thought may imagine an incarnation perfectly distinguished from inspiration, but the theology of the ancient church did not dare to do so. Luther was the first, who endeavoured to think out such a doctrine of incarnation, and he did this by means of his idea of Christ's bodily ubiquity, which began with the first moment of his conception and remained even during the time when Christ's corpse lay in the grave. However, by following this line of thought, we arrive at mere absurdities. And if thus the endeavour to think out the idea, that the *Logos* assumed the manhood in his ὑπόστασις, leads us to absurdities, then we must go further back than the first beginnings of this doctrine, which are made by nothing other than the introduction of popular mythological views into the Christian theology. Only by returning to the lines of the Antiochian theology, . . . can we arrive at an understanding of the

Johannine ' ὁ λόγος σὰρξ ἐγένετο,' which is in harmony with the New Testament and avoids theological and rational impossibilities.[1]

Dr. Loofs is in this passage criticising the theology of Cyril, and not the actual definition of Chalcedon, but his point of view is the opposite of that of Harnack. We must, he would tell us, go back and take our starting-point in the human personality of Christ.

It may be suggested that if we get two modern theologians criticising the formula from two separate sides, it really preserves the balance between different false teachings. But another form of criticism we find, as for example in Mr. Temple's essay in *Foundations*. Mr. Temple does not seem to have studied the subject in the original authorities and is largely dependent upon Harnack's exposition. His complaint is that the formula of Chalcedon does not explain anything.

The formula of Chalcedon is, in fact, a confession of the bankruptcy of Greek Patristic Theology. The Fathers had done the best that could be done with the intellectual apparatus at their disposal. Their formula had the right devotional value ; it excluded what was known to be fatal to the faith ; but it explained nothing. To the Latin mind there was little or nothing to be explained ; the same man may be both consul and augur, the same Christ may be both God and Man. This is true if one is thinking of functions, but is irrelevant if one is thinking of substances. The formula merely stated the fact which constituted the problem ; it did not attempt solution. It was therefore unscientific ; and as theology is the science of religion, it represented the breakdown of theology.

That breakdown was inevitable, because the spiritual cannot be expressed in terms of substance at all. The whole of Greek Theology, noble as it is, suffers from a latent

[1] Loofs, *Nestorius*, pp. 129–130.

materialism; its doctrine of substance is in essence materialistic.[1]

We need not follow Mr. Temple in his attempts at reconstruction, but one sentence is perhaps interesting to quote. 'In fact,' he says, when he is approaching the end of his paper, 'any attempt to state in terms of ordinary thought the whole meaning of the Divinity of Christ must be inadequate.'[2] If any attempt must be inadequate, are we justified in saying that Chalcedon represented the breakdown of theology because it could not fully state the whole meaning of the nature of Christ?

In contrast to this Dr. Bright, in *The Age of the Fathers,* gives a different judgment:

The Definition has been criticised as not explaining *how* the unity of person and the duality of natures can coexist as elements in the Incarnation of our Lord. Perhaps a theological formula is none the worse for exhibiting somewhat of that modest self-restraint in which theologians have sometimes been found wanting. There are many points as to which we have no warrant for asking 'how,' still less for attempting an answer. And if it is thought that the necessary unity of the Incarnate Christ is obscured by supposing Him, in the terms of the Definition, to exist 'in' two distinct spheres of life and action, 'inseparable' yet 'unconfused,' and that it needs to be safeguarded by the idea of a *literal* 'communication of properties' between the two natures, such as would practically mould them into one or fuse one in the other, this is the old Monophysite objection, although it may be urged in support of what amounts to a Monophysitism inverted, according to which it is not the Manhood which gives way, wholly or partially, to the Godhead, but the Godhead which gives way to the Manhood by the temporary abandonment of certain so-called divine 'attributes' —which in truth are plural only in an 'economic' sense, as modes of representing, in human thought and speech, so

---

[1] *Foundations*, pp. 230–1. [2] *Op. cit.*, p. 252.

many aspects of that indivisible perfection which makes up the divine essence, and *is* God. After all, if Christ is believed in as One, yet as both truly God and truly Man— however little we can comprehend the relation thus created —that belief is all that the Chalcedonian terminology implies : to hold it is to be at one with the Fourth Council.[1]

It may be added that, speaking from my personal experience, I should consider that Dr. Bright's *Age of the Fathers*, though without the ' viewiness ' which is so attractive to some modern minds in Professor Harnack, is a much sounder guide to the great controversies of the fourth and fifth centuries. He knows his history far better ; he has lived among the Fathers in a way that few other moderns have done ; and he has the sympathy and the reverence which enable him to understand, instead of merely criticising from outside.

Let us now ask what this formula which is so much condemned, and yet so widely accepted, really says.

It begins by quoting the Creed of the Council of Nicæa, and that creed which we now call the Nicene Creed, which is used in our Communion Service, which is ascribed to the Council of Constantinople, though probably incorrectly, and has become the œcumenical creed ; and it concludes with the following statement of belief :

Wherefore, after the example of the holy Fathers, we all with one voice confess our Lord Jesus Christ one and the same Son, the same perfect in Godhead, the same perfect in manhood, very God and very man, the same consisting of a reasonable soul and a body, of one substance with the Father as touching the Godhead, the same of one substance with us as touching the manhood, like us in all things, sin

[1] Bright, *Age of the Fathers*, vol. ii. p. 550.

XV

except; begotten of the Father before the worlds as touching the Godhead, the same in these last days, for us and for our salvation, born of the Virgin Mary, the Mother of God, as touching the manhood, one and the same Christ, Son, Lord, Only-begotten, to be acknowledged of two natures, without confusion, without conversion, without division, never to be separated, (ἀσυγχύτως, ἀτρέπτως, ἀδιαιρέτως, ἀχωρίστως); the distinction of natures being in no wise done away because of the union, but rather the characteristic property of each nature being preserved, and concurring into one Person and one subsistence, not as if Christ were parted or divided into two Persons, but one and the same Son and Only-begotten God, Word, Lord, Jesus Christ; even as the Prophets from the beginning spake concerning Him, and our Lord Jesus Christ hath instructed us, and the Symbol of the Fathers hath handed down to us.[1]

Now what exactly does this formula teach? It says that our Lord was one Person; that is to say, you cannot think of Jesus on earth being in any way personally different from the Son of God. Is there any possibility of holding any other view? But He exists in two natures. Now here I think that probably from the beginning there has been all the confusion which inevitably arises from different meanings of terms. What do we mean by the nature of a thing? We mean the sum of those attributes which go to make up any particular thing. The nature of a man is humanity. Now we may think of this nature in two ways. To us at the present day, and to a large extent to the ancients, the abstract term 'the nature' expresses something logical. It was the way that you defined anything. But there was always an element of realism running through all ancient thought. They could not think of the nature of anything as being merely an abstraction

[1] Heurtley, *On Faith and the Creed*, p. 216.

xvi

of thought. They were convinced somehow or other it had a real existence. The term nature, then, may be used either formally or materially. It may merely be used to express a logical conception ; it may equally well be used to express some reality which was supposed to make up the abstract qualities (for example) of a man.

Now supposing we take the term ' nature ' in the second sense. It will at once be seen that the expression may leave itself open to all sorts of difficulties. Here is a Person, a divine Person, who has attached to Him, so to speak, a human nature. He has also, of course, a divine nature attached to Him. And so we get not only a fundamental dualism, but an entirely artificial combination ; and, as people were quite acute enough to point out, this human nature attached to our Lord had no real human personality, and therefore, could you really say our Lord was man, if He was only the divine Logos with human nature attached to Him, even though you said that His human nature was quite complete ?

But there is another way of looking at the formula, and that is, taking the term ' nature ' as implying a merely logical definition. If you want to say that our Lord was really God, the way you must do it is to say that He had all the nature of the Godhead. If you want to say that He was really man, you would say that He had all the nature of manhood, the sum of those qualities which make up man— in fact, humanity. It did not mean that He had certain other things added to Him, but that He was God and became man. The language is only formal. If that be so, all the criticism against the formula vanishes. It only means to say, in rather exact language, that the one Person was God and man, and that He had the full human nature and the full divine nature in Himself. But it does not say that these natures were something apart ; they were attributes of Him ; for He, who was God, became man.

Now I think that we can say that this was really what was meant by the Chalcedon formula, and that the reason why it was felt so widely to be satisfactory was that it was thought of as nothing more than an explanation of the Creed. And what the Creed implies is that the Divine Person was also a human person when it says, ' Who for us men, and for our salvation came down from heaven, and was incarnate by the Holy Ghost of the Virgin Mary, and was made man.' The definition then does not attempt —and rightly—to explain what God is—clearly a mystery beyond human comprehension—but it does guard quite well the true tradition of the Christian Church, and it does give language as accurate as you can get to express that tradition.

We need not follow the long tale of controversy which only really ended in the final formularisation of Eastern theology by John of Damascus. It will be sufficient to dwell upon the term ' the Enhypostasia,' which Dr. Relton has made the centre of his essay, and which he has rescued from the criticism to which it has been exposed. I am afraid that to many people the use of such a term will not make things better. It will only be adding another technicality, and therefore I want, as far as possible, to keep in untechnical language. Dr. Relton himself has given us ample opportunity by quotations from the writings of Leontius of Byzantium and of John of Damascus to understand the technical meaning of this phrase ' hypostasia.' It seems to me to come to this. That the formula of Chalcedon is to be taken in the first manner that I suggested, as merely a logical definition, and that it thus guards and expresses just what every one of us really thinks about Christ. Technically it says : that the human nature of Christ was not without an *hypostasis* or Person to whom it belonged, but it had its personality, which was necessary for it, in the divine Christ. The way I should rather put it for us is this : that it says just what we think ; that Jesus Christ, who was God, became man.

This thesis Dr. Relton develops by a very full analysis of divine and human personality and their relation to one another. ' The basis of the doctrine is,' he says, ' the fact that the Divine Logos, prior to the Incarnation, already possessed everything needful to enable Him to live a truly human life.' [1] That means, of course, that as man is created in the image of God, so there is in God everything that goes to make up what is most perfect in man. ' The Divine Logos,' he goes on, ' was capable of being the Ego, not only of His Divine, but also of His human Nature ; because His Personality in virtue of its Divinity already embraced all that is most distinctive of a truly human personality.' [2]

Or we may look at the matter from the other side, how does man attain his real perfection ? Only ' in Christ.' Therefore, clearly, if Christ was to be perfect man, He could not be that except through His Godhead. It was because He was God that He was capable of being the ideal man. As Dr. Relton puts it : ' Human nature as we know it is never

[1] P. 226.
[2] P. 227.

complete, never perfect. Herein lies the fatal error of those who, thinking to secure the reality and completeness of Christ's manhood, speak of His self-consciousness as purely human. Had it been so it could not have been either perfect or complete.' [1] And again : ' If we are to judge of what a perfect manhood is we must go outside human experience, for we have no knowledge of it in ourselves.' ' He was perfect man because He was perfect God. He, and He alone, could live a truly human life, because at every moment of His earthly career He was also the Divine Son of God.' ' What was wanted was a revelation of One Who was Divine, and therefore perfectly and completely human, even if infinitely more than this. The human Ego in man is incomplete. The manhood of Christ, if it had possessed a human Ego only, would have been incomplete.' [2]

He further points out that ' we need not assign one set of experiences to His human nature and another to His Divine, nor deny that the Divine could experience all that we know Jesus Christ did experience during His earthly life. The Incarnation, if it means anything, means God living a truly human life under all the conditions and limitations of a finite and creaturely existence.' [3]

And further this conception of our Lord interprets just the record that we have in the New Testament :

The Gospels, then, reveal the Christ as having lived a truly human life, perfect at every stage of its growth and development. Our Christology enables us to accept this picture with the fullest possible frankness. Every limitation which the Son of Man can be shown to have lived under,

[1] P. 227. [2] P. 228. [3] P 232.

PREFACE

every detail of a circumscribed existence to which Kenotic
Christology has drawn our attention, including, of course,
the fact of Christ's human knowledge being limited, upon
which Gore laid such stress in the famous ' Bampton Lectures,'
and later in the dissertation on ' The Consciousness of Our
Lord,' we can accept without hesitation. All that is involved
in the Christ's possession, not simply of intelligence, but of
intelligence moulded by a certain training and education
as a Jew, and which was circumscribed within the limits
of the scientific knowledge and mental equipment of the
age in which He lived, we can accept as the necessary conditions essential to His human life.[1]

And then the other side :

But when we have said this, we have drawn attention
to but half the truth contained in the Gospel portrait. To
admit that the Christ had a mind moulded by the environment of a Jew's life in Palestine in the first century is not to
deny the equally vital truth revealed in the Gospels, that His
whole earthly life was so truly human as to be capable of
transcending its historical setting, if we may so put it, and
of revealing itself as absolute, archetypal, universal ; incapable, therefore, of being identified with, or confined to,
any particular age, but recognised to be for all time.[2]

He then analyses very fully the divine characteristics of Christ, and he points out that ' the Godhead
is revealed none the less in any and every word and
act of His truly human life.' ' His whole character
is a revelation of God in manhood.'

His conclusion is that :

The Incarnate Christ possessed a Divine and unlimited
self-consciousness.

Is this conclusion absolutely inconsistent with that
[previously] reached, where the fact of His being truly Man,
and truly a man, forced us to conclude that He must have
possessed a truly human and limited self-consciousness ?
We point in answer to the Gospels themselves, which give

[1] P. 247. [2] P. 247.

us the data from which we deduce both conclusions. However incredible or logically impossible such a phenomenon may appear, the fact remains that in the Person of Jesus Christ is revealed One Who was a particular man, and yet the Universal Man; One, moreover, Whose consciousness was at once limited and unlimited, finite and circumscribed, yet infinite and uncircumscribed in its range, human and yet Divine, Divine and yet human. If we say that it is intellectually inconceivable and historically impossible, the facts reprove us. Faith can grasp it. The Gospels record it. Is there any hypothesis which will cover it? The doctrine of the Enhypostasia is the one which we venture to suggest. It is based upon grounds which make it at least conceivable to the human mind. It does not solve the problem, because the problem is ultimately unsolvable by any finite mind. It postulates a logical impossibility—the particular cannot embody its own universal. But the Person of Christ is the bankruptcy of human logic. And it is better for us to face this last fact than to endeavour to gain intellectual consistency at the cost of explaining away or reducing the Christ within the categories of human finite reasoning. [1]

Now I do not know how far it has been possible to put what has to be said simply. But does not this really represent exactly what the ordinary simple religious man always believes? He believes simply that God came down upon earth and lived as man; that He was really God and really man. And he does not feel much difficulty in harmonising the two conceptions. The whole narrative, as he reads it, seems quite real. It will always be found, as Dr. Mozley once said, that the simplest and most ordinary uneducated conception is more likely to be true than the more philosophical one. For the natural human mind, he argues, is not afraid of inconsistency. It recognises facts, and is not too anxious to fit them

[1] Pp. 264-5.

into a theory. Many partial philosophies leave out one side or the other. The higher the philosophical explanation to be attained, the more nearly it corresponds to the simplest religious conviction. The term Enhypostasia is a means of explaining what the religious consciousness has always felt.

One more point on which I would dwell in conclusion. It has been often urged that all this speculation is useless, and people should turn away from the study of ecclesiastical controversy to what it is claimed is more practical. Of course in a sense all ecclesiastical controversy should be unnecessary. But a right notion about Christ is not unimportant or unnecessary. Clearly it makes all the difference to our whole conception of human nature whether we believe in Christ as God. Simple faith, when it has learnt to believe, is satisfied. But our minds must raise questions. As soon as people turn their attention to these things they will give us this or that crude answer, and often cause much perplexity. All the different difficulties were thrashed out and debated in the controversies of the fourth, fifth, and sixth centuries, and if we have the patience to make ourselves masters of the terminology and thought, we can find an answer to whatever difficulty we may have about the Person of Christ. It is the business of a technical theologian to master as fully as he can the controversy, and to put the results before us. It is the business of the clergy to have made themselves as fully acquainted as they can with what the Church has achieved and taught, for they will, directly or indirectly, have many of these questions to answer. I feel that Dr. Relton's thesis marks a distinct step in advance on current methods of dealing with the

PREFACE

problem, and I believe the teaching which lays stress on the reality of Christ as God and man, without attempting to distinguish in the way that modern divines do distinguish, between His Divine and human consciousness, represents a more healthy and a more satisfactory solution than some of those offered to us.

ARTHUR C. HEADLAM.

CONTENTS

PART ONE

PART TWO

CONTENTS

INTRODUCTION

THE object of this thesis is to study afresh one aspect of the Christological problem, viz. the relation of the Human and the Divine in the Person of Christ.

A study of Christian theology in any one of its branches reveals the never-ending conflict between tradition and life, upon which depends the progress of dogma. That this must be so is clear when we remember that Christian theology in any age represents the attempt at full intellectual expression of every aspect of the truth revealed in the central fact of the Incarnation. This intellectual expression tends to crystallise into dogma. Thus dogmas mark the different stages reached from time to time by the intellectual activity of many minds in the persistent endeavour after a fuller interpretation of the truth.

Now, the conservative mind tends to acquiesce in dogma and to cling tenaciously to tradition. It thus finds itself in perpetual conflict with the liberal mind, which is ever endeavouring to reinterpret dogma in terms of current intellectual concepts, and thus to keep it alive. In every age men are found seeking in Christianity a solution of the problems of their own time and attempting to reinterpret the Christ in terms of ' modern ' thought. But in so doing they are always in danger of going beyond dogma, or of setting it aside in their impatience at the restrictions and restraints which it imposes upon intellectual speculation. But at the same time were it not for such intellectual activity, dogmas would rapidly degenerate into lifeless and meaningless incumbrances and prove a stumbling-block to all further advance in the progress of Christian thought.

Because Christianity itself is not a system but a Life we must expect to find its history, from the doctrinal standpoint, bound up with this struggle between the old and the new, the liberal and the conservative, tradition and life.

Our own age is painfully aware of the intensity of this struggle, and its effects are being felt not least in the field of Christology to-day. The problem of the Person of Christ continues to baffle the human intellect, and is thus a perpetual challenge to the mind of man. We are so constituted that we can never be content to acquiesce in intellectual bankruptcy. The more we attempt to analyse the Christ, and the more we struggle to define Him in terms of human reason, the more He continues to baffle our intellectual efforts and to transcend all our endeavours to comprehend Him. But this fact by no means forces us to give up the attempt, nor must we refrain from further effort in despair of a solution. Rather do we accept afresh the challenge His Person constitutes for human intellect. We gather up the best results of previous efforts and press on to a fuller comprehension. Such intellectual activity is wholesome and, if exercised with due reverence and caution, cannot but prove life-giving. By it we preserve the past efforts of previous ages from degenerating into lifeless and outworn dogmas, which have long ceased to convey any helpful meaning to the minds of men in our own time.

The struggle between the liberal and conservative minds in the field of Christology is very pronounced. The student inherits a rich deposit from the past. We venture to think that the value of the ancient Christology, as this reaches us in the creeds and dogmatic utterances of the Councils, cannot be too highly estimated. In it we find preserved the finest results attained by the most acute intellects of the past, and we benefit from the warnings which they give and which they learned as the fruit of much painful controversy and conflict with heretical opinion. Such a deposit is not lightly to be estimated nor hastily to be set aside as outworn dogma. The impatience of the modern mind has its dangers. There are not wanting voices in our midst crying out against the restrictions and restraints which it is supposed that the ancient Christology imposes upon all modern efforts at Christological reconstruction. Something in the nature of a widespread revolt against the ancient Christology is observable, and the particular form which this is taking is a determined attack upon what is called the ' Two Natures ' hypothesis, which by some is erroneously attributed to the Chalcedonian Christology. And this revolt is not confined to those of the liberal school of theologians who have pronounced sceptical views, but is found prevalent also among many whose loyalty to the Person of Christ is above suspicion. Men who are whole-hearted in their allegiance to Jesus as their Lord and Master, men whose lives are hid with Christ in God and who gladly acknowledge Him to be the centre of their religious life and the object of their worship, nevertheless find it difficult, if not impossible, to express their belief in terms of the dogmatic formularies of the ancient Church. Hence the cry to be rid of the ancient Christology with its doctrine of the 'Two Natures' and its self-contradictory postulates. Schweitzer's indictment against the 'Two Natures' hypothesis is typical of the kind of language employed by a body of theologians to-day when they speak of the Chalcedonian Christology :

When at Chalcedon the West overcame the East, its doctrine of the two natures dissolved the unity of the Person, and thereby cut off the last possibility of a return to the historical Jesus. The self-contradiction was elevated into a law. But the Manhood was so far admitted as to preserve, in appearance, the rights of history. Thus by a deception the formula kept the Life prisoner and prevented the leading spirits of the Reformation from grasping the idea of a return to the historical Jesus.

This dogma had first to be shattered before men could once more go out in quest of the historical Jesus, before they could even grasp the thought of His existence. That the historic Jesus is something different from the Jesus Christ of the doctrine of the Two Natures seems to us now self-evident. We can, at the present day, scarcely imagine the long agony in which the historical view of the life of Jesus came to birth. And even when He was once more recalled to life, He was still, like Lazarus of old, bound hand and foot with grave-clothes—the grave-clothes of the dogma of the Dual Nature.—*Quest of the Historical Jesus*, pp. 3–4 (E.T.[2]).

A further point to note in this attack upon the Chalcedonian Christology is a persistent opposition to the doctrine of the impersonality of Christ's manhood, which is rightly perceived to be an inevitable deduction from the Cyrilline Christology, but which in the light of modern psychology is pronounced to be a meaningless abstraction.

xxx

INTRODUCTION

Moreover, a perusal of modern works on the Person of Christ reveals a demand for the abandonment of the particular phraseology employed by the Fathers, whose task it was to define the Church's belief in the language of their own time and with the aid of the best philosophical conceptions then available. We to-day are supposed to have outgrown their philosophy, and modern scientific investigation has revolutionised our whole mode of thought and method of expression. Hence the demand for a new interpretation of the ancient belief in terms of modern thought, and with the aid of the best philosophical concepts which this age possesses. We observe, further, that the modern mind, in spite of all our enormous strides in knowledge, is still struggling between the Scylla of a duplex personality and the Charybdis of an impersonal manhood in its attempts to solve the Christological problem. The same difficulties confront us to-day which were faced by those who endeavoured to steer a middle course between Nestorianism and Monophysitism.

We are encouraged, therefore, in this thesis to endeavour to show the true value and significance of the ancient Christology, and especially to estimate the importance and right place of the Chalcedonian Definition as against modern attacks upon it. We wish to show that the doctrine of the Two Natures must still be an integral and essential factor in any Christology which claims to be based upon the New Testament and tradition.

But this is not the only nor the most important aim of our thesis. We wish to demonstrate the value of the doctrine of the Enhypostasia for modern Christology.

INTRODUCTION

Leontius of Byzantium, in his day, had to defend the Chalcedonian Christology, especially against the attacks of those who repudiated the doctrine of the impersonality of Christ's manhood, which was clearly perceived to be an inevitable deduction from the theology of Cyril of Alexandria. Precisely the same difficulties which Leontius endeavoured to meet by his doctrine of the Enhypostasia are confronting us to-day in the task of Christological reconstruction. The Chalcedonian Christology is being subjected to attacks from all sides, and a work similar to that done by Leontius is needed to-day in defence of the Church's belief. This thesis is offered as a tentative contribution to that work. We venture to think that the contribution to Christology made by Leontius has not received that full recognition which its merits deserve, nor has its true significance for modern thought hitherto been demonstrated. This thesis is an attempt at a full appreciation of the work of Leontius, and such a reinterpretation of his doctrine as we hope may commend it and secure for it a more careful consideration than it has yet received at the hands of theologians.

The thesis divides itself naturally into three parts.

In Part I we review the ancient Christology. Taking Apollinarianism as our starting-point, we trace the course of Christological speculation down to the Chalcedonian Definition, and we endeavour to estimate aright the true value and significance of that formula. We point out its merits and limitations, and we trace its interpretation in the Christology of Cyril and Leo, representing East and West. We then show how the doctrine of the impersonal manhood is the weak point against which attacks were made by those who were unable to accept the Chalcedonian Christology, and who were tempted in either a Nestorian or Monophysite direction.

We then review the theology of Leontius of Byzantium, and endeavour to estimate the precise meaning and significance of his doctrine of the Enhypostasia. We show how this represents the furthest point reached by the ancient Christology in the attempt to fathom the mystery of Christ's Person, and how the importance of the contribution made by Leontius was recognised in its incorporation into the final formulation of Greek theology made by John of Damascus.

In Part II we pass to the second great Christological epoch in which we find ourselves living to-day. We consider carefully the modern revolt against the Chalcedonian Christology, and more particularly the objections raised against the ' Two Natures ' hypothesis and the impersonality of Christ's manhood. We indicate the way in which these objections can be met by the doctrine of the Enhypostasia, and we proceed to show how this doctrine is rooted and grounded in the very nature of both man and God. This leads us to a careful examination of human nature in the light of modern psychology, and we attempt to analyse human personality. We further consider the Nature of God as this is revealed to us, and we fix upon Lotze's treatment of Personality, human and Divine, as one of the keys for a modern reinterpretation of the doctrine of the Enhypostasia. We review the relationship between the human and the Divine in us, and incidentally we endeavour to refute conclusively the modern attempt to argue from the analogy of the relation between the human and the Divine in us, to their relation in the Person of Christ. We give reasons for rejecting this analogy as fundamentally unsound, and as the source of much erroneous teaching in Christology to-day.

The true significance of Part II in its relationship to the whole thesis may easily be missed, but those who will study carefully our treatment of dualism, and the analysis of the human and the Divine both in themselves and in their relationship, will be able to appreciate more fully in the light of the results adduced in Part III how we have endeavoured to find the basis of the doctrine of the Enhypostasia in the very constitution of both natures in the Person of Christ.

In Part III we review some recent attempts at Christological reconstruction, and indicate the general drift of speculation. We see the difficulties under which these attempts labour, and we thus pave the way for our reinterpretation of the doctrine of the Enhypostasia, which we put forward as capable of meeting these difficulties so far as they can be met. We draw out at some length the advantages offered by this theory, and we finally appeal to the Gospel narratives for confirmation of our hypothesis. We conclude that whilst no theory will ever succeed in solving the problem of Christ's Person, which baffles all our ' explanations ' and transcends the capacities of our intellect, remaining thus as much a ' mystery ' for the twentieth-century mind as it was for the first-century mind, yet, amongst the many theories offered to-day for our acceptance, the doctrine of the Enhypostasia, as we have interpreted it, is at least entitled to a more favourable consideration than it has so far received at the hands of theologians. It is true that it fails to carry us much further than the furthest point reached by the ancient theologians, but it offers to us to-day, as it did to the men of the age of Leontius, a theory by which we can continue to defend the Chalcedonian Christology against its many opponents, and by which we can offer to the modern mind an attempt at Christological reconstruction which involves no break with the past and no repudiation of any factor essential to the truth of the New Testament portrait of Jesus Christ.

PART ONE

B

1.

APOLLINARIANISM

THE Apollinarian Controversy is a useful starting-point for our investigation, since it raised for the first time in an acute form the question of the complete humanity of Christ's Person. The result of the Arian Controversy was the vindication of the Church's belief in the full Divinity of her Lord and Master. The Arian negation of this fundamental postulate of the Christian faith had inevitably led to a vehement emphasis upon the Divine character of the God-Man. So zealous had been the defenders of the Nicene Creed in demonstrating the Divine nature of Christ, that they had tended if anything to exalt His Divinity at the expense of His humanity. Christ was so truly and thoroughly Divine that He could not have been, so it was felt, truly and thoroughly human. All the weaknesses and limitations of a common human nature, if applied to Christ, seemed derogatory to one Who was so gloriously Divine. The Arians had emphasised the sufferings of Christ as a proof of His inferiority. Their opponents had in consequence to offer some apology for the Passion. Men like Hilary of Poitiers were so concerned at the seeming incongruity of the Divine Christ suffering on the Cross, and so hard pressed by the conclusions which their Arian opponents were drawing from this picture of a suffering Messiah, that they inevitably tended to seek to minimise the purely human aspects of the Passion and almost

unconsciously drifted into Docetic language. This
Docetic tendency in Hilary's thought can be seen,
for example, reflected in the following quotations
from the *De Trinitate*, Book X, where the language
employed seems to reveal a weakened grasp of the
truth of all that is involved in the real humanity of
Christ. Passages might be quoted which at first
sight seem to be wholly of a Docetic character, but
these have to be balanced by other passages in
Hilary's works of a more orthodox character.

C. 23. He had a body to suffer, and He suffered : but He
had not a nature which could feel pain. For His body
possessed a unique nature of its own; it was transformed
into heavenly glory on the Mount, it put fevers to flight by
its touch, it gave new eyesight by its spittle.

C. 24. It may perhaps be said, ' We find Him giving way
to weeping, to hunger and thirst : must we not suppose Him
liable to all the other affections of human nature ? ' But if
we do not understand the mystery of His tears, hunger, and
thirst, let us remember that He Who wept also raised the dead
to life : that He did not weep for the death of Lazarus, but
rejoiced ; that He Who thirsted, gave from Himself rivers of
living water. He could not be parched with thirst, if He was
able to give the thirsty drink. . . . And if, beside the mystery
of weeping, hunger, and thirst, the flesh He assumed, that is
His entire manhood, was exposed to our weaknesses : even
then it was not left to suffer from their indignities. His
weeping was not for Himself ; His thirst needed no water to
quench it; His hunger no food to stay it. It is never said
that the Lord ate or drank or wept when He was hungry,
or thirsty, or sorrowful. He conformed to the habits of the
body to prove the reality of His own body, to satisfy the
custom of human bodies by doing as our nature does. When
He ate and drank, it was a concession, not to His own
necessities, but to our habits.

C. 25. For Christ had indeed a body, but unique, as
befitted His origin.—' Hilary of Poitiers,' *Nicene and Post-
Nicene Fathers.*

4

Hilary by this line of thought seeks to overthrow the Arian contention that the Passion was a proof of the inferiority of Christ. He points to the Lord's humanity which, even in the days of His flesh and in the state of humiliation, manifested a power which marked it as endowed with Divine properties. But in his anxiety to demonstrate the uniqueness of the humanity of Christ and its Divine endowments, Hilary can hardly be said to escape the dangers of Docetism, and towards this he is drawn by his theory of the impassibility of the God-Man—a theory which, if pursued to its logical conclusion, and rigidly applied to the Gospel portrait of Jesus, results in hopeless contradictions and absurdities. Even in New Testament times the dangers of Docetism had been felt,[1] and the emphasis of Ignatius upon the reality of the truly human experience of Christ, in the days of His flesh, shows us that the Church in his time was faced with the same difficulty. In fact, the Docetic tendency was prevalent whenever undue emphasis was laid upon the Divine character and full Deity of the God-Man. The more the minds of men dwelt upon the Deity of Christ, the more endangered was their grip upon the reality of His appearance in the flesh. So prevalent was this tendency to Docetism in the third and fourth centuries that Harnack has ventured to suggest that down to the beginning of the fourth century ' no single outstanding Church teacher really accepted the humanity in a perfectly unqualified way.' This perhaps is an exaggeration, and the Docetic tendency observable even in writers of a thoroughly orthodox character and wholly loyal in

---

[1] Cf. 1 John i. 1-4 ; iv. 1-3 ; Heb. ii. 9-18 ; 2 John, verses 7-11.

their allegiance to the Scriptural presentation of Christ's life may be due rather to immature thinking, and a failure to follow out to its logical conclusion the result of their belief in the complete humanity of the God-Man. The Apollinarian Controversy, however, raised the problem in an acute form, and forced men to consider more fully all that was involved in the thought of Christ's complete manhood.

Thus attention was directed to the relation of the Two Natures in Christ rather than to the relation of Christ to God. Once the proper Deity of Christ had been vindicated, the course of theological thought was diverted from the Trinitarian to the Christological problem. The price of victory which orthodoxy had to pay for the downfall of Arianism was a weakening of the Church's grasp upon the truly human character of the Word made flesh. The question at issue was this : How can the *Logos* have assumed human nature in its completeness ? If Christ were truly Divine could He be completely human ? Was complete manhood compatible with sinless Godhead in the One Christ ? Did the presence of the Divine Nature exclude that of a fully human nature ? What effect, if any, was brought about by their action and reaction, the one upon the other ? The relation of the Two Natures might be solved in one or other of two directions, leading either to Nestorianism or Eutychianism, according as over-emphasis was laid upon one or other of the two factors, the humanity or the Divinity of the God-Man.

(1) Apollinaris was led to formulate his theory in opposition to Arianism, and both he and the Arians found a common starting-point in a psychology which was Platonic in its origin and had gained currency

in Christian thought through the writings of Origen. That great thinker, in the attempt to reconcile Christian doctrine with Greek thought, and to defend the Christian religion as a philosophy, had necessarily employed current philosophical phraseology. He had found the Platonic tripartite division of human nature particularly helpful to him in the exposition of his doctrine of the pre-existence of the soul.

Origen had retained the trichotomy of Plato which other Greek Fathers also, with the sanction, as they supposed, of St. Paul (1 Thess. v. 23), had adopted. 'Body,' 'soul,' and 'spirit,' or Plato's 'body,' 'unreasoning' and 'reasoning soul,' had helped Origen to explain how the last, the pre-existent soul (the spirit, or the conscience, as he sometimes calls it—*Comment. in Rom.* ii. 9, p. 486), could ever have come to live in the flesh. The second, the soul proper, is as it were a mediating ground on which the spirit can meet the flesh. The celestial mind, 'the real man fallen from on high,' rules by the power of conscience or of will over this soul, where the merely animal functions and the natural appetites reside ; and through this soul over the body. How the celestial mind can act at all upon this purely animal soul which lies between it and the body, Origen leaves unexplained. But this division was necessary for him in order to represent the spirit as remaining itself unchanged in its heavenly nature, though weakened by its long captivity in the body. The middle soul (in which he sometimes places the will) is the scene of contamination and disorder ; the spirit is free, it can always rejoice at what is well done in the soul, and yet is not touched by the evil in it ; it chooses, convicts, and punishes. Such was Origen's psychology.—*Prolegomena*, p. 18, 'Gregory of Nyssa,' *Nicene and Post-Nicene Fathers.*

Although the Church rejected Origen's doctrine of the pre-existence of the soul, yet the thought of the advent of a pre-existent soul into the created body offered to the Arians, and later to Apollinaris, an analogy of a helpful character when they tried to

conceive of the advent of the pre-existent Logos
into human nature. Arius built up a Christological
theory with this tripartite division of human nature
as its basis.

Man was made up of (1) Body (σῶμα); (2) Animal,
or vital soul (ψυχή); (3) Rational, or intellectual soul
(νοῦς). This last, the *nous*, was considered to be the
seat of sinful instincts. Origen, for example, had upheld the freedom of the human will, and looked to this
for the origin of evil, and not to any inherent evil
inevitably bound up with the lower nature of man.
In this respect he was in opposition to the general
tendency of Eastern philosophic thought to regard
human nature as in itself necessarily evil, because of
the corrupt character of the ' body ' in which the
human ' spirit ' was imprisoned. Arius adopted this
psychology, and applied it to the question of the
Person of Christ. His human nature was considered
to be imperfect in that it lacked the third or higher
element, the rational or intellectual soul. This, in
the case of Christ, was supplied by the Logos, Who
united to Himself a human body with an animal or
vital soul. By this theory the Arians tried to prove
conclusively the imperfection not only of Christ's
human nature, but of His Divine nature. In their
view the Logos Himself was a creature, and they
denied His immutability. Because He was a creature and mutable (τρεπτός), between Him and the
Father there was a great gulf fixed. The Logos,
according to Arius, was a creature capable of, and
subject to, creaturely vicissitudes (τρεπτὸς φύσει ὡς
τὰ κτίσματα), One Who, in His incarnate state, could
have sinned. The Arians employed the texts which
related to His human nature as proofs of the imper-

8

fections of the Logos Himself. This imperfect Logos united Himself to an imperfect human nature. Thus the Arian Christ was neither fully Divine nor fully human.

Apollinaris, in opposition to the Arians, was concerned to prove the sinlessness of Christ.

He accordingly abandoned the dichotomic view of man's nature which he originally held, and took as his starting-point the same threefold division of human nature which Arius had adopted, and the same imperfection of the human nature assumed by the Logos.[1]

He agreed with Arius that in Christ the Logos was united to a human body with an animal or vital soul. He differed from Arius in that he maintained that the Logos thus united was not a creature, was not τρεπτὸς φύσει ὡς τὰ κτίσματα, was not imperfect. The very fact that Christ lacked a human *nous*, the seat of free will, free choice and mutability, the seat, therefore, of sinful instinct and the source of sin, secured His sinlessness. There could be no element of free choice in Christ's humanity just because, as Arius agreed, He lacked a human *nous*, and so was not capable of sin. The place of the human *nous* was taken by the Divine immutable and infallible Logos Who, as the ruling principle (τὸ ἡγεμονικόν), secured for the humanity of Christ immunity from just those weaknesses, and just that liability to creaturely vicissitudes which in other men followed from their possession of a human *nous*. Thus Apollinaris tried to turn Arius' own Christological theory against him. He accepted his premises and drew an exactly opposite conclusion.

[1] Petavius, *De Incarnatione*, i. 5, §§ 5–8 ; Athanasius, *Contra Apoll.* ii. 3.

(2) The Christological theory of Apollinaris, how-ever, was not only influenced by his opposition to Arian-ism : the main difficulty was his desire to secure a real union of the Two Natures, the Divine and the human, in the one Person of Christ. Could this be done on the psychological basis of a tripartite division of human nature ? This was the problem Apollinaris tried to solve.

Two perfect natures seemed to him to involve a dual personality. The union of full Divinity and full humanity in one person seemed to him to be an impossible amalgam. Two complete natures meant two persons. It was this fear of what ultimately became Nestorianism which drove him to seek to find an organic unity between the two natures in an incarnation which resulted in the creation of a new nature, Divine-human — ' God made flesh ' — θεὸς σαρκωθείς. In this way he hoped to escape from the impossible dualism at the very centre of person-ality, which seemed to be involved in the conception of a union of two complete natures in one person. If Christ were perfect God and perfect man there would be two natures, and therefore two persons. This involved a conflict of two wills, the Divine and the human, and therefore the possibility of a division between the Logos, the ruling personality in the God-Man, and the human *nous*, the ruling principle in man. To have maintained the completeness of the humanity, and its consequent possession of a human *nous*, meant a conflict for rulership of the manhood which seemed to involve division at the very centre of the being of the God-Man, and con-sequently the impossibility of an organic unity of Person. The only way out of this difficulty was to deny to Christ the possession of a human *nous* at all. This was really to teach that Christ's human nature was impersonal. Apollinaris was seeking to secure a true Incarnation, as opposed to the idea of a mere connection between the Logos and the man Jesus. He was seeking a basis for an organic unity, and he secured this by postulating the Divine Logos as the centre of personality in the God-Man. In this he was right, but, according to his psychology, it involved the rejection of the personality of the human nature, the most important constituent of man. He secured his organic unity between the human and the Divine only by a mutilation of the human. ' He reaches only a θεὸς σαρκοφόρος, as Nestorianism only an ἄνθρωπος θεοφόρος, instead of the proper θεάνθρωπος.' [1] Undoubtedly the threefold partition of human nature which was the basis of his psychology helped Apollinaris to conceive of the advent of the Logos into human nature, as it had helped Origen to formulate his doctrine of the advent of the pre-existent soul into the created human body. The difficulty of the Incarnation was the union of the infinite and pre-existent with the finite and created. Apollinaris solves this by postulating the advent of the Logos into the highest and deepest division of our tripartite nature, the *nous*. Hilary, e.g., says that Apollinaris taught—

that as the body and soul of Adam both sinned, so the Lord must have taken the soul and body of Adam from the Virgin, and that it was not the whole man that she conceived from the Holy Ghost.

He fell back upon the thought that the Christ received from the Virgin Mary His body and irrational soul

[1] Schaff, *Hist. of Christian Church*, Div. ii. p. 708 ff.

11

(finite and created), whilst the higher part of His human nature was supplied by the Logos—i.e. His rational soul (*nous*) was Divine in its origin (infinite and pre-existent).

(3) Notwithstanding the laudable motives which underlay this attempt of Apollinaris to outline a Christological theory which should be proof against the insidious attacks of Arianism, the Church instinctively felt that the price demanded for its acceptance was too great. Although Apollinarianism seemed to secure the unity of Christ's Person and His sinlessness, yet it suffered, so it was felt, from two fatal defects :

The completeness of Christ's human nature was impaired, and, as a consequence, the whole redemption wrought by Christ was defective, since, if the God-Man assumed not human nature in its completeness, ' what was not assumed was not redeemed.'

These two defects secured the condemnation of Apollinarianism at the Council of Alexandria in the year 362 A.D. The faithfulness of the Church to Christian tradition and the New Testament portrait of Christ was vindicated at the Council of Constantinople in 381 A.D., which upheld the full and complete humanity of the God-Man, Who was held to be not only ἀληθῶς θεός, but also τελέως ἄνθρωπος.

(4) But is it quite certain that Apollinaris could not have answered satisfactorily these objections to his Christological theory ? Is it quite certain that his opponents did full justice to all sides of his thought, or fully grasped all that he was striving to teach ? These questions are raised in view of the fact that there is one line of thought in his writings to which

12

more attention perhaps ought to be paid when an attempt is made to describe his theological position. The chief opponents of Apollinaris were Athanasius, the Cappadocian Fathers (the two Gregories),[1] and Epiphanius. It can scarcely be said that Gregory of Nazianzum does full justice to the grander and deeper thoughts suggested by Apollinaris in the development of his Christological theory. The faith of the Church naturally rebelled against the mutilated and stunted humanity which seemed to be implied by his teaching. The Arian Christ had been condemned because He was neither man nor God; but a demi-God, partly Divine, partly human. Apollinaris himself revolted against such a conception, but it seemed to his opponents that his theory of the Christ, as a being resulting from an amalgam of two parts human fused into the unity of a new nature by the advent into it of one part Divine, was open to the same objection. The union of the Logos with a truncated human nature produced a being more like one of the monsters of ancient mythology than even the Arian Christ was considered to be.

But Apollinaris seems to have been fully conscious of these grave objections to his theory, and to have endeavoured to meet them more than half-way. We have to remember that we are largely dependent for our knowledge of his teaching on fragments of his works preserved for us in the writings of his

---

[1] The two Epistles of Basil of Cæsarea (Ep. 243 and 245) may be dismissed, since (a) he himself admits that he has scarcely read the works of Apollinaris; (b) the letters contain little but personal abuse, with no attempt at serious argument, and (c) Apollinaris' teaching is condemned chiefly because ' the theological works of Apollinaris are not founded on Scriptural proofs, but are based on a human origin ' (i.e. grounded upon intellectual reasoning, or upon *a priori* assumptions).

opponents.[1] But even from these extracts we can
see that there were grander and deeper sides of the
truth reflected in his teaching, and certainly one
line of thought in particular, which went far to meet
the objections raised against his theory. How far,
however, these deeper truths are the fruit of his
more mature reflections, reached as the result of the
controversy in which he found himself involved, or
how far they are due to the school of thought which
sprung from his teaching is doubtful. In any case,
they seem to go far towards meeting the objections
raised against his earlier and cruder suggestions,
which were the real cause of his condemnation.
Dr. Ottley gives a very useful and lucid summary
of these more refined and subtler thoughts underlying his teaching :

> The sketch of Apollinaris' theology would be incom-
> plete [he says] without some allusion to an idea of special
> interest, and even grandeur, which underlay his teaching ;
> the idea, namely, of an essential connection between the
> Divine and human natures, which first reached its embodi-
> ment and fulfilment in the Incarnation. A union between
> God and man seemed to be ' demanded by the essence or
> conception of both natures.' In this union Apollinaris
> conceived that both natures—human and Divine—for the
> first time reached a predestined goal : humanity, because
> it remained in a sense imperfect, without the Incarnation ;
> deity, because the Divine love must needs remain unsatisfied
> till God had actually become man.
> According to Apollinaris, the Logos is not only the image

---

[1] Dräseke ('Apollinarios von Laodicea' in *Texte u. Untersuchungen*,
vol. vii. p. 381 ff.) has conveniently brought together all that is left
of the dogmatic writings of Apollinaris, viz. seven larger and some
short fragments from an *Exposition of the Divine Incarnation in the
Likeness of Man*. These fragments have been preserved for us as
quotations in Gregory of Nyssa, *Adv. Apollinarem*. See especially
cap. 48-55 for the passages dealing with the affinity of the Divine and
human natures.

of God but the archetype of manhood. He was eternally
predestined to become man, and bore within Himself, so to
speak, the 'potency' of Incarnation. In this sense Apollinaris
spoke of Christ's human nature as pre-existent. Christ was
the pre-existent heavenly man, as being destined for the
Incarnation. So Apollinaris understood the expression of
S. Jo. iii. 13, *The Son of man which is in heaven,* and the
statement of S. Paul (1 Cor. xv. 47), *The second man is
from heaven.* The Logos, who supplied the place of the
human soul in Christ, was in no sense foreign to the essence
of humanity ; rather He was ' the truth of human nature '—
that without which it could not attain the goal of its
development. Accordingly, from this point of view, human
nature (σάρξ in the wider sense of the term, i.e. ἄνθρωπος)
was in a sense coeternal with the Logos, not something
adventitious, but something essentially ' consubstantial and
connatural ' ; man's nature pre-existed in God. The human
birth of the Son of God was indeed an act of self-humiliation
(κένωσις), but only in the sense that to be the archetypal
man is a higher state of existence than to be actually man
and to pass through the stages of a human history.—Ottley,
Doct. of Incarnation, pp. 376–7.

That the full significance of this line of thought
was not grasped is shown, e.g., by the fact that
his opponents misunderstood him to mean that the
actual *flesh* of Christ pre-existed. How little Gregory
of Nazianzum understood the point which Apollinaris
was trying to make, is clear from the Epistles to
Cledonius, where he says :—

Do not let the men deceive themselves and others with the
assertion that the ' Man of the Lord,' as they called Him, Who
is rather our Lord and God, is without human mind. For
we do not sever the Man from the Godhead, but we lay down
as a dogma the Unity and Identity of Person, Who of old
was not Man but God, and the Only Son before all ages,
unmingled with body or anything corporeal ; but Who in
these last days has assumed Manhood also for our salvation ;
passible in his Flesh, impassible in His Godhead ; circum-
script in the body, uncircumscript in the Spirit ; at once

15

earthly and heavenly, tangible and intangible, comprehensible and incomprehensible ; that by One and the Same Person, Who was perfect Man and also God, the entire humanity fallen through sin might be created anew.—'Gregory Nazianzen,' *Nicene and Post-Nicene Fathers*, p. 439.

The whole Epistle is taken up with answering obvious objections to the theory of Apollinaris, but nowhere can we find a trace of any real appreciation of the full force of that other line of thought indicated above which Gregory apparently so little grasped that he thinks it necessary to deny the descent of the σάρξ from heaven, an idea which Apollinaris never intended to teach.

(5) It is in the light of this thought of Christ as ' the new,' ' the heavenly man,' ' the archetype,' ' the perfect image,' that we must consider what is sometimes spoken of as the Manichæan tendency observable in the teaching of Apollinaris.

In this same Epistle to Cledonius we find Gregory quoting (without naming) Apollinaris as having said ' our mind is subject to condemnation,' and in the treatise of Athanasius against Apollinaris the statement is made, ' For where there is perfect (or complete) manhood there is sin ' (ὅπου γὰρ τέλειος ἄνθρωπος ἐκεῖ καὶ ἁμαρτία).

The assumption is that Apollinaris held a Manichæan view of human nature as inherently and essentially, in itself, sinful ; and that it was because he regarded the human *nous* as the seat of sinful instincts, that he hesitated to attribute to Christ this element which would invalidate His sinlessness.

May it not have been that what Apollinaris was really trying to teach was the necessary imperfection of our human nature as such, in view of the fact that

16

the Fall had mutilated the Divine image in man and that, in this sense, where there is perfect or complete manhood there is imperfect manhood in comparison with the Archetypal Man, Who alone exhibits the true archetype and pattern, i.e., what God intended that man should be, and what man can never become without being re-created ?

It is quite possible that the charge of a tendency to a Manichæan conception of our human nature is really due to a *distortion* of Apollinaris' teaching.[1] But further, if, in comparison with the archetype, Apollinaris regarded even our complete manhood as imperfect, we can begin to appreciate his reason for advocating his theory that the Divine Logos— Who was not only truly God, but also the Archetypal Man—should take the place of the human *nous* in the God-Man. Far from this leaving a truncated humanity, the advent of the Logos brought to the humanity in the person of the Archetypal Man just that essential ' perfected manhood' which alone could make the human nature He took *complete*. The possession of a human *nous* would have made the human nature of Christ incomplete. The re-placing of this by the Logos—the Man from Heaven —made the human nature of Christ complete.

When the opponents of Apollinaris urged that his theory taught a ' mindless Christ ' and an imper-fect humanity, he could have met this objection by dwelling upon the nature of the pre-Incarnate Logos as already possessing in Himself all that was most distinctive of humanity in its highest aspects. Not that His *flesh* pre-existed, but that in some sense, as the second Adam, He was possessed, *before the*

---

[1] *Vide* Ottley, *op. cit.*, note, p. 377.

Incarnation, of all that was most distinctive of man, and was Himself the ' Image,' which, when incarnate, could alone be singled out from amongst the sons of men as being perfectly and completely human, in a sense in which no other man was, and in a manner in which no other man could hope to be, unless He, the God-Man, entered into possession of their manhood, just as He had become Incarnate in His own Person.

The common objections urged against Apollinarianism are so obvious, and his teaching as commonly outlined is so crude, that we may well hesitate to believe that we know what he really did teach.

Epiphanius tells us how he himself hesitated to believe that such a man would put such a doctrine into circulation. ' We supposed,' he says, ' that the disciples had not understood the deep thoughts of so learned and so discerning a man, and had themselves fabricated things which he did not teach.' So acute and profound a thinker can scarcely be thought to have launched a theory of the Person of Christ which could be so easily criticised, and so justly condemned, as that with which we usually associate the name of Apollinaris. And we may well suppose that in this further line of thought with which we have been dealing, and to which scant justice seems to have been done by his contemporaries, we have a hint of some far profounder and more illuminating thoughts concerning the Christological problem, to which he himself would point us as better expressing what he really taught, than any outline of his theory which we have gathered from the writings of his opponents, and from their

18

quotations from his works. Be this, however, as it may, one thing is clear, namely, that his opponents did not succeed in answering his main difficulty : *How could two perfect natures be united in one person, since two natures involve two personalities?* Apollinaris tried to solve this problem by postulating the Logos as the centre of personality of the God-Man. This involved a rejection of the personality of the human nature, i.e. Apollinaris made Christ's human nature impersonal.

Now in these two particulars, as we shall see, Apollinaris was in harmony with the ultimate verdict of the Church. For the moment the Church was content to vindicate the reality and completeness of the human nature of Christ, and to emphasise the essential unity of His Person ; but *the real problem as to how two complete natures could be united in one person without involving a dual personality, was not answered when the Apollinarian solution was rejected.* Apollinaris considered that the union of two complete natures in one person was an impossibility. Such a union he describes as ἀνθρωπόθεος, and stigmatises it as a monstrosity. Here was a very real difficulty, and it arose from an inability to conceive of a *complete* nature without personality.

2.

THE ANTIOCHENE AND ALEXANDRIAN SCHOOLS

THE subsequent development of Christological thought is bound up with the divergent tendencies noticeable in the two great schools of theology, the Antiochene and the Alexandrian. An exaggeration of the truths for which each of these schools contended, resulted in the two great heresies of Nestorianism and Eutychianism (Monophysitism).

For our present purpose it will be sufficient if we notice what these tendencies were.

(A) The Antiochene School was led, in opposition to Apollinarianism, to lay special stress upon the reality and completeness of Christ's manhood ; and it met the Monophysite tendency, in Apollinarian theology, by an insistence upon the distinctness of the manhood from the Godhead in the One Person. It wished to guard against the Pantheistic tendency of the Alexandrian School to confuse the Two Natures, or to think of the Divine transforming the human. This insistence upon the distinctness and completeness of the manhood, if over-emphasised, logically led to its being conceived of as a separate personality, and this, in turn, resulted in Nestorianism, which so pressed the distinction as to separate the Persons. Diodore, e.g., distinguished in the One Person of Christ two Sons, the Son of God and the Son of Mary. Theodore used language which led Cyril of Alexandria later to regard both him and Diodore as the parents

20

of Nestorianism: and Theodore has been named ' A
Nestorian before Nestorius.'   Marius Mercator, later,
denounced him as the real author of Pelagianism, and
the precursor of Nestorianism.   The real strength and
value of the Antiochene School all through, was its
splendid vindication of the historical Christ and the
loving attention paid to the historical portrait in the
Gospels.   In this way it strove to rescue the Man
Jesus from the hands of those who, having found a
place for Him as the Logos within the categories of
their philosophy, were reluctant to admit any historical fact about Him which seemed to clash with
their philosophical data.

A further tendency in Antiochene theology is the
insistence upon a real moral growth and development
in Christ during His earthly life.   Theodore dwells
upon the fact of Christ possessing a free will, which
necessarily involved His having undergone a process
of development in His human nature.   In a very
real sense He underwent probation.

So the life of Christ, according to this school,
was a continual progress, and at every stage of
this advance the Christ proved triumphant over
all temptation, as the result of His union with the
Divine Logos ; until finally He overcame death and
entered upon His glorious inheritance.   The sinlessness and ultimate perfection of His manhood was due
to the fact that in Him the Logos dwelt, and He
received of the Spirit ' without measure.'

The Antiochene theology breaks down when the
question as to the manner of the union between the
Two Natures in the One Person is discussed.   Theodore tries to solve this problem by distinguishing
between three possible modes of indwelling—(a)

essential, ἐνοίκησις κατ᾽ οὐσίαν; (*b*) *effectual*; κατ᾽ ἐνέργειαν; or (*c*) *moral,* κατ᾽ εὐδοκίαν, and fails, because he selects of these three the third, which precludes a real Incarnation.

Commenting upon his theology Dr. Ottley says :

> In effect this view substitutes for the Incarnation the indwelling of a man by the Logos. The Logos assumed the man Jesus from the moment of His conception, and brought Him through trial and probation to perfection.

We have here not an essential union of the human and the Divine, not an Incarnation, but a moral union of grace between the Two Natures. They commonly speak of God as dwelling in Christ ; the Logos assuming human nature, rather than of God becoming man or the Word made flesh. The real reason why Theodore rejected what Cyril later insisted upon, an ἕνωσις καθ᾽ ὑπόστασιν, was the same difficulty which gave rise to all these erroneous solutions, viz. the inability to conceive of ' nature ' without ' personality ' as its necessary and essential part ; and, further, the consequent idea that a complete human nature involves a distinct human personality. This difficulty led Theodore and the later Nestorians into all kinds of inconsistencies. So long as they conceived of the human nature as personal, and having a distinct personality of its own, so long they could hardly avoid speaking of Two Persons when they outlined their Christological theory.

> When we distinguish the natures [says Theodore] we maintain that the Nature of God the Word is perfect, perfect too the Person (πρόσωπον)—for it is not possible to speak of a distinct existence (ὑπόστασιν) which is impersonal (ἀπρόσωπον)—perfect too the nature of the man ; and the person likewise (πρόσωπον). But when we look to the

22

conjunction of the two, then we say that there is one person (πρόσωπον).[1]

The Antiochenes repudiated the charge of teaching ' Two Sons,' ' Two Persons,' and yet their fear of Apollinarianism (' a man without person ') made them insist upon the human nature of Christ as ' personal,' lest by speaking of the impersonality of His manhood they should seem to be denying to His human nature one of its integral and essential constituents, without which it could not be perfect. So they speak of the Logos having assumed *Him* not *It*, i.e. a perfect human nature, and therefore a person.

The man is Son only by virtue of His indissoluble union with the Divine Logos ; when we call Christ the Son of God we think principally of Him who is truly and essentially Son, but we include in our conceptions the Man, who is indissolubly One with Him and therefore shares His Honours and His Name.

So we find them using language, concerning the perfect human nature which the Logos assumed, of a confusing and perplexing character—e.g. ἄνθρωπος ἀναληφθείς : ὁ λαβών : ὁ ληφθείς : τὸ ἀνθρώπινον ὄργανον : Forma Servi : σάρξ : quod assumptum est : Natura assumpta.

Cf. Diodore : ' We worship the purple for the sake of Him who is clothed in it, and the temple because of Him who dwells in it ; the form of the servant because of the form of God ; the lamb because of the High-Priest ; him who was assumed because of Him who assumed him ; him who was formed of the Virgin because of the Maker of all. Confessing this offer one worship.'

---

[1] (ὅταν μὲν γὰρ τὰς φύσεις διακρίνωμεν, τελείαν τὴν φύσιν τοῦ θεοῦ λόγου φαμέν, καὶ τέλειον τὸ πρόσωπον· οὐδὲ γὰρ ἀπρόσωπον ἔστιν ὑπόστασιν εἰπεῖν· τελείαν δὲ καὶ τὴν τοῦ ἀνθρώπου φύσιν, καὶ τὸ πρόσωπον ὁμοίως· ὅταν μέντοι ἐπὶ τὴν συνάφειαν ἀπίδωμεν, ἓν πρόσωπον τότε φαμέν.—Fragment of the Treatise on the Incarnation, Περὶ τῆς ἐνανθρωπήσεως, Book VIII.)

23

(B) By way of contrast we may note briefly the Alexandrian theology and its tendencies. This school started from the Divine aspect of Christ's Person— the pre-Incarnate Logos manifested in time and space through an Incarnation which was a real revelation of God to man.

In the Person of Christ it is not a man who is assumed, but the humanity is that of the Logos, His very own, fashioned for Him ' Who was Incarnate by the Holy Ghost of the Virgin Mary, and was made Man.'

He Who assumed human nature assumed not a person whom He took into union with Him, but He was Himself personally the Son of God and took human nature into vital union with Himself.

The merits and defects of the two schools of thought are well illustrated in the following brief summary taken from the article ' Antiochene Theology.' [1]

The permanent service of the Antiochene school lies in its effort to correct a one-sided view of the factors and methods of revelation. To the emotional, mystical religion, which tended to lose the human element in the Divine, whether in inspiration, or the Person of Christ, or the relations of grace and free-will, it opposed conceptions which endeavoured to do justice to the dignity and worth of human nature.

While the Alexandrian theology started from the Divine side, and deduced all its conclusions from that as its source, the Antiochenes followed the inductive and rationalistic method, which consisted in a careful examination of the facts of human nature and experience. The philosophical basis of the one was Platonist, while that of the other was Aristotelian.

In Christology the school of Antioch centred attention

[1] Hastings' *Encyclopædia of Religion and Ethics,* vol. i. p. 593.

upon the historical Christ ; in its doctrine of inspiration it affirmed the immediate and historical reference of Scripture ; in anthropology it insisted upon the reality of human freedom. It regarded the purpose of the Incarnation as the accomplishment of man's destiny rather than as the deliverance of him from the consequences of sin.   The struggle and conflict provoked by the commandment became a means of educating man to realise his freedom of choice and his weakness, and so of raising him out of the stage of subjection to the passions and mortality into the higher life of immortality and sinlessness which has been won for him by Christ.   The two standpoints, the Alexandrian and the Antiochene, represent complementary aspects of Christian theology.   If the Alexandrian and mystical standpoint has found fuller expression in the later thought and teaching of Christendom, the problems of modern thought, and the evolutionary view of the universe, have once more called attention to the point of view which underlies the teaching of the Antiochenes.

3.

NESTORIANISM

THE Christology of the Antiochene School appears in its developed and exaggerated form in Nestorianism.

We are not directly concerned to enquire how far Nestorius himself was a Nestorian. We have given reasons elsewhere, as the result of an independent enquiry, for believing that he cannot be acquitted of the charges brought against him by the theologians of his time.[1] But in any case, Nestorianism as a developed Christological theory is a fact of history, and with this we are concerned in our enquiry only so far as it professed to be a satisfactory solution of the Christological problem.

(1) What, then, is Nestorianism ? The charges brought against Nestorius by the theologians were :

That he so distinguished between the Godhead and the manhood of our Lord as to treat them as separate personal existences, as though a man and God were joined together, so that our Lord was not one Person but two Persons, and no real union of God and man was effected in Him. It was supposed that he held the Word to be a Person distinct from Jesus, and the Son of God distinct from the Son of Man, and that therefore he avoided the term which expressed the real union of both and preferred to speak of a ' conjunction ' between them. And so some of the old charges against

[1] Vide *Church Quarterly Review*, No. 146, January 1912, *Nestorius the Nestorian*, H. M. Relton. Compare the subsequent treatment of this question in Dr. Loofs' *Nestorius and his Place in the History of Christian Doctrine*, 1914, and Dr. A. C. Headlam's article in *Church Quarterly Review*, No. 160, July 1915, *Nestorius and Orthodoxy*.

the Gnostics and Paul of Samosata were raked up again and he was said, in teaching 'Two Sons,' to introduce a fourth person into the Godhead, and 'to transform the Trinity into a Quaternity.'[1]

Apart from the question as to how far these charges were just, as applied to the teaching of Nestorius himself, we find here undoubtedly the essential features of Nestorianism itself; and the root difficulty at the bottom of it was the failure to conceive of 'human nature' without personality as its essential characteristic, and without which it could not, strictly speaking, be called a 'complete nature.' It is more than significant, as pointing to the close relationship between the theology of the Antiochenes and Nestorians, that we find a use of terms and a phraseology common to both: e.g. ἐνοίκησις in distinction from ἐνσάρκωσις; συνάφεια in distinction from ἕνωσις; 'the Word' and 'the Man assumed by Him'; Mary bore 'the man who is the instrument of the Godhead' (θεότητος ὄργανον), 'the temple which He might inhabit'; the Man Christ as θεοφόρος, God-bearer, or κτήτωρ τῆς θεότητος, 'possessor of the Godhead' and other phrases, all of which leave in our minds the impression that in Nestorian thought the 'manhood' was so distinctively 'personal' as to be in the God-Man a distinct and distinguishable 'individuality,' if only in an abstract sense.

(2) That the danger of such phraseology was vividly present to the minds of those who had to combat Nestorianism is abundantly evident from a perusal of Cyril of Alexandria's writings. To take

[1] *Vide* Bethune-Baker, *Nestorius and His Teaching.*

but one of several passages which might be quoted from Cyril's letters to Nestorius :

> We refuse also [says Cyril] to say of Christ, ' For the sake of Him who assumes I worship Him who is assumed ; for the sake of Him who is invisible I worship Him who is visible.' It shocks me also to say, ' He that is assumed shares the name of God with Him who assumes.' For he who so speaks again makes two several Christs, one God and one Man. For he confessedly denies the union, according to which there is understood one Christ Jesus—not one jointly worshipped with another, or jointly sharing the name of God with another, but one Christ Jesus, one only-begotten Son, honoured with one worship with His own flesh.'—Heurtley, *De Fide et Symbolo*, in which Cyril's ' Epistles to Nestorius ' are given in full.

We are led to enquire whether phraseology, so open to misconstruction, would have been employed, unless the men who used it had been forced to do so because they felt in duty bound in this way to do justice to the truth of the completeness and integrity of the manhood which Apollinarianism threatened.

Was it possible, whilst avoiding the Apollinarian error, yet at the same time to accept another element in his teaching, viz. the ' impersonal nature of the manhood,' by which alone such phraseology as the Antiochenes and Nestorians had been forced to use, could be avoided ? Did the acceptance of the ' impersonal nature of the manhood ' impair its completeness and integrity ? The answer to this question is forced upon us by the fact that the Church did ultimately accept this element in the teaching of Apollinaris. How did theologians reconcile such a step with loyalty to the decision of the Second Ecumenical Council, τελέως ἄνθρωπος ? The first danger to be overcome was the Monophysite alternative.

4.

EUTYCHIANISM

HAVING rejected the Nestorian solution, the Church was faced with the task of defining her position in opposition to Eutychianism. Cyril had battled hard for the ἕνωσις καθ᾽ ὑπόστασιν, as the only one capable of securing such an organic unity between the Two Natures as would safeguard the integrity of the One Christ. But the connotation of this term was by no means fixed. Dr. Bethune-Baker has shown how ambiguous the phrase was. Did such a union admit of a Monophysite interpretation? The opposition of Nestorius and his reluctance to accept the term witnesses to his real belief that it involved a confusion of the manhood and the Godhead with a resultant One Nature after the union.[1] Whilst Cyril's letters to Nestorius, in our opinion, clearly show in what sense he held the 'Hypostatic Union,' and how its acceptance did *not* involve that confusion of the manhood and the Godhead which Nestorius so much dreaded, yet at the same time the subsequent Monophysite heresy in itself shows that his protest was justified, and that he was right in challenging the phrase, and demanding that its meaning should be more clearly defined in view of its ambiguity. The Eutychian Controversy was, in its origin, a reaction from Nestorianism,

---

[1] Cf. Cyril's third anathema and the counter-anathema of Nestorius, where it is quite clear that this was the real point at issue between them.

but, in its results, the logical outcome of an exaggerated emphasis upon that side of the truth
for which the Alexandrian School was contending.
Monophysitism justified the worst fears of Nestorius,
just as Nestorianism justified the worst fears of
Cyril.

Any over-emphasis upon the union of the Two
Natures imperilled their distinctness and involved
their possible confusion. Could the manhood retain
its independence when indissolubly united with so
glorious an element as Godhead? Catholic teaching
allowed it a relative independence as a passive and
receptive instrument of the Logos. But the Eutychian monk, with his vision of salvation through absorption, inevitably tended to apply his pantheistic
conceptions to the relation not only of his own soul
to Deity, but of Christ's humanity to His Divinity,
and the outcome was a return in thought to the
teaching of Apollinaris that 'the Godhead without
constraint swayed the manhood' ($\dot{a}\beta\iota\dot{a}\sigma\tau\omega s,\ \phi\eta\sigma\acute{\iota}\nu,\ \dot{\eta}$
$\theta\epsilon\acute{o}\tau\dot{\eta}s\ \tau\dot{\eta}\nu\ \sigma\acute{a}\rho\kappa\alpha\ \pi\rho\sigma\acute{a}\gamma\epsilon\tau\alpha\iota$), and its result, the latter's
own exclamation, 'O new creation and wondrous
mingling! God and flesh produced One Nature'
($\dot{\omega}\ \kappa\alpha\iota\nu\dot{\eta}\ \kappa\tau\acute{\iota}\sigma\iota s\ \kappa\alpha\grave{\iota}\ \mu\acute{\iota}\xi\iota s\ \theta\epsilon\sigma\pi\epsilon\sigma\acute{\iota}\alpha,\ \theta\epsilon\grave{o}s\ \kappa\alpha\grave{\iota}\ \sigma\grave{a}\rho\xi\ \mu\acute{\iota}\alpha\nu$
$\dot{a}\pi\epsilon\tau\acute{\epsilon}\lambda\epsilon\sigma\alpha\nu\ \phi\acute{\upsilon}\sigma\iota\nu$). This was practically the $\mu\acute{\iota}\alpha\ \phi\acute{\upsilon}\sigma\iota s$
$\sigma\epsilon\sigma\alpha\rho\kappa\omega\mu\acute{\epsilon}\nu\eta$ for which Eutyches contended, and with its
acceptance went the denial of what was felt to be one
essential truth of the Incarnation, namely, that His
manhood was consubstantial with ours. How could it
be if its union with His Godhead meant its absorption?
If at any time after the Incarnation Christ ceased
to be Man, and His manhood once assumed became
merged in His Godhead, the whole purpose of the
Incarnation, both in its redemptive and exemplary

aspects, was lost. No matter, therefore, how zealous the Eutychian monks were not to impair the single-ness of the Divine personality in the One Christ, this could never justify their denial of His real and proper manhood.

Here again we see how the Eutychians were led into error, because of this same difficulty which was involved in the conception of Two Natures and yet One Christ. They persuaded themselves that although Two Natures might be admitted before the Incar-nation, yet to admit of Two Natures after the union was inevitably to bring back Nestorianism, and to undo the work of the Council of Ephesus. Why? Because in their view Two Natures meant two Persons, two Sons. They could not conceive of ' nature ' without personality. So to preserve the unity of Christ's Person they were prepared to go the length of practically denying one whole side of the Incarnation mystery, viz. that which is summed up for us in the phrase ὁμοούσιος ἡμῖν κατὰ τὴν ἀνθρωπότητα. All that circle of ideas which centre round the truth of Christ's human nature ; one with us in all His work on our behalf as the Pattern Man, the Elder Brother, the High Priest, ' like unto His brethren in all things, sin excepted,' ' touched with the feeling of our infirmities,' experiencing in His human nature the full force of temptation up to and beyond anything yet endured by the sons of men ; ' knowing what was in man ' with a knowledge that could only be His in virtue of the reality of His human nature and His experiences in the days of His flesh—this whole circle of ideas was imperilled by the Eutychian insistence upon their formula ' That there were two natures before

31

the union, but only one after it.' [1]   It is not surprising, therefore, to find that Eutyches in his anti-Nestorian zeal laid himself open to the charge of reviving, in its most subtle and dangerous form, the Apollinarian denial of the real and complete humanity of Christ. The Synod which examined him insisted upon his acceptance of the belief that Christ was consubstantial with us as touching His manhood.

[1] Cf. Eutyches : ὁμολογῶ ἐκ δύο φύσεων γεγενῆσθαι τὸν κύριον ἡμῶν πρὸ τῆς ἑνώσεως, μετὰ δὲ τὴν ἕνωσιν μίαν φύσιν. Cf. Bright, *Age of the Fathers*, vol. ii. pp. 431–2.

5.

THE CHALCEDONIAN DEFINITION

THE Church's task was indeed a difficult one when so much was at stake. The famous ' Tome ' of Leo embodies for us the careful and cautious utterance of the Western Church in its attempt to preserve the truth intact as against the errors and confusion of thought which the more daring and speculative spirit of Eastern theologians had brought about. Leo's vindication of the truth of the reality and permanence of the manhood of Christ after the Incarnation was a service of vital importance rendered to the Church.

How hard a task it was for theologians to preserve the truth from over-emphasis in either a Nestorian or a Monophysite direction, can be more fully appreciated when we bear in mind what Cyril of Alexandria more than once points out, namely, that the Incarnation is a stupendous fact and an unutterable mystery.

Between the Nestorian and Monophysite alternatives, both of which seriously impaired the doctrine of the Incarnation in one or other of its essential features, the Church had to steer a middle course : and far from attempting to offer a satisfactory and logical solution for intellectual apprehension, she had to be content simply—(a) positively, to state the problem with the aid of the best language which the categories of thought of that time supplied ; and (b) negatively, to safeguard the whole truth from exaggerated emphasis upon any one factor in it to the detriment of the rest. Nestorianism and Monophysitism were both offered as solutions of a problem which in the ultimate analysis is insolvable. Both solutions were only reached by an over-emphasis upon one factor in the problem, to the detriment of the whole truth. The Church rejected both solutions, and in doing so was forced to make her own position more explicit, and to define her doctrine more fully perhaps than she would otherwise have been inclined to do. The result was the Chalcedonian Definition, embodying as it does the carefully guarded language of Leo's ' Tome.'

In our own day the Chalcedonian Definition has been subjected to criticism from many different points of view. Much of this criticism arises from a mistaken idea as to what the Definition professes to be, and what may be legitimately expected from it of a positive character in the elucidation of the Christological problem.

(1) In the first place, it does not profess to explain the mystery of the Incarnation, nor does it claim to be adding anything fresh to the Church's Creed. The Symbols of Nicæa and Constantinople are quoted and accepted as containing the whole Faith. But—

(2) Inasmuch as the Nestorian and Eutychian heresies have given rise to much confusion of thought and widespread error, a more careful explanation of the Church's teaching is demanded, with a view to safeguarding the truth of the Incarnation against these two forms of error, both of which are shown to be inadequate and to endanger the Church's belief by a one-sided exaggeration of one or other element in it.

(3) The second letter of Cyril to Nestorius, and his epistle to John of Antioch, are accepted because of their value as confuting the Nestorian error, and as being helpful in the explication of the Faith. Leo's ' Tome ' also is accepted because of its value as confuting Eutyches, and also because it is a common monument erected against heretics :

for it confutes (*a*) those who presume to rend asunder the mystery of the Incarnation into a double Sonship, and it deposes from the priesthood (*b*) those who dare to say that the Godhead of the Only-begotten is passible ; and it withstands (*c*) those who imagine a mixture or confusion of the two natures of Christ ; and it drives away (*d*) those who fondly teach that the form of a servant which He took from us was of a heavenly or some other substance ; and it anathematises (*e*) those who feign that the Lord had two natures before the union, and that these were moulded into one after the union.

By setting its seal thus to these documents the Definition defines its own position negatively.

(4) Positively, the Definition goes on to formulate a confession which claims in no way to depart from the hitherto accepted belief of the Church, and which deals in turn with :

(*a*) The Unity of Christ's Person.
(*b*) The reality and permanence of each Nature.
(*c*) The relationship between the Two Natures.

Wherefore, after the example of the Holy Fathers, we all with one voice confess our Lord Jesus Christ one and the same Son, the same perfect in Godhead, the same perfect in manhood, very God and very Man, the same consisting of a reasonable soul and a body ($\tau \grave{o} \nu$ $\alpha \mathring{v} \tau \grave{o} \nu$ $\mathring{\epsilon} \kappa$ $\psi v \chi \hat{\eta} s$ $\lambda o \gamma \iota \kappa \hat{\eta} s$ $\kappa \alpha \grave{\iota}$ $\sigma \acute{\omega} \mu \alpha \tau o s$), of one substance with the Father as touching the Godhead, the same of one substance with us as touching the manhood ($\acute{o} \mu o o \acute{v} \sigma \iota o \nu$ $\tau \hat{\omega}$ $\Pi \alpha \tau \rho \grave{\iota}$ $\kappa \alpha \tau \grave{\alpha}$ $\tau \grave{\eta} \nu$ $\theta \epsilon \acute{o} \tau \eta \tau \alpha$, $\kappa \alpha \grave{\iota}$

35

ὁμοούσιον τὸν αὐτὸν ἡμῖν κατὰ τὴν ἀνθρωπότητα), like us in all things, sin except; begotten of the Father before the worlds as touching the Godhead, the same in these last days, for us and for our salvation, born of the Virgin Mary, the Mother of God, as touching the manhood, one and the same Christ, Son, Lord, Only-begotten, to be acknowledged of two natures (ἐκ δύο φύσεων. Old Latin and Evagrius, ii. 4; ἐν δύο φύσεσιν, vide Routh, Opusc. ii. p. 119); without confusion, without conversion, without division, never to be separated (ἀσυγχύτως, ἀτρέπτως, ἀδιαιρέτως, ἀχωρίστως); the distinction of natures being in no wise done away because of the union, but rather the characteristic property of each nature being preserved, and concurring into one Person and one subsistence, not as if Christ were parted or divided into Two Persons, but one and the same Son and Only-begotten God, Word, Lord, Jesus Christ; even as the Prophets from the beginning spake concerning Him, and our Lord Jesus Christ hath instructed us, and the Symbol of the Fathers hath handed down to us.

Such is the famous Chalcedonian Definition, which a modern writer thinks is ' a confession of the bankruptcy of Greek Patristic theology.' [1]

(5) It may be conceded at once that the Definition is not an explanation of the mystery of the Incarnation. The very failure of the Definition to solve the insolvable is its best recommendation to our careful consideration. The framers of the Definition were not concerned so much to formulate a theory as to safeguard the truth from two attempted solutions of an erroneous character, and to preserve for us the truth hidden in both those errors.

The keynote of the Alexandrian theology was One Christ and He Divine.

[1] Temple, *Foundations*, Essay V, p. 230. The formula [he tells us] merely stated the fact which constituted the problem; it did not attempt solution. It was therefore unscientific; and as theology is the science of religion, it represented the breakdown of theology.

The keynote of the Antiochene theology was the reality and permanence of the complete manhood of Christ.

Both these truths are preserved in the Definition : the unity of the Person, the reality of the two complete Natures in the One Person. Eutyches would have sacrificed the latter to the former, Nestorius the former to the latter. The Chalcedonian Definition sacrifices neither, but preserves both.

(6) But is it at the cost of consistency ? Does it involve the Definition in hopeless contradictions ? Taken at its face-value no doubt it is open to these charges, but we have to remember that its authors, if pressed, would doubtless have fallen back upon the Alexandrian theology as expounded by Cyril, and pointed to this for an ' explanation,' which the Definition itself did not profess to contain. The Chalcedonian formula admirably fulfilled the purpose for which it was drawn up, namely, to exclude two possible explanations of the mystery, and to provide a convenient summary of essential facts which must be borne in mind by all those who attempted to penetrate still further into the mystery. The four characteristic words, ἀσυγχύτως, ἀτρέπτως, ἀδιαιρέτως, ἀχωρίστως, were four convenient sign-posts, each with a warning to the traveller that he might know what to avoid in his journey as a seeker after the truth. But these sign-posts were in no sense intended to bar the path for future seekers.[1] The Chalcedonian Definition warns us what to avoid ; it leaves us free within the limits of this warning to pursue our own road towards a solution of the problem, which it defines and safeguards, but in no sense solves. If the problem as thus defined contained

---

[1] Cf. A. J. Mason, *The Chalcedonian Doctrine of the Incarnation.*

no inconsistencies and seeming contradictions, there would be no need for further investigation. It would be solved! That the Definition, therefore, is accused of being a mass of contradictions, is in itself a proof of how well and adequately its framers adhered to the task they had set themselves to accomplish, namely, not to 'explain,' but to 'define' and 'safeguard' a mystery.

We expect, then, to find in the Definition a series of contradictory or complementary truths, the very existence of which in the Church's belief gave rise to various heresies which represent different attempts on the part of theologians either to reconcile them to or get rid of one or other.

The very antagonism of the two schools of thought—the Alexandrian and the Antiochene—in Christology witnesses to the fact that the problem contained two complementary or contradictory sides of the whole truth, as this was reflected in the Gospel narratives and had been handed down by Christian tradition. These two truths are focused in the doctrine of the 'Two Natures' in Christ—a doctrine which the Chalcedonian Fathers did not create, but which was received by them from the past, and for the origin of which we must look to the Gospel portrait of the God-Man. Far from the 'Two Natures' hypothesis being the creation of the Chalcedonian Definition, its very existence in that formula vindicates the claim of those who drew up the latter, that they were but reproducing what the Church had always believed and consistently taught. To attempt to eliminate the Two-Natured Christ from the New Testament would be to mutilate every page of the Gospel narratives. That this portrait involved seeming contradictions

has been the discovery of thinkers in every age whenever men have attempted to confine that portrait
within the limits of the categories of a consistent
intellectual or philosophic system. That it should
be left to thinkers in our own time to discover in the
Chalcedonian Definition traces of inconsistency, is
but proof of the faithfulness with which that Definition
reflects the New Testament portrait !

(7) But Harnack's criticism of the Definition is
even more uncompromising than the complaints of
those who find it inconsistent, and whose objections
to it really spring from their reluctance to accept
the doctrine of the ' Two Natures,' the origin of which
they erroneously ascribe to the Chalcedonian formula.

Harnack attacks it from a different standpoint,
and sees in it the cause of an ' arrested development '
in the progress of Alexandrian theology. But this
is to foist upon Athanasius, Cyril of Alexandria, and
the Eastern theologians generally, just those exaggera-
tions which misled the few into the Monophysite
error. If it can be shown that the true development
of Eastern theology lay in the direction of a consistent Monophysitism, then the Chalcedonian Definition
proved in a very real sense a stumbling-block and a
barrier to the future progress of Greek theology ; but
Harnack is practically alone in advocating such a
view, and we may well rest content with the hitherto
unchallenged opinion that the Chalcedonian Definition
conserved the best elements in Alexandrian theology,
and not the worst. Undoubtedly there were elements
in the speculative theology of the Easterns which
were subversive of Christian truth, not only in
Christology but also in Soteriology and Anthropology,
but these were not representative of the best side of

Eastern theology as exhibited in the writings of
Athanasius and Cyril of Alexandria. Did Christ
take human nature and make it Divine?—i.e. was His
humanity lost, or merged in His Divinity? Does
this really represent the teaching of Athanasius, even
admitting that it is possible to trace in Cyril's anti-
Nestorian writings a Monophysite tendency? For
what was at stake? If Christ's humanity was redeemed by absorption, the inevitable conclusion is
that our redemption will be effected in like manner,
and this is surely a one-sided idea of redemption, which
can scarcely be credited as the consistent teaching
of Eastern theologians. It may represent the un-
healthy influence of Eastern asceticism, with its
morbid teaching of the inherent evil of the flesh and
its consequent redemption only by destruction. That
such ideas should be found amongst the monks is not
surprising, but in no sense can it be claimed as representative of the best side of Eastern thought. Moreover, it is inconsistent with the Christian ideal, which
starts with the thought of our human nature as made
in the image of God, and therefore having essential
affinity with God apart from sin, which has marred
and degraded it.

Redemption, according to this view, is not the
destruction of human nature, but its restoration to
what it was always in the Divine thought, and to
what it may yet become as the result of Christ's
work for it and in it.

Christian thought does not lead us to believe that
the future holds for us the destruction of our human
nature, but its final and complete purification and
restoration. And this belief is bound up with the
Church's teaching as to the reality and permanence of

the manhood of Christ after the Incarnation. Christ took not our human nature to destroy it, but to purify and to uplift it. After the union, therefore, in His one Person His perfect humanity persists and is preserved.

Our Christian hope of redemption is bound up with the Church's belief in the perfection and permanence of Christ's manhood. This truth was preserved and safeguarded in the Chalcedonian Definition, in opposition not to the true line of Alexandrian theological thought, but as against the perversion of this in Eutychianism and the pantheistic tendencies of Eastern asceticism in the form in which this endeavoured to assert itself within the confines of the Church. In excluding it the Chalcedonian Definition was faithful not only to Church teaching, but also to the best traditions of Eastern theological thought. As Dr. Ottley says:

> The permanence and perfection of Christ's manhood; the reality of His brotherhood with men in suffering and temptation; the fulfilment of man's ideal destiny in His Person, —all these necessary conditions of a true redemption are secured by the assertion of His 'consubstantiality with us.'

This being so, the conservation of the truth of Christ's being ὁμοούσιος ἡμῖν κατὰ τὴν ἀνθρωπότητα by the Definition of Chalcedon, rendered as great a service to the Church as did the Nicene Creed in its insistence upon the complementary truth of Christ's being ὁμοούσιος τῷ Πατρὶ κατὰ τὴν θεότητα.

If the Nicene formula safeguarded the truth of Christ's essential Divinity, the Chalcedonian Definition equally safeguarded the truth of His essential humanity. Both these truths are vital for any Christology

41

which claims the New Testament and Christian tradition as its foundation. (See further Appendix A, p. 97.)

Reviewing the results of our investigation so far, we see (1) that the whole problem is overshadowed by the fear of Apollinarianism. If the West feared Arianism, the East feared Apollinarianism.

(2) The fear of Apollinarianism resulted in Nestorianism and Eutychianism. Both these heresies, though diverse in origin, were nevertheless the fruit of the same difficulty which Apollinaris had tried to overcome, viz. how can Two Complete Natures be united in One Person ? Nestorianism answers the question by postulating Two Persons as the result of the union ; Eutychianism solves the problem by eliminating one of the Natures, and so secures the unity of the Person.

(3) The Chalcedonian Definition offers no solution, but safeguards the unity of the Person as against Nestorianism, and the completeness of the Two Natures as against Eutychianism. Thus the Church conserves both aspects of truth for which the Alexandrian and Antiochene Schools were contending.

(4) We have seen that the Chalcedonian Definition states but does not solve the problem. The question remains in what way was the Definition to be interpreted ? In an Alexandrian or in an Antiochene direction ? The answer is, in both ; so far, and only so far, as these both contained an element of the truth.

This is shown by the fact that the Council set its seal both upon Cyril's two letters, and also upon Leo's ' Tome.'

42

What was the essential point of Cyril's letters ?
The Unity of the Person, the One Christ, as against
Nestorianism.

What was the essential point of Leo's ' Tome ' ?
The reality, integrity, and completeness of Christ's
manhood, as against Eutychianism.

The Council's acceptance of these documents
is its acceptance of these two truths, both vital for
a true Christology.

But the Chalcedonian Christology itself needed
interpretation. What further advance did the
Church make ?

The question brings us to a more careful consideration of the teaching of those documents which
received synodical sanction at the Council of
Chalcedon, viz. :

(1) The ' Tome ' of St. Leo.

(2) The Second Letter of Cyril to Nestorius.

(3) The Letter of Cyril to John of Antioch.

6.

THE SYNODICAL LETTERS

IF the Chalcedonian Definition is itself simply a statement, rather than an attempted solution, of the Christological problem, we have to remember that the Council which drew it up set its seal at the same time upon certain documents which go beyond a mere statement, and may themselves be taken as reflecting the mind of the Church at that time. If the Definition itself needs interpretation, these documents, though prior to it in time, may legitimately be considered as commentaries upon it, since the same body of men who drew up the Definition accepted also as authoritative Cyril's second letter to Nestorius, his letter to John of Antioch, and Leo's letter to Flavian (The 'Tome'). These letters were accepted on their merits as being fully in accord with Church teaching. Leo's 'Tome,' it is true, provoked some discussion, but when certain passages had been explained it also was received as the Faith of the Fathers—'Peter has spoken by Leo; thus Cyril taught!' Had these letters not been available it is quite possible that the Definition might have been more elaborated, and something further by way of explanation and elucidation added; but the Council preferred to accept these letters as the best embodiment of what they believed to be the teaching of the Church, rather than to attempt in their own words a more elaborate explanation.

The authoritative character of these letters enables

us to turn to them in order to see how the Church would have defended the Definition, and upon what lines she would have interpreted it. In these documents we find crystallised (*a*) the teaching of the Western Church generally, and (*b*) the theology of the Nicene party as this had been expounded by Athanasius, elaborated by the Cappadocians, and developed by the Alexandrian School under the leadership of Cyril.

I. *The ' Tome ' of Leo.*—In this we have a typical example of the merits and defects of Western theology.

Leo's letter [says Dr. Ottley] exhibits all the characteristics of an understanding practical, strong, and sagacious, but unversed in the subtle distinctions which occupied the Greek mind, and incapable of contributing more to the solution of the problem than a clear antithetic statement of its factors. It is virtually a reproduction of current Western theology in terms already adopted and fixed by Tertullian. It exhibits the uniform tone and tendency of the Roman Church; its tenacious hold upon the faith; its practical rather than speculative interest in theology.

The following passages may be quoted as bringing out the distinctive characteristics of this Christology :

(1) The Unity of the Person. The Logos and the Christ are not two but one and the same Person.

C. 3. Accordingly, the same who, remaining in the form of God made man, was made man in the form of a servant. For each of the natures retains its proper character without defect ; and as the form of God does not take away the form of a servant, so the form of a servant does not impair the form of God.[1]

C. 4. For the selfsame who is very God, is also very Man ;

[1] Proinde qui manens in forma Dei fecit hominem, idem in forma servi factus est homo. Tenet enim sine defectu proprietatem suam utraque natura : et sicut formam servi Dei forma non adimit, ita formam Dei servi forma non minuit.

and there is no illusion in this union, while the lowliness of man and the loftiness of God meet together. . . . For, as we must often be saying, he is one and the same, truly Son of God, and truly Son of Man.[1]

(2) In the One Person are found Two Natures without confusion and without division.

C. 3. Accordingly, while the distinctness of both natures and substances was preserved, and both met in one Person, lowliness was assumed by majesty, weakness by power, mortality by eternity; and, in order to pay the debt of our condition, the inviolable nature was united to the passible, so that, as the appropriate remedy for our ills, one and the same 'Mediator between God and man, the Man Christ Jesus,' might from one element be capable of dying and also from the other be incapable. Therefore in the entire and perfect nature of very man was born very God, whole in what was His, whole in what was ours.[2]

(3) In spite of the distinctness of the Two Natures, their union in one Person makes it possible to predicate the properties of each nature as belonging to the one Person, and in this sense Leo teaches the doctrine of the Communicatio Idiomatum. Not that there is an actual interpenetration of the Two Natures, resulting in such a confusion or mixture between them as to make it a matter of indifference whether the human properties are predicated of the Divine nature, or the Divine attributed to the human, but

---

[1] Qui enim verus est Deus, idem verus est homo : et nullum est in hac unitate mendacium, dum invicem sunt et humilitas hominis et altitudo Deitatis. . . . Unus enim idemque est, quod saepe dicendum est, vere Dei filius, et vere hominis filius.

[2] Salva igitur proprietate utriusque naturae et substantiae, et in unam coeunte personam, suscepta est a majestate humilitas, a virtute infirmitas, ab aeternitate mortalitas : et ad resolvendum conditionis nostrae debitum, natura inviolabilis naturae est unita passibili : ut, quod nostris remediis congruebat, unus atque idem mediator Dei et hominum, homo Jesus Christus, et mori posset ex uno, et mori non posset ex altero. In integra ergo veri hominis perfectaque natura verus natus est Deus, totus in suis, totus in nostris.

simply the fact that the Divine Subject of both natures being one and the same, His experiences, whether in His Divine or in His human natures, may be predicated of the same Subject, i.e., Himself.

C. 4. For as ' God ' is not changed by the compassion, so ' Man ' is not consumed by the dignity. For each ' form ' does the acts which belong to it, in communion with the other ; the Word, that is, performing what belongs to the Word, and the flesh carrying out what belongs to the flesh ; the one of these shines out in miracles, the other succumbs to injuries. And as the Word does not withdraw from equality with the Father in glory, so the flesh does not abandon the nature of our kind.[1]

Leo is clear that the Communicatio Idiomatum is not a refined form of Monophysitism.

Compare also the following passages which illustrate the doctrine :—

C. 4, 5. As then—to pass by many points—it does not belong to the same nature to weep with feelings of pity over a dead friend and, after the mass of stone had been removed from the grave where he had lain four days, by a voice of command to raise him up to life again ; or to hang on the wood, and to make all the elements tremble after daylight had been turned into night ; or to be transfixed with nails, and to open the gates of paradise to the faith of the robber ; so it does not belong to the same nature to say, ' I and the Father are one,' and to say, ' The Father is greater than I.' For although in the Lord Jesus Christ there is one Person of God and man, yet that whereby contumely attaches to both is one thing, and that whereby glory attaches to both is another ; for from what belongs to us He has that manhood which is inferior to the Father ;

---

[1] Sicut enim Deus non mutatur miseratione, ita homo non consumitur dignitate. Agit enim utraque forma cum alterius communione quod proprium est ; Verbo scilicet operante quod Verbi est, et carne exequente quod carnis est. Unum horum coruscat miraculis, aliud succumbit injuriis. Et sicut Verbum ab aequalitate paternae gloriae non recedit, ita caro naturam nostri generis non relinquit.

while from the Father He has equal Godhead with the Father. Accordingly, on account of this Unity of Person which is to be understood as existing in both the natures, we read, on the one hand, that ' the Son of Man came down from Heaven,' inasmuch as the Son of God took flesh from that Virgin of whom He was born; and on the other hand, the Son of God is said to have been crucified and buried, inasmuch as He underwent this, not in his actual Godhead, wherein the Only-begotten is co-eternal and consubstantial with the Father, but in the weakness of human nature.   Wherefore we all, in the very Creed, confess that ' the Only-begotten Son of God was crucified and buried,' according to that saying of the Apostle, ' for if they had known it, they would not have crucified the Lord of Majesty.'

The important points for us to notice are these :—

(1) The clear absence of speculation as to the mode and manner of the union between the Two Natures. Leo is quite content to state the two sides of the problem involved in the Incarnation, and this he does with clearness and precision, but with no attempt to grapple with the contradiction involved in the duality of Natures united in the Unity of the One Person.

This is exactly the attitude adopted in the Chalcedonian Definition.

(2) He insists upon the reality, integrity, and permanence of Christ's manhood after the union. He is quite clear that our human nature was not impaired by its union with the Divine in the Person of Christ.   Herein lies the real value of Leo's ' Tome,' and it is the incorporation of this great truth into the Chalcedonian Definition which, as we have seen, gives to the latter its permanent and abiding value. Herein the element of truth enshrined in the Antiochene theology gains permanent recognition and is securely incorporated into Catholic teaching.

Sicut enim Deus non mutatur miseratione, ita homo non consumitur dignitate. . . . Et sicut Verbum ab aequalitate paternae gloriae non recedit, ita caro naturam nostri generis non relinquit.

It was Leo's clear grip upon the redemptive work of Christ which makes him emphasise so strongly the reality and integrity of both natures, and he is quite clear that the ' forma servi ' did not detract from the ' forma dei.' The condescension of God, the Logos, did not impair or change either His Nature or the nature which He assumed.

As Redeemer of weak and fallen man He must be the all-powerful and fully Divine Saviour, Totus in suis.

As Redeemer He must be equally and wholly one with those whom He came to redeem, Totus in nostris.

For [as Leo says] we could not have overcome the author of sin and death, unless He who could neither be contaminated by sin, nor detained by death, had taken upon Himself our nature, and made it His own. . . . [Compare also the passage C. 3, quoted on p. 45.]

This shows how entirely from the Soteriological standpoint Leo approaches the problem of the Person of Christ, and in this he is at one not only with the practical side of Western theology but also with the best side of Alexandrian theology as exhibited in the writings of Athanasius.

(3) Leo's doctrine of the ' Communicatio Idiomatum ' is the most questionable part of his theology as found in this letter, because by it he preserves so rigid a distinction between the two natures as seriously to imperil the reality of their true union.

We postpone our consideration of this point until

49   E

we have examined Cyril's theology, with which we must now deal.

II. *The Second Letter of Cyril to Nestorius.*—Here in this letter we have Cyril's Christology, as this commended itself to the mind of those who framed the Chalcedonian Definition. Its authoritative character as a standard of orthodoxy is further enhanced when we remember that, before its acceptance by the Council of Chalcedon, it had been approved by a Council of the Egyptian Churches held at Alexandria, by another Council held at Rome, and by the Council of Ephesus at which it was publicly read and formally accepted.[1]

In this letter Cyril outlines the doctrine of the Incarnation, with special reference to the Nestorian danger, and in doing so he gives us a very clear and distinct statement of the chief points of his own Christology. For the chief passages of the letter, see Appendix B, p. 98.

(1) This Christology is in line with that of Athanasius and the Cappadocian Fathers. Cyril's starting-point is that of the Alexandrian School who approach the Incarnation from the Divine side. The infinite pity and condescension of God results in the Eternal Divine Logos, begotten of the Father before all worlds, becoming Man. ' The Word was made flesh.' The Incarnation is an exhibition of Divine Power for redemptive purposes.

(2) The resultant Incarnation is an assumption by the Logos of our manhood in its entirety. For us men and for our salvation He personally unites to Himself manhood, and by so doing undergoes no change in His inmost essence but remains what He

---

[1] Labbe, *Council. Ephes.* iii. 462–492.

ever was before.   The Incarnation makes Him
ὁ Λόγος σαρκωθείς.

(3) Cyril, in accordance with the Alexandrian
line of thought, escapes the Nestorian difficulty by
teaching that the Logos assumed not the person of
a man whom He took into union with Himself, but
manhood in its completeness and integrity, including
the rational soul and its powers, which He makes
His own.   The whole point of his Anti-Nestorian
teaching is one Christ and He Divine.   The humanity
is incorporated into His Person, appropriated by
Him and united with His own substance or φύσις.
The Incarnation was a condescension of God, not
the exaltation of a man into union with the Logos.
This condescension found its expression in the
appropriation by the Logos of all that constitutes
manhood and its incorporation within the unity of
His own Person.

(4) This union baffles analysis. One of the
strongest points in Cyril's Christology is his clear
recognition of the fact that the manner of the Incarnation is a mystery baffling human comprehension,
and therefore never to be fully explained in terms of
human thought.   ' The Word, having in an ineffable
and inconceivable manner personally united to Himself flesh instinct with a living soul, became Man and
was called the Son of Man.'

(5) Though the union baffles analysis Cyril is
clear that it resulted in no confusion of substance,
and equally clear that the manhood continued to
retain its integrity.   Cyril was saved from Monophysitism by his firm grip upon the thought of the
essential difference between the Two Natures in the
one Person.   ' While the natures which were brought

51

into this union were diverse,' he says, ' there was of
both one Christ and one Son : not as though the
diverseness of the natures were done away by this
union, but rather that the Godhead and manhood
completed for us the one Lord and Christ and Son by
their unutterable and unspeakable concurrence and
unity.' The very clearness with which Cyril held this
diverseness between the Two Natures made the resultant union, in his view, all the more wonderful and
staggering to human thought.

(6) Cyril escapes Monophysitism by his insistence
upon the completeness and integrity of Christ's
manhood after the union ; but if it be asked how in
doing this he escapes the opposite error of Nestorianism, the answer must be sought in his conception of
the unity and continuity of the One Logos in His pre-
Incarnate and Incarnate state. A consequence of
great significance follows from this conception. In
some sense or other for Cyril the manhood of Christ
received its personality from the Logos Who assumed
it, since He was the personal subject of the God-Man.
Clearly for Cyril the manhood never had an independent hypostasis or personality of its own.   If the union
of the Two Natures was hypostatic, ἕνωσις καθ᾽ ὑπόστασιν,
a union in a person, the one Person Who thus formed
the subject of the God-Man was the Logos.   The manhood which He assumed became personal only by His
assumption of it.   It received its subsistence from Him.

Apparently Cyril only succeeds in avoiding the
Nestorian conclusion by holding in some form the
doctrine of the impersonality of Christ's manhood.
This is a point to which we shall return again.

(7) In what sense does Cyril hold the doctrine
of the Communicatio Idiomatum ?

52

If we compare his treatment in this letter with that of Leo in the ' Tome,' we can find no essential difference between the two. Both draw a rigid distinction between the Two Natures, and maintain that the Logos underwent no change in His essential attributes when He became Man. This view they held in common with Origen and Athanasius before them. Whatever form of κένωσις Cyril held, it certainly did not include the thought of the abandonment on the part of the Logos of any essential part of His Divine Nature. When He lowered Himself to a condition of self-renunciation (καθεὶς ἑαυτὸν εἰς κένωσιν) He did not put away from Him or lose what He was. Both for Leo and for Cyril it is the unlimited Logos Who is the centre of the God-Man. It follows that, in the Incarnate Christ, His Divine Nature, having undergone no change, is incapable of suffering, and remains unchangeable and unalterable through all the experiences He undergoes in His Incarnate life. Consequently, although these experiences may be predicated of Him as being the subject of both Natures, and in virtue of the fact that they are the experiences of the One Person, nevertheless in reality they were the experiences of His human and not of His Divine Nature. This is all apparently that both Leo and Cyril mean to imply in those passages in the ' Tome ' and the second letter from which the doctrine of the 'Communicatio Idiomatum' is derived. The properties of the one Nature may be predicated of the other, *not* because the Divine was capable of experiencing the human, nor because there was in any sense so close an interpenetration between the two as to render their distinction of no value, but in virtue of

53

the fact that the One Person is the subject of both
natures. Thus stated, the doctrine of the 'Communicatio Idiomatum' seems to be a question merely
of phraseology, and a convenient method of con-
cealing a radical dualism which really underlies the
teaching of both Cyril and Leo. Indeed it becomes
doubtful whether Cyril, even with his doctrine of the
hypostatic union, was very much more successful
than Nestorius in achieving a real union between
the Two Natures, such as Catholic thought was
seeking. Whilst undoubtedly the ἔνωσις καθ᾽ ὑπόστασιν
secured an infinitely more vital and indissoluble
union than any mere σχετικὴ συνάφεια or ἐνοίκησις κατ᾽
εὐδοκίαν, yet at the same time it is open to question
whether Cyril ever really succeeded in securing such
a unity of person as Catholic thought demanded.

(8) This conclusion is forced upon us when we
come to examine the underlying presuppositions of a
philosophic character which form the basis of Cyril's
Christology.

We have seen that Cyril is saved from Monophysitism by his rigid distinction between the Two Natures.
In his view Godhead and manhood are diverse, and
their union therefore in the Incarnate Christ does not
extinguish their diverseness. From this standpoint
Cyril is led to his doctrine of the 'Communicatio
Idiomatum.' The basis of this doctrine is evidently
a dualism, which in Leo's 'Tome' and in Cyril's
letters, seems to be skilfully concealed by a literary
style and an aptness of phraseology which enables
them both to present an apparently sound Christology.

It is true that such a dualism is essential in the
interests of Catholic theology as against the Monophysite tendency, but what is the basis of it in

Cyril's Christology ?   The answer is his doctrine of
the impassibility of the Divine Logos.   The effort to
maintain this doctrine leads Cyril into all kinds of
difficulties and even contradictions ;   it vitiates his
whole Christology ;   it seriously endangers that unity
of Person in the God-Man for which he had so strenuously fought against Nestorianism.

What then is the philosophic basis of this doctrine
of the impassibility of the Divine Logos ?   Surely
the Platonic doctrine of the absolute rather than the
Christian doctrine of God.   To be invisible, increate,
immortal, belongs to the Divine essence ;   these are
attributes which differentiate the Divine from the
human.   Is the attribute of impassibility to be included in this catalogue ?   So long as God is thought
of exclusively within the categories supplied by an
abstract deistic monotheism, so long will the gulf
between the human and the Divine, the creature and
the Creator, the finite and the Infinite, the relative
and the Absolute, remain unbridged, and the doctrine
of the impassibility of God render an Incarnation
inconceivable.   But the Incarnation itself forced men
to widen and to deepen their conception of the being
and nature of God as well as that of man.   The
prevailing idea of God such as Cyril held when he
spoke of an ἄνισος, ἀνόμοιος, ἑτέρα φύσις of God and
man,[1] had to undergo a transformation as the result
of the revelation in Christ.   This transformation
was accelerated by the Arian controversy, which
itself helped theologians to grip more firmly the
doctrine of the Trinity and thus led them to a truer
conception of God.   But the influence of the Platonic
philosophy was very powerful even upon theologians

[1] Dorner, *Person of Christ*, Div. II. vol. i. p. 65.

whose belief in the Incarnation should have emancipated them from it. The Alexandrian School especially was so influenced, and to this cause possibly may be traced the defects in Cyril's Christology. So long as men clung to an Ante-Christian conception of God, emphasising His physical attributes ; so long would they dwell upon His unlikeness to man and tend to widen the gulf between the Creator and His creatures. Thus they would be liable to miss the significance of that fuller revelation of the Divine and human natures in their affinity and likeness which the Incarnation was meant to teach. Moreover a deeper comprehension of the Incarnation with its revelation of love as the very being and essence of God would challenge the doctrine of His impassibility. Yet it is curious to notice with what insistence men clung to this doctrine as containing one of the essential marks which differentiated the Divine from the human, and no modification of it was acceptable. When the Patripassians, for example, having emancipated themselves from the more rigid Platonic conceptions of the Deity, dared to attribute change and suffering to the Godhead, Catholic theologians shrank from the consequences of a doctrine which so transformed the prevalent ideas of the Deity and seemed so derogatory to Him. Again, in the later Arian controversy, the defenders of the full Divinity of the God-Man considered their task accomplished when they had demonstrated the immutability and impassibility of the Logos. In their view, His possession of these attributes proved conclusively His oneness with the essence of the Deity and His distinction from all created things. Possibly it was this very fear of Arianism which led men like Cyril to uphold, at whatever cost, the impassibility of the Logos in His Divine Nature, and consequently to assign to His human nature the hunger, the thirst, the suffering, the dying : in short all those creaturely vicissitudes so characteristic of a distinctively human, so seemingly derogatory to a distinctively Divine, experience. Nevertheless the Patripassians, however defective their theories from another point of view, came very near to one great truth the Incarnation was meant to teach, viz. that in Christ, God did enter into so intimate a fellowship with our human nature as to share the distress of our finitude and the sufferings which fall to the lot of our creaturely existence.

In this sense the revelation of God in Christ was for ever a refutation of His ' impassibility,' since it was a revelation of Love Himself Incarnate.

Cyril's difficulties arose from his unethical conception of God. Although he regards the Incarnation as a movement of Divine pity which found its expression in a redemptive act, yet he fails to realise fully all the consequences which follow from this revelation through Christ of the very essence of God as Love. Love is an ethical attribute, not a physical, and the Incarnation was the advent of Love Himself. Such a conception of the inmost being of the Logos, as Love Incarnate, precludes the rigid application of the attribute of impassibility to Him in His Incarnate state. God is in His Nature impassible, but He is Love and therefore capable of suffering.

Tertullian clearly perceived in his controversy with Praxeas that if God is capable of sympathy, He is capable of suffering ; if He is Love, He can suffer. This is the very heart of the mystery of Calvary : Love Himself crucified, Love Himself suffering. If

the Incarnation revealed God as Love Incarnate,
and capable therefore of suffering, the Cross revealed
the extent to which He did suffer ; the measure of
His suffering being the measure of His love, and
the measure of His love being the measure of His
suffering.

Once full weight is given to the revelation in
Christ of God not only as possessing the ethical
attribute of love, but as being in His very essence
Love Himself, the *a priori* theory of His impassibility
fades into insignificance before the tremendous historical fact of Love Himself crucified, a revelation in
time and space of an eternal truth.

The Cyrillian theology, which presents us with
the picture of an impassible and immutable Logos
clothing Himself with our humanity, incorporating
into the unity of His Person our manhood in its
distinctness and completeness, and yet withal remaining untouched in His inmost being by the sufferings of the flesh which He had assumed, and at the
most, sympathising with those human experiences
He Himself was incapable of feeling, not only gives
to the whole life and experience of the God-Man a
refined docetic unreality, but fails to do justice to
the height and depth both of the Being of God and
the nature of humanity, of which the Incarnation
itself was at once the revelation and the proof.

The infinite condescension of God in the Incarnation is revealed in that very self-limitation whereby
He consented to experience a truly human life with
all its limitations, and so utterly to identify Himself
with man as to become in all points like as we are,
sin excepted. But such a condescension were to no
purpose if the gulf between the human and the

Divine precluded the possibility of the Logos ever
in His inmost nature being touched with the feeling
of our infirmities.

Here is the root difficulty of Cyril's Christology.
He thinks too exclusively of the Divine Nature in
terms of a Platonic rather than a Christian philosophy.
He defines the Being of God in metaphysical rather
than in ethical terms, dwelling upon those attributes
which differentiate God from man, rather than upon
the revelation in Christ of God's very essence, Love,
which alone made an Incarnation possible and
which alone can bridge the gulf between the Creator
and the creature. Love itself is in its very essence
a creative act; and Love Himself, in His creation
of man, made a being to that extent not unlike, but
like Himself, and, therefore, capable of becoming a
partaker of the Divine Nature. The Incarnation
itself was a revelation of this fact and proved the
possibility of its being accomplished. This indeed
was a revelation of an essential affinity between the
Divine and the human, and showed that the gulf
between them could be bridged, and in fact was
bridged, when the Divine and the human were
united in the person of the One Christ. The possibility of such a union could only be found in the fact
that not only was man made in the image of God,
but that there was in God a human element. The
possibility, therefore, of a real Incarnation was to be
sought, not in an over-emphasis upon certain physical
attributes possessed by God which differentiate Him
from man, but in the fact that He was Love Himself, and therefore related to man by a community of
essence, since man himself was the result of a creative
act on the part of God. A real basis for a sound

Christology will be found only in a full recognition of the very nature of God as Love, and a full recognition of the very nature of man as created in His Image. If the Chalcedonian Definition places manhood and Godhead in a real and vital union, theologians are left to explain the conditions under which such a union is possible or even conceivable. The problem resolves itself into one of a deeper comprehension of both factors, the human in its essential nature and the Divine. Cyril's Christology fails because his analysis of the latter does not do full justice to the Nature of God as in His very essence Love.

III. *The Letter of Cyril to John of Antioch.*—This document is interesting as embodying the Creed of Union (A.D. 433) which formed the basis of the reconciliation effected between the Alexandrian and Antiochene Schools in the persons of Cyril and John of Antioch respectively.

This Union Creed is quoted in full in the letter and contains the element of truth for which both schools were contending. The Alexandrian position is vindicated in the use of the term θεοτόκος and in the phrase δύο γὰρ φύσεων ἔνωσις γέγονε, the word συνάφεια being rejected.

The Antiochene position, however, is safeguarded in spite of these admissions by the fact that the distinctness of the manhood and the Godhead in the One Person is explicitly dwelt upon.

We confess, therefore, our Lord Jesus Christ, the Only-begotten Son of God, perfect God and perfect Man, of a reasonable soul and flesh consisting; begotten before the ages of the Father according to His Divinity, and in the last days, for us and for our salvation, of Mary the Virgin,

60

according to His humanity, of the same substance with His Father, according to His Divinity, and of the same substance with us according to His humanity; for there became a union of two natures.   Wherefore we confess one Christ, one Son, one Lord.

According to this understanding of this unmixed union, we confess the holy Virgin to be Mother of God; because God the Word was incarnate and became Man, and from this conception He united the temple taken from her with Himself.

However strong a Monophysite tendency may be discoverable in Cyril's Christology, this letter shows us that he himself strove hard to convince his opponents not only that he upheld the integrity of Christ's manhood and was not an Apollinarian, but that he denied that there was a crasis, or mingling or mixture between God the Word and flesh.   And the reason he gives for this repudiation of the Monophysite error is his belief in the immutability and impassibility of the Logos.

For He remains that which He always was, and has not been changed, nor is He capable of change.   For we all confess, in addition to this, that the Word of God is impassible, even though when He dispenses most wisely this mystery, He appears to ascribe to Himself the sufferings endured in His own flesh. . . . In order that He should be believed to be the Saviour of all, by an economic appropriation to Himself, as just said, He assumed the sufferings of His own Flesh.

The contents of this letter confirm the impression of Cyril's Christology which we have formed from an examination of his previous letter to Nestorius.

Our examination of the Synodical letters gives us the following results.

(1) In Leo's ' Tome ' we find a typical example of the spirit of ecclesiastical orthodoxy.   Leo is content simply with preserving the traditional faith which in

the Chalcedonian Definition is expressed in a series
of antithetical statements admirably adapted to
maintain the balance of religious truth.   We find an
entire absence of that speculative spirit so characteristic of Eastern theologians, and we look in vain to
Leo's ' Tome ' for any ' theory ' of a helpful character
in our endeavour to penetrate deeper into the mystery
of the Incarnation.   Leo succeeds in preserving the
balance of religious truth but does not contribute to
its advancement.   If we ask what positive contribution he makes, we find it in his conservation of the
truth of Christ's manhood ; a truth for which the
Antiochene School had strenuously fought and to
which Leo's ' Tome ' does full justice.

(2) In Cyril's second letter, which we have taken
as embodying in outline his Christological position,
we find a clear recognition of the unity of Christ's
Person, but the doctrine of the ' impassibility ' of the
Logos prevents him from securing a unity deep enough
to satisfy all the requirements of the New Testament
portrait of the God-Man.   If anything Cyril secures
the unity of Christ's Person at the expense of His
humanity, in this sense, that he scarcely does full
justice to the Antiochene endeavour to secure for the
human factor a relative independence.   Cyril, instead
of conceding to the manhood of Christ a relative
independence and an existence of its own, regards
Christ's humanity rather as a congeries of attributes
appropriated by the Logos and incorporated into His
φύσις, or substance.   The result for Cyril is μία φύσις
τοῦ Λόγου σεσαρκωμένη, a formula which was not intended by him to teach a ' confusion ' or ' mixture '
of the substances, but which, nevertheless, at least
meant that ' the manhood of Christ ' was in some

sense or other ' impersonal.' The strength of Cyril's Christology lies in his refutation of the Nestorian error. But looking at his second letter with a view to gaining from it any theory of a helpful character in the elucidation of the problem which the Chalcedonian Definition states but does not solve, we must confess that Cyril fails us, and the reason for this failure lies in his philosophical presuppositions concerning the Nature of God which prevent him from entering more fully into the real meaning of the Incarnation.

(3) We have examined the Synodical letters in some detail with a view to discovering what light they shed upon the Chalcedonian Definition, and whether they reflect for us the lines upon which the Church would have interpreted that formula. The Chalcedonian Definition was the work of men who were powerfully influenced by the writings of Cyril and Leo, and who shared to a large extent the views reflected therein. The result of our enquiry has revealed at once the strength and the weakness of both Western and Cyrillian theology. It is legitimate therefore to question whether the Council of Chalcedon, in accepting the Synodical letters, thereby set the seal of its authority as an Ecumenical Council upon the letters in their entirety, or upon those distinctive points in each which the Council felt to be in accordance with Catholic tradition and New Testament teaching. Was Cyril's letter accepted because of the tremendous truth so forcibly demonstrated therein of the unity of Christ's Person ? Was Leo's ' Tome ' accepted because of its splendid vindication of the completeness and permanence of Christ's manhood ? If these were the points which won for

the Synodical letters their authoritative status, it follows that the Council did not thereby bind itself to the acceptance of other features in the letters, and especially the doctrine of the ' Communicatio Idiomatum.' To this extent we are not bound to accept the latter as the authoritative teaching of the Church, even though it is found in letters to which the Church in Council has set its seal.

Cyril himself, in accepting the Union Creed which is contained in one of these letters (to John of Antioch), did not bind himself thereby to any stronger statement than is contained in the closing paragraphs of that Creed where it is said :—

And as to the expressions concerning the Lord in the Gospels and Epistles, we are aware that divines understand some as common, as relating to one Person, and others distinguish, as relating to two natures, explaining those that befit the Divine nature in reference to the Godhead of Christ, and those of a humble sort in reference to His manhood.

This shows us (1) that there was a division of opinion amongst divines as to which particular usage they should employ. (2) The question was one really of phraseology. (3) The assertion that some of the passages in the Gospels and Epistles referred to the Divine Nature, and others to the human nature, was not a denial that in the case of both sets of passages the reference was to the actions and experiences of the One Christ.

At the most therefore the Council, by its acceptance of the Synodical letters, cannot be charged with having committed itself to more than these three points. And if Cyril and Leo by this usage introduce a doctrine of Communicatio Idiomatum which is subversive of the unity of Christ's Person, the Council can scarcely be charged with endorsing their error when it recognises the usages to which the error owes its origin.

We conclude then that even if the Council is held to have bound itself to the doctrine of the ' Communicatio Idiomatum,' which is at least open to question, it can only be in the sense that it countenances a usage of phraseology current among some divines, and is not thereby committed to an acceptance of the dualism, which, as we have tried to show, really underlies this usage in the minds of some who employed it.

7.

MONOPHYSITISM

IF the West, with its love for ecclesiastical orthodoxy, was content to leave the problem at the
point to which the Chalcedonian Definition had
carried it, the speculative spirit of Eastern theologians
urged them to further effort in their endeavours to
unravel the mystery.

A reaction set in after Chalcedon, parallel in some
respects to that which had followed the Nicene Council.
A work corresponding to that which the Cappadocian
Fathers did for the Nicene theology was needed to
commend the Chalcedonian Definition and to win for
it full acceptance.

Monophysitism persisted and made headway
amongst Eastern theologians; but, as we have seen,
this was not the true line of development for Alexandrian Christology. The real value of the Monophysite and Monothelite controversies lies in the fact that
they forced Church teachers to make more explicit
exactly how much was contained in that complete
manhood which the Logos assumed. Cyril had
clearly shown that Nestorianism excluded a real
Incarnation. His own Christology had found room
for the retention within the unity of Christ's Person
of a complete manhood; but he had failed to show
how this was consistent with his further fundamental
postulate that the centre of personality in the God-
Man was the unlimited Divine Logos unchanged by
His Incarnation. If, as Cyril maintained, the man-

66

hood remained after the union in its completeness and integrity, what had become of *its* personality ? He failed to define how this manhood could still remain in its completeness and integrity when it had as its subject the Divine Logos.

The question still to be settled then was this : what constitutes a complete manhood ? What is the minimum which it must retain if it is still to be called complete ? If the Logos had become the Ego of the manhood, in what sense could the manhood be said to have retained all its parts ?

The Church was clear that Monophysitism offered no true solution. The manhood must be preserved in its integrity in the interests of a true Soteriology. But did this involve a dual personality ? Cyril had successfully contended against this supposition and refuted Nestorianism. But at what cost ? For him, in some sense, the manhood was impersonal. In what sense ? If pressed he would have preferred to speak of the Divine personality of Christ rather than of His impersonality *quâ* man. Even if by this means he escaped the Nestorian dual personality, the question still remained to define more clearly exactly how much the manhood retained, and the extent of its relative independence within the unity of the One Person.

Was there a dual will ? Was there one energy or operation of Christ's will or two ? All these questions arise in any attempt to harmonise the duality of natures with the unity of person. The Monophysite and Monothelite controversies drove the Church to face the question which Cyril had not fully answered, namely : *How the human nature of Christ could retain its identity and integrity as*

67

completely human, when its centre of personality was the Divine Logos, and when its very subsistence was dependent upon Him and it had no independent subsistence apart from Him. How could it then in any true sense be termed complete ? The doctrine of the impersonality of Christ's manhood had to be defined and elaborated in a much more satisfactory way than Cyril had attempted if the truth for which the Antiochene school had contended was not after all to be lost in favour of a Monophysite solution.

(1) How did the Church defend Cyril's Christology from the charge of Monophysitism ? (2) How did she commend Leo's ' Tome ' and the Chalcedonian Definition to Catholic thought in spite of their apparent dualism ?

The answer lies in a study of the theology of Leontius of Byzantium, whose importance in the history of Christological thought cannot be overemphasised.

8.

THE THEOLOGY OF LEONTIUS OF BYZANTIUM

I

THE Life and Work of Leontius.—Little, if anything, is known for certain of Leontius, but the researches of Dr. Loofs in recent times have thrown some helpful light upon his life and work. His date may be approximately fixed *c.* 485–543 (Harnack). He appears to have been born at Byzantium, of noble parentage, and he himself tells us that in Scythia he came under Nestorian influence, from which he succeeded in emancipating himself, and thenceforth he became an ardent defender of the Chalcedonian theology. Other details of his life of a more or less authentic character may be added.

He is said to have been at Constantinople and Rome in 519 in the company of Scythian monks, and to have retired later to the monastery of St. Saba in the vicinity of Jerusalem. He took part in a conference arranged by Justinian at Constantinople between the Catholics and Severians in 531, and he appears to have made more than one journey from his cloister to the capital, which may explain the titles by which he is designated—Monachus Hierosolymitanus and Monachus Byzantinus. He is, however, frequently confused with others of the same name, and the genuineness of the works ascribed to him is in many cases doubtful.

69

But happily for our present purpose we are only concerned with two of these,[1] both of which are accepted as genuine by most scholars.

The first of these two treatises alone would secure for Leontius a very high place as a clever and acute theologian, and by itself, apart from other treatises, justifies the encomium of Cardinal Mai, who first edited his works and declared him to be 'in theologica scientia aevo suo facile princeps.'[2]

Leontius earned for himself the title of Scholasticus, the first 'schoolman,' because he was the first to introduce Aristotelianism into theology as an aid in the reconciliation of the Chalcedonian theology with Greek religious feeling.

In the course of the transition from the fifth to the sixth century [says Harnack], Aristotelianism once more became the fashion in science. This revolution helped to bring about the naturalisation of the Chalcedonian Creed in the Church, or what amounts to the same thing, contributed towards reconciling Greek religious feeling to it. Leontius was helped to accommodate himself as a theologian of the school of Cyril to the Chalcedonian Creed by the Aristotelian conceptual distinctions, and therefore by scholasticism. Leontius was the first scholastic. In his works we have an exposition of doctrine based on philosophical conceptions. He treated of substance, genus, species, individual being, of the attributes which constitute the substance, of inseparable accidents and of separable accidents.

What then is the distinctive contribution of Leontius to the elucidation of the Christological problem ?

We find it in his doctrine of *the Enhypostasia.*

It is in his writings that we first meet with the

---

[1] 1. *Tres libri adversus Nestorianos et Eutychianos,* Migne, P. G., 86, i. 1267-1396.   2. *Adversus Argumenta Severi,* Migne, P. G., 86, ii. 1915-1945.   [2] Bardenhewer, *Patrology,* p. 546.

term ἐνυπόστατος as applied to the human nature
of Christ, which he regards as neither ὑπόστασις
nor ἀνυπόστατος but ἐνυπόστατος,[1] i.e. ἐν τῷ λόγῳ
ὑποστᾶσα.[2] As we have seen, the outstanding difficulty all through these controversies was the inability to conceive of 'nature' apart from 'personality,' and this led to one or other of two errors
according as the hypothesis was, as in Nestorianism, δύο ὑποστάσεις, or, as in Eutychianism, μία φύσις.
Both these hypotheses were designed to get over the
same difficulty. Two Natures, therefore Two Persons,
was the Nestorian error. The negation of One
Nature, so as to avoid Two Persons, was the
Eutychian error. Leontius endeavoured to escape
the Nestorian error and the Eutychian error in the
following way : he agrees with the Monophysites
that there can be no such thing as a φύσις
ἀνυπόστατος,[3] which seemed to be suggested by the
Cyrillian doctrine of the impersonality of Christ's
manhood. At the same time he escaped the Nestorian conclusion that the manhood of Christ had a
distinct personality of its own by postulating a φύσις
ἐνυπόστατος, i.e. a nature which receives its hypostasis from another, or which has its hypostasis in
another. τὸ δὲ ἐνυπόστατον, τὸ μὴ εἶναι αὐτὸ συμβεβηκὸς
δηλοῖ, ὃ ἐν ἑτέρῳ ἔχει τὸ εἶναι, καὶ οὐκ ἐν ἑαυτῷ θεωρεῖται.[4]

II. *His Doctrine considered in its Relation to the
Aristotelian Terminology he Employed.*—Leontius was
desirous of reproducing and reinterpreting the
thoughts of the Fathers for the men of his own generation. For this purpose he employed the best philosophical system he knew as an aid in defending the

[1] *Adv. N. et E.* i. 1277 D.   [2] *Adv. Sev.* ii. 1944 C.
[3] i. 1280 A.   [4] i. 1277 D.

71

Chalcedonian Definition. He was evidently well acquainted with Porphyry's classification of the predicables—genus, species, differentia, proprium, accidens—and with the Aristotelian Linea Predicamentalis. It may be objected that the doctrine of the Enhypostasia stands or falls with the validity or otherwise of the Aristotelian categories which he employs to illustrate it. But we hope to show that his doctrine is entirely independent of the Aristotelian setting in which it is found, and can be restated as an idea in terms of modern thought stript of all the Aristotelian terminology which Leontius himself used in his elaborate treatise against the Nestorians and Monophysites. It is true that in this work he treats at length of οὐσία, γένος, εἶδος, εἰδοποιοὶ διαφοραί, ποιότητες οὐσιώδεις, and it is more than probable that in his treatment of the relationship between φύσις or οὐσία and ὑπόστασις, he had in mind Aristotle's division of substances into primary (πρῶται) and secondary (δεύτεραι). In the 'Categories' (C. 5), Aristotle thus defines these two :

Substance which is properly, primarily, and especially so called, is that which is neither a predicate of a subject nor inherent in a subject : for example, a particular man, or a particular horse. Secondary substances so called are the species ; for example, a particular man is in a species, man, the genus of which is animal : these then are called secondary substances, man and animal.'

And in the same chapter Aristotle lays down his fundamental postulate that ' without primary substances it is impossible for anything to be.' If Leontius accepted Aristotle's Realism and this philosophy of substantial things in contrast to the Platonic doctrine of universal forms (εἴδη), we can understand how he would readily agree with the Monophysites that there can be no such thing as a φύσις ἀνυπόστατος. Zeller, in his masterly treatise on *Aristotle and the Earlier Peripatetics*, has shown that the central point about which revolves the whole Aristotelian attack on Plato's metaphysics lies in just this insistence that what is essential and in the last resort actual, is not the universal ideas but the individual things.   Plato considered that it is only the Universal, as such, which can be actual, and that it must exist for itself as something substantial beyond phenomena. In opposition to this Platonic Idealism Aristotle formulated his philosophy of individual substances. He attacks Plato's Ideal theory on the ground that ' Substance cannot be separate from that whereof it is the Substance, nor Genus from that which (as forming part of the Essence) it belongs.   This proposition, in fact, summarises the whole difference between the Platonic and Aristotelian systems.' [1]

A follower of Aristotle therefore, having his treatment of the κοινὸν in view, would naturally refuse to consider an abstraction like φύσις ἀνυπόστατος, and insist that it is only conceivable in a concrete shape and form as the nature of an individual person in which it subsists.   The doctrine of the impersonality of Christ's manhood, which was involved in the Cyrillian Christology, was open to attack upon these lines, and Leontius recognised the difficulty.   But he was not bound therefore to accept the Nestorian alternative.   There was in the Aristotelian system, as expounded in the treatise on the 'Categories,' a philosophical conception of which Leontius thought he might make use to illustrate his theory of the Enhypostasia, and which might commend it to his

[1] Zeller, *op. cit.* vol. i. p. 316 ff.

opponents.   Aristotle, in spite of his insistence upon
the reality of individual substances, admitted, in
deference to Plato's teaching, that genera and species
might be called ' substances ' in a derivative sense
as 'secondary substances' (δεύτεραι, in contrast to
πρῶται οὐσίαι).¹ These ' secondary substances ' were
a kind of half-way house between Substance and
Accident.   As Zeller says :

> The so-called secondary substance of Aristotle cannot
> be treated as exactly identical with quality, but neither can
> it properly be considered substance.   It denotes substance
> on the side of its qualities only.   For it is the combination
> of the essential properties of a definite class of substances.
> (*Cat.* c. 5, 3, *b*, 18.)   In contrast with it, it is the individual
> substances alone which are of that self-sufficient and inde-
> pendently subsisting nature to which the name of substance,
> in its original sense, belongs.'—*Op. cit.* pp. 333–4.

Now Dr. Loofs has examined the doctrine of the
Enhypostasia very carefully in connection with the
Aristotelian terminology, and he shows what use
Leontius made of this ' secondary substance ' of
Aristotle.   He points out that Leontius regards the
πᾶσαι αἱ ποιότητες, αἵ τε οὐσιώδεις καὶ ἐπουσιώδεις καλούμεναι
as equivalent to ἐνυπόστατον εἶναι, because they are
neither συμβεβηκότα nor πράγματα ὑφεστῶτα, since they
have much more τὴν τοῦ εἶναι κοινωνίαν with the οὐσία
to which they belong as συμπληρωτικὰ τῆς οὐσίας.²
Leontius remembered that these ποιότητες οὐσιώδεις
in Aristotle's system occupied a middle position
between substances and qualities, and he sought
to make use of this point in his treatment of the
relationship between the Two Natures and the One
Hypostasis in the Person of Christ.   Unfortunately

---

¹ See *Categories*, c. 5, quoted above.
² Cf. Loofs, *Leontius von Byzanz*, pp. 65–68.

he has it in mind in the illustrations he uses, and
this casts suspicion upon his theology, which seems
to be bound up with the validity, or otherwise,
of these particular conceptual distinctions. Aristotle's classification of universals as predicates of
individuals involves many difficulties, and led to the
later scholastic controversy between Nominalism and
Realism, which arose from a chance sentence in
Porphyry's Introduction (Isagoge) to Aristotle's
'Categories.' His doctrine of 'secondary substances'
is considered to be one of the weak points in his
system, and is due to his efforts to come to terms
with Plato's doctrine of Ideas.

According to Zeller, this unsafe position of the
generic notion, midway between substances and
qualities, is one of the root errors derived from Platonic
influences. It results in a contradiction between the
'Categories,' and the 'Metaphysics.' In the 'Categories,' in deference to Plato, as we have seen, Aristotle
says that genera and species are 'secondary substances.' This, however, contradicts his whole treatment of the subject in Book VII of his 'Metaphysics,'
where he shows that substance is that which is not
predicated of a subject, but of which all else is predicated ; and he goes on to deny that a universal can
be a substance at all, since it is a predicate and belongs
to a subject.

For primary substance is that kind of substance which
is peculiar to an individual, which does not belong to anything else ; but the universal is common, since that is called
universal which naturally belongs to more than one thing.
. . . Further, substance means that which is not predicable
of a subject, but the universal is predicable of some subject
always. — Book VII, c. 13, 10–15. Transl. Smith and
Ross, vol. viii. p. 1038b.

The writer of the article ' Aristotle ' in the eleventh edition of the *Ency. Brit.* (vol. ii. pp. 510–511) deals very fully and clearly with the difference between the two treatises, the ' Categories ' and the ' Metaphysics,' and shows that the former, being nearer to Plato,

forms a kind of transition from Platonism to the ' Metaphysics,' which is the reverse : to call universals ' secondary substances ' is half-way between Plato's calling them the only substances and Aristotle's denial in the ' Metaphysics ' that they are substances at all.

There can be little doubt that Leontius is following Aristotle's ' Categories,' c. 8, in his treatment of the concept of ποιότης, and that he accepts the doctrine of the δεύτεραι οὐσίαι. Dr. Loofs is right therefore in saying that the theology of Leontius adheres to this error, and that ' his idea of φύσις or οὐσία is that of the Aristotelian δευτέρα οὐσία ; the idea of the ὑπόστασις corresponds to the Aristotelian πρώτη οὐσία. Just as with Aristotle the genus and the διαφοραί, which constitute the δευτέρα οὐσία, are individualised through the εἶναι ἐν τῇ οὐσίᾳ, so with our author the human nature in Christ is individualised through the εἶναι ἐν τῇ ὑποστάσει τοῦ λόγου, through the ὑποστῆναι ἐν τῷ λόγῳ.'[1]

But when we have admitted this, we have not condemned the doctrine of the Enhypostasia, because, after all, even though Leontius makes use of a weak point in Aristotelianism, it is only by way of illustration, and his idea is not bound up with the validity or otherwise of these conceptual distinctions. He only employs the Aristotelian terminology as an aid to commend his idea, which in itself is quite distinct and independent of the philosophical setting in which its

[1] Loofs, *op. cit.* p. 68.

author places it. This will be seen more clearly when we examine the way in which Leontius works it out. Let us see how he does it.

III. *The Doctrine of the Enhypostasia as thus Illustrated.*—(1) We have seen that he agrees with the Monophysites from the Aristotelian standpoint, that there can be no such thing as a φύσις ἀνυπόστατος. Nature can only exist individually in an individual, and hence a nature without hypostasis would be an abstraction. ἀνυπόστατος μὲν οὖν φύσις, τουτέστιν οὐσία, οὐκ ἂν εἴη ποτέ. (i. 1280 A.)

(2) Must Two Natures then involve Two Persons? Not necessarily so, for just as Aristotle allows between substance (πρώτη οὐσία) and accidents (συμβεβηκότα) a third term, 'secondary substance' (δευτέρα οὐσία), so between an ὑπόστασις and a φύσις ἀνυπόστατος there may be a φύσις ἐνυπόστατος. Nature might in a sense exist as a distinct φύσις or οὐσία, without an independent ὑπόστασις of its own, provided it possessed an ὑπόστασις in a derivative sense in virtue of its inherence in a subject. An independent φύσις is related to an ὑπόστασις as qualities to a substance, as the ποιότητες οὐσιώδεις to the οὐσία.

The human nature of Christ was not without hypostasis, but became hypostatic in the Person of the Logos. It was not an hypostasis because it never existed, καθ' ἑαυτήν, but it was ὑποστῆναι ἐν τῷ λόγῳ.

We may quote the following extract, which gives us a very good example of the kind of argument employed by Leontius in his treatment of both Nestorians and Monophysites.

Hypostasis (ὑπόστασις) is not the same as enhypostatic (ἐνυπόστατος) any more than essence is the same as essential. For hypostasis points to a certain thing, enhypostatic to its existence; hypostasis distinguishes an individual by its characteristic properties, enhypostatic shows that it is not an attribute, which has existence in something else and is not seen in itself. Such are all qualities, both those called 'essential' and those called 'non-essential,' none of which is an essence, i.e. a self-subsistent thing, but one which is always seen in connection with the essence, as colour in the body and knowledge in the soul. So that the man who says, 'Nature does not exist without hypostasis,' speaks truth: he draws a false conclusion however when he makes 'not being without hypostasis' equivalent to 'being an hypostasis.' It is just as if a man were to say—and truly—that the body is not without form, and then go on to conclude that the form is the body, instead of something seen in the body. Nature, then, that is, essence, could never exist without hypostasis. Yet nature is not hypostasis, because the terms are not convertible; hypostasis is nature, but nature is not hypostasis. For nature admits the principle of existence; hypostasis, that of existence by itself. Nature holds the principle of form; hypostasis points out an individual thing. Nature shows the distinctive mark of a universal; hypostasis divides the particular from the common. In short, things that are of the same essence, and that have a common principle of existence, are rightly said to be of one nature. But definition is concerned with hypostasis—either in the case of things that are the same in nature but differ in number; or that are composed of different natures but possess a common existence in and together with each other. I say 'common existence,' not as being complementary to each other's essence, as can be seen in the case of essences and the things that are essentially predicated of them (which are called qualities), but as being each of diverse nature and essence, yet not seen by itself, but in combination and unity with the other. You will find this exemplified in many things, but not least in the soul and body, which have a common hypostasis, particular natures, and different principles.—*Adv. N. et E.* i. 1277 D, ff.

The examples given in the above passage, where Leontius illustrates his idea by a reference to the qualities (ποιότητες οὐσιώδεις) in an object, e.g.

colour in a body, or knowledge in a rational soul, are criticised by Dr. Ottley, who considers that the simile fails since ' ποιότητες cannot subsist independently of the object to which they belong, whereas *ex hypothesi* human nature can subsist apart from personality (e.g. that of Christ).'   Dr. Harnack also indicates the same objection.[1] 'Leontius refers to the mode of the existence of the ποιότητες οὐσιώδεις in the *ousia*.   The comparison is defective, since these ποιότητες do not in themselves constitute a φύσις.'

(3) Leontius proceeds to illustrate his ideas in the following way :

Of things that have essential existence and are combined in essence, some preserve even in combination the peculiar principle of their existence, while others are intermingled and so injured as to destroy their distinct identity.   With the first kind the behaviour of the constituent parts, when seen with and in each other, produces from both a single thing, and, as one may say, shows it to be one in number, preserving the difference of existence in the sameness of the combination.   An illustration of this in the class of animals is man, and among simple or natural bodies the behaviour towards each other of things which have hypostasis of their own and are able to exist by themselves.   You can see this in the case of a torch.   The stem is one thing, the flamy essence of fire another; but when they are with and in each other the two make one torch.   And as one may say— though the expression is somewhat forced—fire is made wooden and wood made fiery, the one element partakes of the brightness of fire, while the other shares in the earthy grossness of the torch material; each gives to the other of its peculiar properties, and yet remains in its own permanent and unconfused identity.

And let no stupid person again take exception to our illustration, on the ground that it contains an element inapplicable to the argument ;—as for instance the oil, which is the medium for the union of these two, or the underlying

---

[1] *History of Dogma*, iv. 233, note 3.

quality of oiliness, or the fact that it does not last long but is burnt to ashes ; remembering what we have said before about an illustration, and its definition. The same blending can be found in the case of fire and air, or air and water. For the mixture of earth and water approaches the intermingled kind of combination, since it makes a way for the moist (i.e. water) and the finer particles (i.e. earth), and differs in respect of the alteration of qualities that results from the mutual interaction as a change and alienation of the distinctive characteristics of each. I omit to speak of those qualities which, though their essences are separate, are often found in each other, and are closely connected without mingling ; such as the twinklings of the light-bearing stars which, mingling with each other and with the air, preserve their own proper quantity in quality. This is demonstrated by Art, which imitates nature.

If then a man, to quote from the great Dionysius, were to light many torches and shut them up together in one house, and then plucking one from the group to bring that out of the dwelling, he will fetch out this torch with its light ; it will have left no scrap of its own light to the others. And to speak generally nothing that is combined undergoes alteration or intermingling, except where each element possesses passive qualities. For where this is not so the active one will act but not suffer, while the passive one will suffer but not act. But where there is a common principle of mutual interaction, there each element acts and is acted upon to a greater or less degree in accordance with the superiority or equality of its passive qualities. This is the case with things that melt and with metals, and with everything that can be mingled or melted together by physicians or craftsmen in the exercise of their arts.

Now that we have first distinguished these, we must know that those things which can be changed or transformed into one another, composed out of many forms and diverse essences, do not preserve in its pure form after the synthesis any of those elements which went to make up the synthesis. On the contrary, the synthesis having combined and intermingled the peculiar properties of all, from all to all, has produced a diverse mingled form ; and from many hypostases and natures there has resulted in the combination a confused mixture, which has neither retained the peculiarity of the hypostasis nor the common element of the nature, but has produced another thing which has come from these and yet is not the same as either of its antecedents. If then Divinity and manhood when united in essence do not retain in the unity the natural peculiarities of each, they have been intermingled together, and neither Divinity nor manhood is left, but they have produced a diverse form of existence that came from them and yet was not themselves. And what could be more impious and shocking than even to entertain such an idea, not to speak of holding and teaching it as a dogma? From this examination, then, of the principle of unity in respect of essence, it remains for us to accept the unmingled peculiar nature of both Divinity and manhood, according to the examples given; while at the same time we gather from them all a kind of faint image of the truth that is beyond all, which shows plainly that the product of these is a single thing—call it person, or hypostasis, or undivided unity, or underlying reality—I do not care which. For those who by reason of dignity or authority or some such dividing relationship separate them in their close connection have just now been beaten and put to flight by our argument, which has proved that they are dividing the natures for the hypostases; and that these natures neither admit nor offer mutual communion or exchange of properties.—*Adv. N. and E.* i. 1304 B, ff.

It will be seen from this passage that, according to Leontius, an ἕνωσις φύσεων (ἑτεροειδῶν) may result either in a mixture or confusion of the two, in which case a new εἶδος is produced, or in a conjunction, in which case a numerical unity is formed, and within this unity each nature preserves its own integrity. In the case of the lighted torch, each φύσις remains as such in its distinctness, but there may be an ἀντίδοσις τῶν ἰδιωμάτων. Here we have a case in which by synthesis an ἐνυπόστατον εἶναι is produced. But Dr. Loofs puts his finger on the weak point of the analogy when he says,

'Which of the two parts of the synthesis is the
ἐνυπόστατον, which also in its hypostasis takes the
φύσις of the other, the author does not here say.'[1]

Whatever may be thought of the illustrations
and analogies Leontius employed, we consider that
his main idea of the Enhypostasia is really independent
of the Aristotelian terminology he uses to commend
it. He is not unmindful himself that the illustrations he employs are inadequate when used as analogies of what is admittedly a unique phenomenon.
The Person of Christ baffles analysis and transcends
all analogies. Leontius knew this. He offered his
theory of the Enhypostasia as the only way of escape
from the Nestorian and Monophysite pitfalls, and
as the only theory by which the Chalcedonian
Christology could be defended against the charges
of its opponents.

We have felt it necessary, however, thus to deal
at some length with the philosophical setting in
which the doctrine is found, in order to anticipate
the criticism of some who may be led to think that
the doctrine is worthless because its author bases
it upon conceptual distinctions which have little
or no value for the modern mind. On the contrary,
whilst we admire the skill with which Leontius
employed the Aristotelian terminology to illustrate
his doctrine and to commend it to the mind of his
time, we are not bound to follow him in his illustra-

---

[1] *Op. cit.* p. 67. We are indebted to the Rev. G. W. Butterworth
for kindly furnishing us with a far more accurate translation of this and
the preceding passage from Leontius than we were competent to make.
The very technical character of a good deal of the treatise *Adv. N.
and E.* makes it almost necessary to undertake a preliminary course
in Aristotelian logic and metaphysics if one wishes to catch the full
sense of the arguments Leontius employs, and the illustrations he uses.

tions when we take from him his doctrine. We must endeavour to reinterpret it in such a way as may commend it to-day to those called upon to do for our age a work in defence of the Chalcedonian Christology such as Leontius successfully performed for his age.

The importance of this contribution of Leontius and its precise significance for Christology will appear in what follows.

9.

THE DOCTRINE OF THE ENHYPOSTASIA

HOW important this contribution of Leontius was is shown from the fact that his idea is incorporated in the final formulation of Greek theology as this was drawn up by John of Damascus. John mentions Leontius by name, and borrows directly from him the doctrine of the Enhypostasia, which he elaborates at some length in his great work, περὶ ὀρθοδόξου πίστεως (*De Fide Orthodoxa*, Bk. III). The following passages illustrate John's treatment of the subject :

Bk. III, ch. iii. And therefore we hold that there has been a union of two perfect natures, one Divine and one human ; not with disorder or confusion, or intermixture, or commingling . . . and not in a personal or relative manner, or as a matter of dignity or agreement in will, or equality in honour, or identity in name, or good pleasure . . . but by synthesis, that is, in subsistence, without change or confusion or alteration or difference or separation, and we confess that in two perfect natures there is but one subsistence of the Son of God incarnate ; holding that there is one and the same subsistence belonging to His Divinity and His humanity, and granting that the two natures are preserved in Him after the union, but we do not hold that each is separate and by itself, but that they are united to each other in one compound subsistence. For we look upon the union as essential, that is, as true and not imaginary.

Ch. ix. For although there is no nature without subsistence, nor essence apart from person (since in truth it is in persons and subsistences that essence and nature are to be contemplated), yet it does not necessarily follow that the natures that are united to one another in subsistence should have each its own proper subsistence. For after they have come together into one subsistence, it is possible that neither should they be without subsistence, nor should each have its own peculiar subsistence, but that both should have one and the same subsistence. For since one and the same subsistence of the Word has become the subsistence of the natures, neither of them is permitted to be without subsistence, nor are they allowed to have subsistences that differ from each other, or to have sometimes the subsistence of this nature and sometimes of that, but always without division or separation they both have the same subsistence—a subsistence which is not broken up into parts or divided, so that one part should belong to this, and one to that, but which belongs wholly to this and wholly to that in its absolute entirety. For the flesh of God the Word did not subsist as an independent subsistence, nor did there arise another subsistence besides that of God the Word, but as it existed in that it became rather a subsistence which subsisted in another, than one which was an independent subsistence. Wherefore, neither does it lack subsistence altogether, nor yet is there thus introduced into the Trinity another subsistence.

Ch. xi. For He took on Himself the elements of our compound nature, and these not as having an independent existence or as being originally an individual, and in this way assumed by Him, but as existing in His own subsistence. For the subsistence of God the Word in itself became the subsistence of the flesh, and accordingly ' the Word became flesh ' clearly without any change, and likewise the flesh became Word without alteration, and God became Man.

The Christological position of John is conveniently summarised in Dr. Fisher's *History of Christian Doctrine*, pp. 159–160 :

The unity of the two natures it is attempted to secure by relegating to the divine Logos the formative and controlling agency. It is not a human individual that the Logos assumes, nor is it humanity, or human nature, in general. It is rather a potential human individual, a nature not yet developed into a person or hypostasis. The hypostasis through which this takes place is the personal Logos

through whose union with this potential man, in the womb
of Mary, the potential man acquires a concrete reality, an
individual existence. He has, therefore, no hypostasis of
himself but only in and through the Logos. It is denied
that he is *non-hypostatic* ; it is affirmed that he is *en-hypos-
tatic*. Two natures may form a unity, as the body and
soul in man. So man, both soul and body, is brought into
unity with the Logos ; there being then one hypostasis for
both natures. There is a circumincession (περιχώρησις) of
the divine and human, an interchange of attributes. There
is a communication of divine attributes to the human nature,
so that the latter is deified, and so that we may say that God
has suffered in the flesh. But in this interchange the human
nature is merely receptive and passive. The Son of God—
the humanity, the flesh, included—is to be worshipped.
The will, in accordance with the current psychology, is
regarded as a quality of the nature, and it is said that in
Christ the human will has become the will of the incarnate
God. It is simply the organ of the divine will.

While the Damascene makes distinctions which are
intended to preserve the reality of the human nature
in Christ, the drift of his teaching is in the Monophysite
direction.

Commenting on John Damascene's theology,
Dorner says :

It is evident enough that the Christological result thus
arrived at by the ancient Church, whatever may have been
the extent of its traditional influence even down to recent
times, was far from bringing the matter to a close. The
human nature of Christ was curtailed, in that, after the
manner of Apollinaris, the head of the divine hypostasis
was set upon the trunk of a human nature, and the unity
of the person thus preserved at the cost of the humanity.
Further, and this is simply the reverse side of the same
fault, the entire doctrine of the natures and wills taught
by the ancient Church, admitted of nothing but an external
union of the divine with the human ; and the two natures,
continuing unchanged even as to their attributes, were but,
as it were, inserted into each other in the Person of Christ.
We can, indeed, discover the rudiments of something better ;

86

and they warrant us in supposing that the theory adopted failed, notwithstanding its rounded appearance, to give adequate expression to the image of Christ which hovered before the mind.   The doctrine of the freedom of the humanity of Christ was plainly intended to play a more important part than it actually did, in the system of John of Damascus. He did not mean merely to teach that the humanity of Christ was passively carried and moved hither and thither by the Logos, that it lost its personality in the personality of the Logos ; for it would have contradicted one of his fundamental postulates, which was, that nothing that forms an essential part of any nature—and the hypostasis must without doubt be counted essential both to the Logos and to humanity—can fail, without involving the destruction of that nature, nor be really communicated by another nature, especially if of a different substance.   And, on the other hand, when he laid down the doctrine of the ἀντίδοσις, περιχώρησις, οἰκείωσις, he had in view a much more intimate union between the divine and human natures than he arrived at in his systematic exhibition of the matter—invariably ending, as it does, with denying that either the natures or the attributes were really interchanged.—Div. II, vol. i. pp. 220–221.

It will thus be seen that the doctrine of the Enhypostasia meets with little favour from Dorner, as indeed from any theologian, and it is more than once asserted that this doctrine is at bottom Monophysite, or a refined form of Apollinarianism.   Thus Dr. Ottley quotes with approval Seeberg's comment on the theology of the Damascene, ' The Chalcedonian Definition is victorious, but Apollinaris is not overcome.'   Harnack, commenting upon the theory of Leontius, says: ' A pious Apollinarian monk would probably have been able to say with regard to the ὑποστῆναι ἐν τῷ λόγῳ : " Apollinaris says pretty much the same thing, only in somewhat more intelligent words." ' [1]

[1] *History of Dogma*, iv. 233, note 3.

Again, to take a very recent writer on the Christological problem, Dr. Mackintosh, in his review of the theology of John of Damascus, says: ' He laid stress, moreover, on the " Enhypostasia " of the manhood, thus perpetuating, in spite of the Dyophysite and Dyothelite creeds, a view that has many points of affinity with Apollinaris. The Logos is placed as head on the mere trunk of humanity.' [1]

In spite, however, of this adverse criticism, it is our purpose to rescue this doctrine from the oblivion into which it has been allowed to sink, and to endeavour to show that this solution of Leontius, interpreted in terms of modern thought, carries us deeper into the mystery of the Person of Christ than any other theory yet put forward in the attempt to elucidate a problem which must indeed ever baffle human analysis, but into which the human mind by its very constitution must ever be seeking to probe deeper. At this stage in our enquiry we must simply note, in view of the criticisms of Dorner and others which we have quoted, what exactly was the purpose of Leontius and John of Damascus in elaborating this doctrine of the Enhypostasia.

(1) It seems generally to be overlooked that the doctrine of the impersonality of Christ's manhood is an inevitable deduction from the Chalcedonian Definition, and an integral factor in Chalcedonian Christology.

As we have already seen, for Cyril of Alexandria, in some sense, Christ's human nature was impersonal, since the centre of personal life in the God-Man resided unquestionably in the Divine Logos. The Divine Nature being the root and basis of the personality of Christ, the human nature occupied

[1] *The Person of Jesus Christ*, p. 222.

88

a relatively subordinate place. The tendency of Alexandrian theology was to regard the humanity of Christ as a series of attributes assumed by the Logos and incorporated into the unity of His Person, or as an accident (συμβεβηκός) of the Divine Person Who assumed it.

Those who were concerned to preserve at whatever cost the complete manhood of Christ, felt that this view so reduced the manhood as to make it appear a mere unsubstantial accident of the Godhead, a depressed humanity, and if ' impersonal ' then in what conceivable sense perfect ?

Cyril's Christology thus invited criticism on these lines as a refined form of Apollinarianism, and the same charge was brought against the Chalcedonian theology by those who were keen enough to perceive that, although the Definition did not explicitly state it, nevertheless, in some sense, the impersonality of Christ's manhood was a legitimate deduction from the Definition, and an integral factor in the Chalcedonian Christology.

Once the Cyrillian contention that the pre-existent Divine Logos was the centre of personality in the God-Man was admitted, and, at the same time, the Nestorian contention of an independent personality of the manhood denied, the inevitable conclusion followed that in some sense Christ's manhood was ' impersonal,' even though it had a relatively independent existence of its own.

(2) Now Leontius, and later, John of Damascus, were concerned to defend the Chalcedonian Christology against the charge of Apollinarianism on the one side, and the apparently more logical Monophysite solution on the other.

In the doctrine of the Enhypostasia, Leontius
secures for the manhood of Christ a completeness
which saves it from being regarded as truncated in
an Apollinarian sense.   Leontius secures for the
manhood an hypostasis;   and thus saves it from
being regarded as a mere series of attributes, or a
mere accident of the Godhead.   Although, according
to this theory, the manhood has no independent
personality of its own, and had, in fact, no existence
at all before the Incarnation;   nevertheless it becomes hypostatic in the Person of the Logos and
receives its subsistence from Him.   It thus reaches
its completeness, and comes to self-consciousness in
Him at every stage of its growth and development.
The human nature of the God-Man was from the
very beginning inseparably united with the Divine
Nature, and in virtue of that union received from
the Logos-personality its personality, and thus its
completeness.

John Owen, the Puritan theologian,[1] puts this
point very well : ' In itself it (the human nature
of Christ) is ἀνυπόστατος—that which hath not a subsistence of its own, which should give it individua-
tion and distinction from the same nature in any
other person. But it hath its subsistence in the
person of the Son, which thereby is its own. The
divine nature, as in that Person, is its suppositum.'

(3) It follows from this review that Dorner's
criticism of the Chalcedonian Christology is really
met by the doctrine of the Enhypostasia, which saves
Christ's manhood from degenerating into a series
of attributes attached to the Logos, and secures its
completeness in the One Christ. The doctrine of

[1] Works, vol. i. p. 223.

the impersonality of Christ's manhood is indeed open to grave objection, but this is not the doctrine of the Enhypostasia, which secures for the manhood a personal subsistence. Thus the doctrine of the Enhypostasia is not open to the charge of Apollinarianism. The reality and completeness of the manhood is secured in a better way than Cyril succeeded in doing. Dorner criticises the ancient Christology because, as he says, the human nature of Christ was curtailed; in that, after the manner of Apollinaris, the head of the Divine hypostasis was set upon the trunk of a human nature, and the unity of the person thus preserved at the cost of the humanity. But according to the doctrine of the Enhypostasia, what did the humanity lack in order to its perfection? The answer surely is ' Nothing.' And the reason is that the Logos brought to the humanity every element which it lacked, in order to make it complete. What were these elements? Certainly one was human personality, the most distinctive and characteristic constituent of human nature, without which it could not be said to be human. But could the Logos, Who Himself possessed Divine Personality, give to the human nature He took, human personality?

This is the real crux of the position. Does Divine Personality already contain within itself all that goes to make up what is distinctively human personality? Is the less (the human personality needed to complete the human nature) contained in the greater (the Divine Logos personality which assumed the human nature)?

If the answer to this question is in the affirmative, then in a very true sense Apollinaris came into his own when the doctrine of the Enhypostasia was incorporated by John of Damascus into the final formulation of the later Greek theology ; because, as we have tried to show, it was Apollinaris who strove to prove that there was already in God a human element, and this alone made an Incarnation possible.

(4) This, then, is the line of thought we shall have to pursue if we are to make any further advance in the study of the Christological problem. A deeper analysis of both the human and the Divine Natures is required if we are ever to find the ground of the possibility of their union in the One Christ.

Our review of the Christology of the ancient Church leaves us with the Chalcedonian theology, and the further step in its elucidation taken by Leontius in his doctrine of the Enhypostasia. Beyond this apparently the Church could not go. What was wanted was a deeper analysis of personality, human and Divine.

There was One Person. There were Two Natures. The apparent resultant dualism could only be solved by a careful analysis of all that is involved in (a) the Divine Nature; (b) the human nature. The apparent dualism between these two might resolve itself into a unity deeper down in the depths of each. Was there a meeting-place between the human and the Divine deeper down in the depths of human personality ? Was there a meeting-place between the human and the Divine, in virtue of the fact that deep down in the Being of God Himself was to be found a human element ? Only a deeper analysis of personality, human and Divine, could answer these questions. Have we in modern times better facilities for conducting such an analysis than were available for the theologians of the ancient Church ? This is the question we shall endeavour to answer in the pages which follow ; but before finally leaving the ancient Christology, there is one further step we must note which the Church took in its task of defining more explicitly exactly how much was contained in the human nature of Christ, consistent with its belief in the perfection of His manhood. This step was taken as the result of the Monothelite controversy.

10.

MONOTHELITISM

THE defence of the Chalcedonian theology against the Monothelites was concerned with the answer to the same question raised by the Monophysites. What constitutes a complete manhood ? What is the minimum which it must retain if it is still to be called complete ? Was a dual will essential if the manhood was in any sense to retain a relative independence within the unity of the One Christ ? The Sixth General Council, A.D. 680, at Constantinople, decided in favour of Dyothelitism. Christ was held to have possessed two wills or volitions. Δύο φυσικὰς θελήσεις ἤτοι θελήματα ἐν αὐτῷ καὶ δύο φυσικὰς ἐνεργείας ἀδιαιρέτως, ἀτρέπτως, ἀμερίστως, ἀσυγχύτως . . . κηρύτ-τομεν. It was felt necessary to condemn Monothelitism, and to postulate two wills in Christ in order to preserve the truth of His real manhood and the ethical efficacy of His human temptations and experiences as our example. It was clearly seen, however, that the doctrine of two wills did not necessarily lead to a division at the very centre of the personality of the God-Man, since the Gospel portrait revealed Christ's human will ever to have been in complete harmony with the Divine, and in all things obedient to it. ' Not my will, but Thine be done,' was felt to be not only a revelation of Christ's attitude towards the Father, but also as covering the relationship between His two wills distinct and yet united. Extract from the Definition of the Sixth Ecumenical Council :

We likewise declare that in him are two natural wills
and two natural operations indivisibly, inconvertibly, inseparably, inconfusedly, according to the teaching of the
holy fathers.　And these two natural wills are not contrary
the one to the other (God forbid !) as the impious heretics
assert, but his human will follows and that not as resisting
and reluctant, but rather as subject to his Divine and omnipotent will.　For it was right that the flesh should be moved
but subject to the Divine will, according to the most wise
Athanasius. . . . For as his most holy and immaculate ani-
mated flesh was not destroyed because it was deified but
continued in its own state and nature, so also his human
will, although deified, was not suppressed, but was rather
preserved. . . .

This concludes our review of ancient Christology,
and our task is now to consider it afresh in the light
of modern thought.　It is easy enough to reject the
enormous labour and the acute thought of many
minds in the ancient Church, and to dismiss their
efforts as the outworn results of a discredited philosophy.　We find in some modern writings a tendency
to disparage the work done by the Fathers of the
ancient Church, and to regard the Creeds and
Definitions of the Councils as of comparatively little
value in view of our supposed enormous advances in
knowledge.　Dr. Loofs, in his recent work, entitled
What is the Truth about Jesus Christ? commits
himself to a startling and significant statement
when he writes, ' There is hardly a single learned
theologian (I know of none in Germany) who defends
the orthodox Christology in its unaltered form.'[1]
On all sides we hear the demand for restatement
in terms of modern thought.　But whilst we admit
the need for reviewing the ancient Christology afresh
with the aid of all the light our modern knowledge

[1] P. 184.

95

can possibly shed upon it, nevertheless we refuse to regard the work of the ancients as in any sense a sheer waste of strength, and relatively of little or no value to-day.   On the contrary, we believe that the most our modern thought can add to their labours will be the confirmation in substance of the results they reached.   The reinterpretation of their thought in the language of our own time will not lessen our sense of the debt we owe to them for the contribution they have made towards a solution of the problem.

APPENDIX A

THE following estimates of the value of the Chalcedonian
Definition show how the formula appeals to the minds of
different theologians, according to the standpoint from which
they approach it.

(*a*) Dr. Shedd considers the Chalcedonian Symbol as the *ne
plus ultra* of Christological knowledge, ' beyond which it is probable
the human mind is unable to go, in the endeavour to unfold the
mystery of Christ's complex person, which in some of its aspects
is even more baffling than the mystery of the Trinity.'—*History
of Doctrine*, i. 408.

This estimate reflects that note of reverent caution and
conservatism so typical of Western theology, in contrast
to the bolder and more speculative tone of the Eastern
theologians.

(*b*) Dr. Baur imputes to the Creed ' untenable inconsistency,
equivocal indefiniteness and discordant incompleteness,' but
ascribes to it the merit of insisting upon the human in Christ as
havingequal claims with the Divine, and of thus leaving the possibility of two equally legitimate points of view.—*Geschichte der
Trinitätslehre*, Bd. i. p. 823 f ; cf. Schaff., *Hist. Christ. Ch.* ii. p. 759,
where these passages are quoted.

Here we seem to detect that note of impatience so
characteristic of the rationalistic temper in the presence of
a ' mystery ' which claims to transcend the limits of human
thought.

(*c*) Dr. Bright brings his examination to a close with the
following weighty words :
'The Definition has been criticised as not explaining *how* the
unity of person and the duality of natures can co-exist as elements
in the Incarnation of our Lord.   Perhaps a theological formula is
none the worse for exhibiting somewhat of that modest self-
restraint in which theologians have sometimes been found wanting.
There are many points as to which we have no warrant for asking
' how,' still less for attempting an answer.   And if it is thought
that the necessary unity of the Incarnate Christ is obscured by
supposing Him, in the terms of the Definition, to exist ' in ' two
distinct spheres of life and action, ' inseparable ' yet ' unconfused,'

and that it needs to be safeguarded by the idea of a *literal* ' communication of properties' between the two natures, such as would practically mould them into one or fuse one in the other, this is the old Monophysite objection, although it may be urged in support of what amounts to a Monophysitism inverted, according to which it is not the Manhood which gives way, wholly or partially, to the Godhead, but the Godhead which gives way to the Manhood by the temporary abandonment of certain so-called divine 'attributes' —which in truth are plural only in an ' economic ' sense, as modes of representing, in human thought and speech, so many aspects of that indivisible perfection which makes up the divine essence, and *is* God. After all, if Christ is believed in as One, yet as both truly God and truly Man—however little we can comprehend the relation thus created—that belief is all that the Chalcedonian terminology implies : to hold it is to be at one with the Fourth Council.'—*Age of the Fathers*, vol. ii. p. 550.

This appeals to us as a truer estimate of the value of the Definition, as against Harnack's criticism on the one hand, and certain aspects of modern Kenotic theories on the other.

APPENDIX B

It may be well to give this outline in Cyril's own words. We quote in full the main portion of this most interesting and instructive letter.

For we do not affirm that the nature of the Word underwent a change and became flesh, or that it was transformed into a whole or perfect man consisting of soul and body ; but we say that the Word, having in an ineffable and inconceivable manner personally united to Himself flesh instinct with a living soul, became man and was called the Son of Man,—yet not of mere will or favour, nor again by the simple taking to Himself of a person (i.e. of a human person to His divine person),—and that while the natures which were brought together into this true unity were diverse, there was of both one Christ and one Son : not as though the diverseness of the natures were done away by this union, but rather that the Godhead and Manhood completed for us the one Lord and Christ and Son by their unutterable and unspeakable concurrence and unity. And thus, although He subsisted and was begotten of the Father before the worlds, He is spoken of as having been born also after the flesh of a woman : not that His divine nature had its beginning of existence in the holy Virgin, or needed of necessity on its own account a second generation after its generation from the Father, for it is foolish and absurd to say that He who subsisted before all worlds, and was co-eternal with the Father, stood in need of a second beginning of existence but, forasmuch as the Word having 'for us and for our salvation,' personally (καθ' ὑπόστασιν) united to Himself human nature (τὸ ἀνθρώπινον, Manhood, or the human element), came forth of a woman,—for this reason He is said to have been born after the flesh (σαρκικῶς). For He was not first born an ordinary man of the holy Virgin, and then the Word descended upon Him, but having been made one (ἑωνθείς) with the flesh from the very womb itself, He is said to have submitted to a birth according to the flesh, as appropriating and making His own the birth of His own flesh.

In like manner we say that He 'suffered' and 'rose again.' Not as though God the Word suffered in His own divine nature either stripes or the piercing of nails, or the other wounds inflicted on Him, for the Godhead is impassible because It is incorporeal. But forasmuch as that which had become His own body suffered these things, therefore again He Himself is said to have suffered them for us. For the Impassible was in the suffering body. So likewise of His Death. For the Word of God is by nature both incorruptible, and Life, and Life-giving, but forasmuch as His own body by the grace of God, as Paul says, 'tasted death for every man,' therefore once more He Himself is said to have suffered death for us. Not as though He experienced death as regards His own (divine) nature—to say or hold which is madness—but that, as I said just now, His flesh tasted death. So likewise when His flesh was raised, the resurrection again is spoken of as His resurrection, not as though He had seen corruption, God forbid, but because once more it was His own body that was raised.

Thus we confess one Christ and Lord, not as worshipping a man conjointly with the Word, that there may not through this phrase 'conjointly' be insinuated the semblance of division (as though we were dividing the one Christ into two Persons)—but as worshipping one and the same Person, because the body of the Lord is not alien from the Lord, with which body also He sits with the Father Himself: not again as though two sons do sit with the Father, but one united to His own flesh. But if we reject this hypostatic union (τὴν καθ' ὑπόστασιν ἕνωσιν) either as impossible or unmeet, we fall into the error of making two sons. For in that case we must needs distinguish and speak of the man severally (the human person) dignified with the appellation of Son, and again of the Word which is of God severally (the divine Person) possessing naturally the Sonship, both name and thing; (i.e. if we reject a union of substances or natures in the one Person, we make two several Sons, and must perforce distinguish—speaking

99

of the One, as merely dignified with the title of Son, the other as Son in reality as well as in name). We must not then divide the one Lord Jesus Christ into two sons. To hold this will nowise contribute to soundness of faith, even though some make a show of acknowledging a union of persons. For Scripture does not say that The Word united to Himself the person (πρόσωπον) of a man, but that ' He became flesh.' But this expression ' The Word became flesh ' is nothing else than that He became partaker of flesh and blood, just as we do, and made our body His own, and was born a man of a woman (ἐκ γυναικός), not casting aside the being God, and the having been begotten of God the Father, but even when taking to Himself flesh still remaining what He was. This is the doctrine which strict orthodoxy everywhere prescribes (literally gives the place of honour to). Thus shall we find the holy Fathers to have held. So did they make bold to call the holy Virgin ' the Mother of God.' Not as though the nature of the Word or His Godhead had its beginning from the holy Virgin, but forasmuch as His holy Body, endued with a rational soul, was born of her, to which Body also the Word was personally (καθ' ὑπόστασιν) united (i.e. the two substances united in one Person, in opposition to the union of two Persons), on this account He is said to have been born after the flesh.—Heurtley, *On Faith and the Creed*, pp. 157–161. Greek in *De Fide et Symbolo*, pp. 183–185. *Cf.* another translation in ' The Seven Ecumenical Councils,' *Nicene and Post-Nicene Fathers*, pp. 197–198.

PART TWO

1. MODERN CRITICISM OF THE ANCIENT CHRISTOLOGY.
2. DUALISM.
3. THE ANALYSIS OF HUMAN NATURE IN THE LIGHT OF MODERN PSYCHOLOGY.
   - (*a*) THE SOUL.
   - (*b*) ITS RELATIONS WITH THE BODY.
   - (*c*) HUMAN PERSONALITY.
4. THE ANALYSIS OF DIVINE NATURE.
   - (*a*) GOD IS LOVE.
   - (*b*) GOD IS PERFECT PERSONALITY.
   - (*c*) THE TRANSCENDENCE AND IMMANENCE OF GOD.
5. HUMAN AND DIVINE IN THEIR RELATIONSHIP.
   - (*a*) RELIGIOUS EXPERIENCE, MYSTICISM, ECSTASY, INSPIRATION AND REVELATION, PROPHECY.
   - (*b*) COMMUNION WITH GOD IN CHRIST.
     GRACE.
     GRACE AND FREE-WILL.
   - (*c*) SUMMARY.

MODERN CRITICISM OF THE ANCIENT CHRISTOLOGY

THE intervening period between the close of the labours of the ancient Church in the field of Christology and the modern period is one of comparative barrenness. The Christological problem receded into the background, and for fourteen centuries became a mere side-issue. The Adoptianist controversy in the Latin Church was but another effort to solve the problem of the relation of the One personality to the Two Natures in the One Christ; and although it was not a revived Nestorianism, yet the motive of it was the same, viz. an endeavour to rescue the manhood of Christ from the Monophysite tendency in the Alexandrian theology. The use made of the doctrine of the Enhypostasia by the Adoptianists is most interesting and instructive, but does not carry us any further beyond the point reached by Leontius of Byzantium.[1]

From this time onwards the centre of interest shifts from Christology to Anthropology, and theological thought is concerned more with the doctrine of the Atonement. In scholastic theology Christology is not the central subject, and even in the later Lutheran controversies the Christological problem was only an incident in the sacramental controversy. We have to wait until modern times for a revived interest in the Christological problem.

[1] See Dorner, Div. II, vol. i. pp. 248-268.

The rationalist movement of the late eighteenth and the beginning of the nineteenth century set the Person of Christ at the centre once more of theological speculation and controversy. This movement raised afresh the issues which had been regarded as finally settled by the dogmatic utterances of the first four General Councils. The central dogma of the Divinity of Christ was challenged afresh, and this challenge created the second great Christological epoch in the history of doctrine, the climax of which we have not yet reached.

A study of the history of Christology from the Council of Chalcedon onwards to our own day reveals a persistent opposition to the doctrine of the Two Natures.

The dualism inherent in the Chalcedonian Definition has in every subsequent age invited criticism, and the miracle of a Two-Natured Christ has challenged opposition. Sooner than acquiesce in this New Testament portrait, of which the Chalcedonian Definition is in the ultimate analysis a faithful reproduction, men have sought by any and every means to reduce the Christ within the categories of thought demanded by rationalism. And this is natural when we consider that the Chalcedonian Definition implies the bankruptcy of rationalism, and is itself a perpetual reminder that the Christ transcends any human intellectual effort to analyse Him. If He could be reduced within the limits of rationalistic thought, if there were no element in Him which could not be explained within the strict limits of the rationalistic creed, He would cease to be the Christ of the New Testament. The stupendous fact of the Incarnation itself implies the doctrine of the Two Natures, and the modern revolt against the latter is really the revolt of scepticism against the former. The issues raised by rationalism inevitably affected Christology, and the tremendous revolt of modern times against the supernatural, which has not yet spent itself, has had an enormous influence upon the problem of the Person of Christ, and has given rise to what Dr. Sanday describes as two types of Christology, the one ' full Christianity,' and the other ' reduced Christianity ' ; though how far the latter is really entitled to the name ' Christianity ' at all is an open question.

The points at issue in the field of Christology centre round the question ' Jesus or Christ ? ' and this question has been, and still is, the battle-cry between orthodoxy and the liberal school of modern times. The very form in which the question is put itself indicates a revolt against the doctrine of the Two Natures : either Divine or human, but not both. Happily we are not called upon to review the results of the negative criticism from the time of the Tübingen School onwards so far as the Person of Christ is concerned. This has been done in Schweitzer's brilliant and instructive book, *The Quest of the Historical Jesus,* and few reading that book will question that if it is legitimate at this stage to postulate any definite results, we may say that (1) the central truth of the Nicene Creed remains unshaken, and (2) the tendency of negative criticism is to a certain degree towards an approximation to the Christ of the Creeds. It would indeed be difficult to find anywhere a more scathing denunciation of the conflicting results of negative criticism in the field of Christology than that contained in Schweitzer's exposure of the bankruptcy of the rationalistic attempt to eliminate the

supernatural from the Person of Christ. A reading
of this review of the course of criticism from Reimarus
to the modernists of our own day, reveals them to
have been united on one point and one point only,
namely, their consistent denial of the possibility of
the supernatural, and consequently their utter failure
to do justice to one side of the problem raised by the
Christ of the New Testament and of the Creeds, viz.
His Divinity. So long as the supernatural is ruled
out of court on *a priori* grounds, so long critics are
forced to eliminate from their enquiry one whole
series of data furnished by the New Testament for
Christology, and the result is a one-sided and to this
extent a distorted picture of the Christ of history.
The Eschatological School, however, in their revolt
against this one-sided liberal criticism, may yet adjust
the balance. Their emphasis upon the Self-Witness
of Christ and the transcendental character of His
claims is of immense significance for Christology.
But it is not to be supposed that this negative criticism
has been unfruitful in results of a positive character
for Christology. On the contrary, one outstanding
contribution of liberal theology has been the tremendous emphasis laid upon the manhood of Christ, and
this at a time when there were many tendencies at
work which threatened to endanger this great truth.
Negative criticism may justly claim to have rescued
the historical Christ from that nebulosity into which
He had almost vanished in the hands of the Docetics,
for whom Christ had become so utterly Divine as to
have ceased to be, in any practical sense, a man
amongst men, the Jesus of the Gospels. If negative
criticism failed to do justice to the full Divinity of
the God-Man, it did more than ample justice to the

reality of His manhood; and further than this, it made it impossible for any future Christology to base itself on any other ground than the historical data supplied by the New Testament and the historical Jesus as its starting-point. If the result of the long controversy with negative criticism should prove— as it shows every sign of doing—the essential historicity of the Gospel-story, then the struggle will not have been labour lost, in that we shall have, as the foundation pillars of the Creed, a definite series of authenticated historical phenomena which have successfully withstood the most searching criticism to which they could possibly have been subjected. And the historical phenomena thus established indirectly by the work of both Liberals and Eschatologists will form a solid basis upon which a sound Christology may safely be built up. The importance of this will be readily grasped when we remember that the doctrine of the Two-Natured Christ of the Creeds is rooted and grounded in New Testament teaching, and in fact is involved in the very thought of an Incarnation. The establishment, therefore, of the historicity of the New Testament is the vindication of the Christ of the Creeds. Given the historicity of the New Testament portrait of Christ, we have the root and basis of the Nicene and Chalcedonian Christology. Dr. Sanday, summing up the results of modern criticism as applied to the Gospels, says:

The common matter of the Synoptic Gospels remains substantially unscathed . . . what is now left us, we may be sure, is built upon the solid rock; the gates of Hades itself will not prevail against it. But what does this rescued matter contain? It contains two things which I believe will be found to be the key to all the rest. . . .

(1) Our Lord really believed Himself to be the Messiah.

(2) He also believed Himself to be in a unique sense Son of God.

There may be dispute over what we mean by 'unique sense.' It is allowed that our Lord Jesus Christ drew a clear distinction between Himself and all the children of men. That is the foundation-stone of the Creeds. Grant us that and the rest will follow. These two concessions are my second ground of hope. They are axioms which I conceive bar the way against any further fall. The Christian faith can, I believe, be reconstructed out of them.

In this enquiry we are not concerned with the modern revolt against the doctrine of the Two Natures, so far as this is a revolt of negative scepticism against the doctrine of the Incarnation, and we may further leave out of account Dr. Sanday's type of 'reduced Christianity,' which fails to do justice to the full Divinity of Christ, and to this extent has not the necessary data for a sound Christology.[1]

When, for example, we are told that it is unthinkable that Godhead and manhood should be united in a single person walking upon the earth, it is legitimate to question the presuppositions on the basis of which the Liberal critics set out to examine the New Testament portrait, and we speedily find that the real difficulty is an *a priori* 'psychological impossibility' of the Two Natures of Christ, which vitiates the whole treatment of the subject, and leads to the inevitable conclusion that, for example, in Mark's account of the historical Christ we have to distinguish two distinct narratives : one giving us the picture of

[1] This point is very well brought out in two articles of a helpful character by Dr. Warfield which appeared in the *American Journal of Theology* (July and October 1911, 'The "Two Natures" and recent Christological Speculation '), and to which we are indebted in what follows.

the human Jesus ; the other, that of the Divine Christ ; and that these two narratives have been so inextricably woven together that modern criticism is faced with the almost insuperable task of disentangling them, and rescuing the ' earlier ' human Jesus from the mass of legendary details by which He has come to be surrounded.

But this whole treatment of Mark's Christology is really a negative vindication of the Two-Natured Christ, since it shows us how utterly impossible it is to eliminate the supernatural elements from the Gospel narrative without destroying the integrity of the Gospel itself. If the Two-Natured Christ can only be eliminated from Mark's narrative by the supposition that the narrative itself is of an extremely complex and composite character, into which have been woven with incomparable skill two entirely different conceptions of the Person and work of Jesus, and we have to choose between this hypothesis and the traditional explanation, we must confess that it is easier to believe the latter. The value of such criticism is the clear recognition that even in Mark's account the portrait of Christ contains elements of a supernatural character, and that therefore, even apart from the fourth Gospel, the Synoptic narratives themselves are amply sufficient as a foundation for the Church's belief in the doctrine of the Two Natures.

Thus Johannes Weiss tells us : [1]

The Christology of the Evangelist himself is very far advanced in the direction of the Johannine ; there can be no doubt that Jesus is to him the Son of God, in the sense of a divine being with divine power and divine knowledge

[1] *Jesus von Nazareth*, pp. 132–133 (quoted by Warfield).

from the beginning on. Nothing is hidden from him : his own destiny, the denial, the betrayal, the fate of Jerusalem —he tells it all exactly beforehand. Nothing is impossible to him : the most marvellous healings, like the sudden cure of the withered hand, of leprosy, of blindness, are performed by him without any difficulty ; he raises a dead person ; he walks on the water, and feeds thousands with a few loaves ; he makes the fig-tree wither—it is all related as if nothing else could be expected ; we see in these accounts neither the bold faith to which all is possible nor the enthusiasm of one beside himself, nor natural intermediation ; Jesus can do just anything. And therefore, to the Evangelist, it is nothing singular that at his death the sun was darkened, and the veil of the temple was rent ; and that he left the grave on the third day—all this follows altogether naturally and of itself from his Christology. But alongside of these stand other traits : his power rests on the Spirit, which was communicated to him at Baptism : we see how this Spirit struggles with the spirits ; his miraculous power is limited by unbelief, he must have faith himself and find faith in others if he is to help ; his dominion over suffering and death has its limits ; he trembles and is afraid, and feels forsaken by God ; he is ignorant of the day and hour ; he will not permit himself to be called ' Good Master ' ; he prays to the Father like a man, and is subject to all human emotions, even anger, and to mistake with reference to his disciples.

Now if this is an accurate summary of the Jesus-portrait in the Markan Gospel, what is the inference ? Are we to suppose that therefore there are in Mark two conceptions—(1) the human Jesus, (2) the Divine Christ, and that the first of these alone is the historical, and the second the mythical ? Or is it not rather obvious that the doctrine of the Two Natures is amply justified by Mark's Christology alone ? In view of the assumption sometimes made in modern times that the ' Two Natures ' doctrine is in some sense the creation of the Chalcedonian Christology, it is well to be reminded by such a passage as this from Weiss that, in the words of Dr. Warfield—

not only is the doctrine of the ' Two Natures ' the synthesis of the entire body of Christological data embodied in the pages of the New Testament ; and not only is it the teaching of all the writers of the New Testament severally ; but the New Testament provides no material whatever for inferring that a different view was ever held by the Christian community. The entire Christian tradition from the beginning, whatever that may be worth, is a tradition of a two-natured (Christ) Jesus, that is to say, of an incarnated God. Of a one-natured Jesus, tradition knows nothing, and supplies no materials from which he may be inferred.

But it would be a mistake to suppose that the revolt against the ' Two Natures' hypothesis, as it is called, comes solely from the negative and sceptical side : on the contrary, one of the most striking phenomena in the modern Christological period is the widespread criticism to which this doctrine has been subjected by men whose loyalty to Christ is unquestioned, but who feel that the Chalcedonian Definition, for example, fails as a vehicle for the expression of their belief. Not that their belief is in question, but that the language of the Chalcedonian Definition fails to express it in terms acceptable to their mode of thought, and the categories in which they prefer to express that thought. With this modern attack upon the Chalcedonian Definition we are intimately concerned, because here we shall find the real difficulties which orthodox theologians experience in their attempts to translate the truth contained in the ancient Creeds into terms of modern thought. As an example of an extreme statement of what the Chalcedonian Definition is supposed to teach, we may take the words of Principal Dykes in a series of papers on ' The Person of our Lord,' written for the *Expository Times* (October 1905–January 1906) :

A Being [he says] who combines in an inscrutable fashion Divine with human properties, and of whom, consequently, contradictory assertions may be made, whose single Person is Divine, while His dual natures hold an undefined relation to one another : this is not a scheme to satisfy either head or heart. It is but the bare skeleton of a dogma, in which one cannot readily recognise either the Jesus of the Gospels or the Christ of the Church's worship. It needs to be filled up with the details of our Saviour's earthly life, and with the meaning of His saving work as Revealer of the Father and Redeemer of man, before we can see in Him the Person whom Christians know and love.

Whilst we shall feel that this does but scant justice to the Chalcedonian Definition, there is no doubt that it represents, to a certain extent, the feeling of some modern theologians in their attitude towards the Chalcedonian Christology.

But the most searching criticism we have been able to find on this question is contained in Dr. Mackintosh's recent work entitled *The Person of Jesus Christ*, and we propose to quote this at length, because in our opinion it affords a useful summary of the chief difficulties which the modern mind experiences in any attempt to accept the ancient Christology, as this is presented to us in the Creeds and dogmatic utterances of the Church.

Dr. Mackintosh tells us that, for modern thought, the chief defect in strictly traditional Christology has been its insistence, not accidentally, but on principle, upon the doctrine of the ' Two Natures ' ; and that this doctrine, as defined, for example, in the Westminster Confession, although it is that in which tradition came to rest, now fails to satisfy the

great bulk of evangelical theologians.   He then goes
on to submit the doctrine to the following searching
criticism :

First, the doctrine of the two natures, in its traditional
form, imports into the life of Christ an incredible and
thoroughgoing dualism.   In place of that perfect unity
which is felt in every impression of Him, the whole is bisected
sharply by the fissure of distinction.   No longer one, He is
divided against Himself.   It has always been perceived
that a dualism of this kind, if more than a form of words,
annuls the very thought of redemption by means of God's
self-manifestation in flesh.   Divine and human alternately
vitiates the truth of incarnation.   The simplicity and
coherence of all that Christ was and did vanishes, for God
is not after all living a human life.   On the contrary, He
is still holding Himself at a distance from its experiences
and conditions.   There has been no saving descent.   Christ
executed this as God, it is said, and suffered that as man.
It could not be otherwise, since in the last resort deity is
impassible.   Now this leaves a profoundly disappointing
impression of unethical mystery and even, in a sense,
duplicity.   It means that the reader of the Gospels has
constantly to be on guard against his own instinctive
intuitions.   The self-consciousness of Jesus, as depicted by
the evangelists, we may call Divine or human as we please ;
to express the whole truth we must call it both at once.   But
it is a single consciousness after all ;   it moves always as a
spiritual unity ;   and separatist or divisive theories do a
grave disservice not merely to clear thinking, but to religious
truth and power.   Always the result has been that deity
and humanity in Christ are joined in ways so external that
either may be contemplated and (so to speak) analysed in
abstraction from the other.   It is an unquestioned merit in
the ecclesiastical Christology that it brings out emphatically
the basal oneness of Christ with God, insisting further that
this oneness is, in ultimate character, mysterious ;   it is a
grave fault, on the other hand, that it should so construe
this mystery as to get wholly out of touch with the actualities
of the New Testament.   Briefly, the doctrine of the two
natures, if taken seriously, gives us two abstractions instead

of one reality, two impotent halves in place of one living whole. It hypostatises falsely two *aspects* of a single concrete life—aspects which are so indubitably real that apart from either the whole fact would be quite other than it is, yet not in themselves distinctly functioning substantialities which may be logically estimated or adjusted to each other, or combined in unspiritual modes.

In the second place, there is a difficulty concerned with the person in which the two natures are held to be ' inseparably joined together.' Once more we are obliged to report unfavourably on the term ' nature,' this time from a rather different point of view. The ancient dogma proceeds on the definite assumption that, in both God and man, there exists a complex whole of attributes and qualities, which can be understood and spoken about as a ' nature ' enjoying some kind of real being apart from the unifying or focal Ego ; whereas nothing is more certain than that it is within personal experience, and only there, that all the varied factors of our human life—intellectual, moral, emotional, social—have any proper existence or reality. To put it frankly, when we abstract from personality—the spirit which gathers the manifold particulars into unity and suffuses each with the glow and intimacy of specifically conscious life—what we vaguely call ' human nature ' is not human nature in the least. It is at most hypothetical raw material, which, if taken up into and shot through with self-consciousness, becomes an organic factor in a real human experience, but in separation, as untenanted or by itself, it is no more human nature than hydrogen by itself is aquatic nature. We must not be tempted into the obvious mistake of regarding one element in a living unity as being the same thing outside the unity as within it. Now in tradition human nature *is* thus taken (even if it be only provisionally) as real apart from personality. According to the technical phrase, the manhood is enhypostatic. What constitutes the person is the Ego of the pre-existent Logos, who assumes into union with His own hypostasis that whole complex briefly described as ' human nature,' conveying to it the properties of His divinity. Certain teachers of the Church, who felt keenly the unreal character of an impersonal humanity, strove to redress the balance by

114

asserting that our Lord's manhood is personal separately or in its own right, with the unavoidable result that two personalities came only too plainly to be predicated of the one Christ.   A twofold personality, however, is not merely something that we fail to understand; it is something we see quite well to be impossible.   In fact, a being in whom now the God acts, now the man, is equally repellent to faith and theory.   It implies that to reach the Godhead we must pass out beyond the manhood, and *vice versa*—the two being so utterly heterogeneous and disparate that no true union is conceivable.

This dilemma, then—the Scylla of a duplex personality and the Charybdis of an impersonal manhood—has invariably proved fatal to the doctrine of two natures.   If it takes Jesus' manhood seriously, as the New Testament of course does by instinct, it makes shipwreck on the notion of a double Self.   If, on the other hand, it insists on the unity of the person, the unavoidable result is to abridge the integrity of the manhood and present a Figure whom it is difficult to identify with the Jesus of the Synoptic Gospels. For tradition the unity of the person is always a problem, and to the last a mystery; for the New Testament it is the first reality we touch.   For tradition it appears as a hypothetical conclusion tentatively posited at the close of intricate processes of reasoning; for the New Testament it is given in a direct and original impression.   For tradition the question is that of uniting two abstractions which have been defined in bare contrast to each other; for a mind which takes its religion from the New Testament the problem is to investigate the grounds which have led Christians in every age to confess this concrete historic person, Jesus Christ, as God.—*The Person of Jesus Christ,* pp. 294–7.

Now, although we may not be very much perturbed by the statement of Dr. Loofs with reference to the attitude of liberal theologians, especially German, towards the ancient Christology, because a knowledge of the premises from which they start makes their conclusions almost inevitable, yet no one, we venture to think, can fail to be deeply impressed by such a criticism of the traditional Christology as that which is offered in the above lengthy quotation from Dr. Mackintosh's most able and reverent work on the Person of Christ. And this the more so when we remember that his criticism voices the judgment of hundreds of the students of Christology in language of a careful and guarded character which they can scarce excel. We have here real difficulties which are felt by those most loyal to the Person of Christ, most anxious to render the homage due unto His Name; and yet for whom the progress of modern thought, and the new categories within which that thought finds itself compelled to move to-day, make the restatement and reinterpretation of the Creeds almost an imperative necessity. And we venture to think that no attempt of a constructive character in Christology to-day will be successful which fails to grapple with these difficulties, or to answer them so far as they can be answered. Not that these difficulties in some cases are entirely new and due solely to the progressive character of modern thought. On the contrary, as we hope to show, Dr. Mackintosh has in some cases simply restated in terms of modern thought objections which have been urged against the received Christology from the first, and which are due not to modern thought, but to the very nature of the subject itself, and to which therefore no answer capable of fully satisfying the human intellect can ever be given. The doctrine of the Incarnation must ever transcend the efforts of finite minds, either to comprehend it, or to express it in human language which will not be open to the charge of inconsistency, or even of containing seemingly contradictory statements. This, however, is due both

116

to the nature of the subject and the failure of human language in every age to express it. Nevertheless, we believe that a restatement of the Christological problem to-day is possible which, to a certain extent, can meet the perplexities which the ancient Christology presents to those who are seeking to make it real to their own minds.

If we enquire in what direction modern thought is capable of grappling with the problem under better conditions, and with more hope of success than was possible to those responsible for the ancient Christology, we shall find the answer in the following considerations :

(1) It is a commonplace to assert that ancient theologians were handicapped in their efforts by a defective conception of ' personality,' and it is a claim of modern thought to have given to the word ' personality ' a fuller and a vastly richer content than it ever possessed for the minds of those upon whom devolved the task of interpreting the one unique Personality which has ever emerged in the history of the world.

In our own day personality is put forward as the supreme fact, the ideal centre of consciousness. And the comparatively new science of psychology is exercising a powerful influence upon the Christological problem.

(2) The modern scientific hypothesis of evolution has been applied not only to the material universe, but also to the realms of the moral and the spiritual, and has even penetrated into the field of metaphysics. In fact, this category of thought threatens to revolutionise our whole religious outlook, and has done so already in almost every field of mental activity. Consequently it has to be reckoned with as a great

factor, not only in the creation of the modern religious outlook, but more especially in the reaffirmation of the Creeds, and not least in the modern restatement of the Christology problem.

The influence of this factor, as one of the four most recent categories moulding present religious thought, is ably dealt with in W. D. McLaren's book entitled *Our Growing Creed*. This is a work which has not yet received that recognition which its outstanding merits deserve.

The four fresh factors which Mr. McLaren selects as the most potent in the process of reshaping and reinterpreting the Creed are :

(*a*) The doctrine of the Universal Fatherhood ; (*b*) the doctrine of Evolution ; (*c*) the Spirit of Collectivism ; (*d*) the Spirit of Historical Criticism. Of these four different trends of thought, the most revolutionary has undoubtedly been the second.

(3) The trend of modern thought, both in philosophy and theology, has brought into ever-increasing prominence the doctrine of the Immanence and Transcendence of God. This is an agelong puzzle with which the human mind has never yet successfully grappled, and the difficulty created for human thought by the conception of the Deity transcending creation, and yet wholly present in the meanest thing that lives, is no new one. Nevertheless for our age this difficulty has, if anything, become more acutely felt by those who have adopted in any degree the reaffirmation of the philosophy of Change, so brilliantly stated by Professor Bergson. One of the outstanding needs, therefore, of theology at the present day is a complete survey of the whole problem of the Being of God in view of the changed

outlook suggested to men's minds by (*a*) the philosophy of the Absolute, and (*b*) the philosophy of Change. We may here perhaps note in passing that although Bergson himself has not gone further than deducing life and the vital impulse as an ultimate reality, nevertheless one of his most sympathetic and acute disciples, Dr. Carr, in his recent work, *A Study of the Fundamental Principle of the Philosophy of Bergson*, claims that the fundamental principle of Bergson's philosophy results in a new conception of Deity. God can be conceived of as ' unceasing life, action, freedom.' This is a necessary deduction from Bergson's fundamental postulate of change as the absolute principle. It would seem to follow from this, that the old theological conception of the Changelessness of God will have to be restated in such a way as to conserve this new truth towards which philosophy is leading us. There is no need to believe that the reconciliation between theology and philosophy on this point is an impossibility. We can quite easily believe in a Changeless God Who Himself is Lord of Change, and is not Himself bound by that principle which He has allowed to prevail within the Universe of which He is the Creator. He Himself, we may well believe, can continue to transcend change, even whilst at the same time He is the Creator of a Universe wherein are infinite possibilities of change, and which is ever in a state of becoming by the never-ending process of creative evolution. But whilst this new conception of God as ' unceasing life, action, freedom,' does not necessarily exclude the old complementary truth of His Changelessness, as transcendent above and yet immanent in His Creation, nevertheless the bearing of this new aspect of

119

the truth of the Being of God upon the doctrine of the Incarnation must be faced by those who seek to reinterpret Christology in terms of modern thought.

And not the least difficult task in such an attempt will be the fullest possible analysis of the Divine Nature and the Being of God both in Himself and in His relations with His Creation. This is fundamental in view of the fact that the difficulties created for Christology have, to a large extent, as we have seen, been due to an imperfect apprehension of the being and nature not only of man but of God. It is pertinent to enquire how many of these difficulties would have vanished if all through full weight had been given to St. Paul's clear grip upon the fundamental principle that ' Of Him and through Him and unto Him are all things ' : a principle which alone affords a secure basis for an Incarnation, and a right apprehension of God in His relationship to the finite creation. This principle secures the two complementary truths of His Transcendence and Immanence, and a false emphasis upon either leads to bankruptcy in the field of Christology. These then are some of the considerations to be borne in mind in the attempt to construct a Christology in terms of modern thought. We shall best secure clearness of treatment if we consider first of all the problem of the dualism created by the doctrine of the Incarnation, and re-emphasised in, e.g., Dr. Mackintosh's criticism of the ancient Christology.

Then we shall pass on to consider more in detail the analysis of human nature and personality in the light of modern psychology. After this we must endeavour to gather up what fresh light has been shed upon the Divine Nature and the Being of God by modern thought. We must then examine the human and the Divine in their relationship. This analysis of the human and the Divine should furnish us with the necessary data for a restatement of the Christological problem, and we shall then be in a position to estimate the gains and losses involved in such a restatement, and so rightly gauge the value of the new in the light of the old, and *vice versa.*

2.

DUALISM

AT the outset we have clearly to recognise that the dualism between the human and the Divine in the Person of Christ is in a very real sense an inevitable factor, and a fundamental postulate involved in the very doctrine of an Incarnation. It is but the recognition, in the field of Christology, of a fundamental fact of all our thinking with reference to the Being and Nature of God in contrast to His Creation. Its origin lies in the very constitution of the finite, which, though contained in, is nevertheless not identical with, the Infinite. The Divine is not the human, nor is the human the Divine, in the ultimate analysis. Between the Creator and the creature there is, and must ever be, a line of demarcation, and Christian Theism, if it attempts to obliterate that line, must inevitably degenerate into Pantheism. And if this be true of God, as Divine, in relation to man, as human, it must hold true also of the Incarnation.

But whilst clearly recognising this as fundamental for a sound Christology, it may well be questioned whether this distinction has not been unduly pressed with dangerous results. The moment attention is fixed upon the distinction of the Two Natures, as clearly set forth in, for example, the Chalcedonian Definition, the inherent dualism involved in such a conception is acutely felt, and inevitably gives rise to a feeling of revolt in favour of the Unity. Thus it is

122

that this charge of dualism has been brought against the received Christology in every age, and it is inevitable that it should be so. And, further, the received Christology cannot escape such criticism. The very fact that it has to steer a middle course between the Scylla of a duplex personality, and the Charybdis of an impersonal manhood, is itself a witness to the faithfulness with which it reflects the doctrine of the Incarnation. The Monophysite solution in comparison is so simple, and yet so fundamentally unfaithful to the deepest revelation we have of the eternal distinction between the Creator and the creature. But once the human mind has clearly grasped this essential distinction, it is quite possible to go on to a fuller apprehension of another great truth of a wonderfully helpful character in toning down, whilst not obliterating, the dualism between the human and the Divine. And this truth is the fact of an essential affinity between the human and the Divine of which the Incarnation itself was both a revelation and a confirmation. And surely for modern thought, the edge of the criticism against the incurable dualism of the Chalcedonian Definition is, to a considerable extent, blunted by allowing due weight to this second equally fundamental postulate of a sound Christology. Christian thought cannot ever abandon the dualism which undoubtedly has impeded its efforts to solve the Christological problem. It must continue to recognise a generic difference between the human and the Divine Natures, but it can go on to a fuller appreciation perhaps than has yet been given to the Biblical truth of an essential affinity between the Divine and the human natures.

And this truth is no modern discovery, although

it may well be re-emphasised in modern Christology. It is, in fact, an idea familiar enough in ancient Greek thought, and one to which both poet and philosopher in pre-Christian times paid tribute. We have only to look, for example, at that exquisite product of Stoicism, the Hymn of Cleanthes, to find a beautiful expression of this truth which St. Paul himself selected as a common meeting-ground of Greek and Christian thought in his famous sermon on Mars Hill.[1]

This great truth, so eloquently advocated by the Apostle of the Gentiles, reaches back to the Hymn of Cleanthes, where it receives poetic expression in the famous lines (4 and 5):

ἐκ σοῦ γὰρ γενόμεσθα, θεοῦ μίμημα λαχόντες
μοῦνοι, ὅσα ζώει τε καὶ ἔρπει θνήτ᾽ ἐπὶ γαῖαν.

We are thy children, we alone, of all
On earth's broad ways that wander to and fro,
Bearing thine image wheresoe'er we go.[2]

It was apparently a familiar Greek idea that men are but ' mortal gods,' and gods ' immortal men '— τί δαὶ οἱ ἄνθρωποι ; θεοὶ θνητοί· τί δαὶ οἱ θεοί ; ἄνθρωποι ἀθάνατοι. This belief was imported into Roman religion, and, in its developed form, as the man-deifying movement culminating in the worship of the Cæsars, formed the most distinctive contribution of Roman religion—the conception of a Man-God—as Dr. Warde Fowler has shown in his recent book, *Roman Ideas of Deity*.

But Plato was the first of the Greeks to make the

---

[1] Acts xvii. 26–28, τοῦ γὰρ καὶ γένος ἐσμέν.
[2] Reading γενόμεσθα for the corrupt γένος ἐσμέν, ἤχου, the conjecture of Meineke.

kinship of the Divine and human natures the basis
of a philosophy of man, and the passages in his writings
bearing upon this doctrine are fully dealt with in
James Adam's delightful book entitled *The Vitality
of Platonism*, where he tells us that it was Plato
who expounded the doctrine with more emphasis
than any pre-Christian body of thinkers except the
Stoics, and with a far greater wealth of philosophic
meaning than any other writer in any age.

The passages in Plato where this idea is distinctively emphasised are worth considering a little more
in detail, because they bring out clearly a thought
which is of special significance in our enquiry. The
doctrine of the essential Divinity of man is, of course,
an underlying conviction of Plato's many writings,
as Mr. Adam points out in the notes to his edition of
the ' Republic ' (501 B), where he says :

> The sure and abiding conviction of the presence of a
> divine element within us, rendering our nature essentially
> and truly human, makes itself felt in nearly all the dialogues
> of Plato.   It is the ultimate source of all his idealism, religious
> and metaphysical, no less than moral and political, and may
> well be considered the most precious and enduring inheritance
> which he has bequeathed to posterity.

From this belief Plato deduces his version of man's
chief end, which is the knowledge of God, and culminates in assimilation to His glorious image—
ὁμοίωσις θεῷ κατὰ τὸ δυνατὸν ἀνθρώπῳ.[1]

But the really helpful thought is this : *that it is just
the presence of this Divine element that makes us specifically human.   Man is most truly man when he most
resembles God.*   Mr. Adam points to two passages in

---

[1] *Theaet.* 176 B.

the ' Republic ' where, in his opinion, this suggestion is most clearly intended.[1]

The argument is, that, e.g., a State can only attain to true happiness if it be sketched by painters who copy the divine original. The true philosopher, who has his eye fixed upon immutable principles, will fashion States after the heavenly image. So also if he has to fashion human nature generally. Where will he find the original ? The answer is in the form and likeness of God.

They will begin by taking the State and the manners of men, from which, as from a tablet, they will rub out the picture, and leave a clean surface. . . . Having effected this, they will proceed to trace an outline of the constitution. . . . And when they are filling in the work, as I conceive, they will often turn their eyes upwards and downwards : I mean that they will first look at absolute justice and beauty and temperance, and again at the human copy ; and will mingle and temper the various elements of life into the image of a man ; and this they will conceive according to that other image, which, when existing among men, Homer calls the form and likeness of God.

If ἀνδρείκελον is nothing but θεοείκελον, man is most manlike when he most resembles God.[2]

Again in the 'Timæus' (90 A) Plato writes :

As concerning the sovereign part of soul within us, that which we say, and say truly, dwells at the top of the body and raises us from earth towards our heavenly kindred, forasmuch as we are a heavenly and not an earthly plant—

---

[1] *Republic*, 501 B, 589 D. The references are to Adam's edition in two vols.

[2] We have followed Jowett's translation, with which compare that of Davies and Vaughan, who translate τὸ ἀνδρείκελον, ' they will work in *the true human complexion*, guided by those realisations of it among men, which . . . even Homer has described as godly and godlike.'

θεοειδές τε καὶ θεοείκελον. The reference seems to be to Iliad i. 131, θεοείκελ' Ἀχιλλεῦ.

φυτὸν οὐκ ἔγγειον, ἀλλ᾽ οὐράνιον—we ought to believe that
God has given it to each of us as a dæmon.[1]

Thus the central thought of Plato's religious teaching
is the essential Divinity of the human soul, and his
deduction from this, that man is truly human just in
proportion as he is Divine, is, as Mr. Adam reminds
us, one which was afterwards taken up by Aristotle
and the Stoics. ' And no one,' he says, ' can fail to
see its hitherto unexhausted, perhaps for ever inex-
haustible, significance for religion.'

Can we make use of this in our effort at a constructive Christology ? The danger to which the
Platonic teaching of the essential Divinity of the
human soul is exposed is, of course, the same to
which we have already referred, viz. the obliteration
of the distinction between the human and the Divine ;
but the clear recognition of an essential affinity
between the two, notwithstanding their eternal distinction, is surely a most fruitful conception. If the
human is never more truly and essentially human
than when it is most Godlike ; if man is most truly
man when he most resembles God, we have here the
possibility of such an indissoluble union between the
two, in virtue of their affinity, as will satisfy Catholic
thought whilst still preserving within their unity the
difference between them. If we consider the essential
affinity between the two as the real basis of their
union, and that by which alone such a union is
rendered possible, we have gone a long way to miti-
gate the dualism which still remains. Applying this

---

[1] Works, vol. vii; Bekker, p. 368. (τὸ δὲ δὴ περὶ τοῦ κυριωτάτου παρ᾽
ἡμῖν ψυχῆς εἴδους διανοεῖσθαι δεῖ τῇδε, ὡς ἄρα αὐτὸ δαίμονα θεὸς ἑκάστῳ δέδωκε,
τοῦτο ὃ δή φαμεν οἰκεῖν μὲν ἡμῶν ἐπ᾽ ἄκρῳ τῷ σώματι, πρὸς δὲ τὴν ἐν οὐρανῷ
ξυγγένειαν ἀπὸ γῆς ἡμᾶς αἴρειν ὡς ὄντας φυτὸν οὐκ ἔγγειον, ἀλλ᾽ οὐράνιον,
ὀρθότατα λέγοντες.

line of thought to the Person of Christ, it follows
that in His Incarnate life He was never more truly
Divine than when He was most really human, and
never more truly human than when He was most
really Divine. Does not such a Christology take us
back at once to the New Testament portrait of Jesus
Christ in His essential unity as the God-Man, Divine
in Human, Human in Divine? How true it is that
the unity of the Person is the first reality we touch
in the New Testament portrait! But does not this
doctrine of an essential affinity between the human
and the Divine continue to secure for us this same
unity of Person, even when we leave the New Testament portrait and submit our impressions to the
searching analysis of human reason? Even though
one line of thought suggested by human reason bids
us remember the essential dualism which must have
prevailed within the unity of Person, so vividly depicted for us in our New Testament portrait; yet
another line of thought, reminding us of the essential
affinity between the human and the Divine, inter-
venes to preserve for us the reality of the unity just
when this is most seriously threatened with disintegration by other considerations. May not this pregnant
thought help human reason to grasp the unity of
Christ's Person in just as real and vivid a way as
faith does? Moving along some such a line of thought
as is here suggested the modern mind may be helped,
if not entirely to banish the obstacle of a dualism
which it is felt is fatal to any intellectual grasp of the
unity of Christ's Person, at any rate so effectively to
balance this by another consideration, as to make it
possible not only for faith, but also for reason, to
retain the reality of the One Christ which the New

Testament presents for our acceptance. But if this doctrine is to play that part in the elucidation of a modern Christology, which we have ventured to suggest that it may play, it will need to be supported not only by the fact that it is rooted in Greek thought and Platonic philosophy—is moreover a fundamental postulate of revealed religion in Judaism, and receives its confirmation in the fact of the Incarnation itself, of which it is the basis ; but it must also be shown to be rooted and grounded in the very nature and being of both man and God. We must turn, therefore, to the consideration of these two factors in order to see whether modern research into the depths of human personality justifies our still clinging to the belief that there is an essential affinity between the human and the Divine. Only upon this basis can we hope to build up a reconstruction of the doctrine of the Enhypostasia, which will commend itself to modern thought with increasing force once it can be shown to be founded upon the nature of God and man. Only if there is an essential affinity between the human and the Divine, is it conceivable that the unique personality of Jesus Christ could be at one and the same time truly human and yet fully Divine ; and that His unique *single* consciousness, which is the true basis of the unity of His Person, could be the central Ego of both natures. This brings us to the second part of our task, viz. the analysis of human nature in the light of modern psychology.

3.

THE ANALYSIS OF HUMAN NATURE IN THE LIGHT OF MODERN PSYCHOLOGY.

(a) THE SOUL.
(b) ITS RELATIONS WITH THE BODY.
(c) HUMAN PERSONALITY.

NOW it is significant that the moment we open a modern book on psychology, we find that the phraseology to which we have grown accustomed in our study of ancient Christology has practically vanished. 'Nature,' 'Substance,' 'Person,' 'Essence' are gone, and we are confronted with a new vocabulary, in which the dominant words seem to be 'Consciousness,' 'Personality,' and 'Ego.' The all-absorbing subject is the unity, continuity, discontinuity of consciousness. We read of the 'sub-conscious,' 'un-conscious,' or 'sub-liminal self,' 'alterations of personality,' 'the stream of thought,' and so on. This vocabulary is a forcible reminder that one of the first needs of a modern Christology, if it is to be in any sense a reinterpretation of the old, will be an endeavour to establish some series of equations between the old and the new terms.[1] Such words as 'Nature,' 'Substance,' 'Person,' need to be thought out afresh, and possibly given a fuller and a richer content in the light of modern psychology. Not that we believe such words to be perfectly useless and meaningless, because even though modern thought

[1] Cf. an article in the *Interpreter*, April 1915, 'An Essay on the Christological Problem.'

prefers a new vocabulary, it is the same truths which find expression, whether in the old or the new phraseologies.   It must not be supposed that psychology is the discovery of our time.   In many respects the analysis of ' Self ' by the ancients was as profound as anything contained in a modern text-book on the subject, and the ideas which it was sought to express by such terms as ' Nature,' ' Substance,' ' Person,' were the same as the modern psychologist expresses in his new vocabulary.[1]   Therefore the acceptance in modern Christology of this new vocabulary is not the acknowledgment of the bankruptcy of the ancient Christology.   It simply means that we are striving to express the same truths in a different way to that employed by the Fathers.   Whether we prefer to think in terms of ' Consciousness ' rather than of ' Nature,' and to speak of ' Two Consciousnesses ' rather than of ' Two Natures,' does not make the Christological problem less easy, as we hope to show, nor does it eliminate that dualism against which the modern mind revolts when it strives to conceive of the union of the human and the Divine in the Person of Christ. We note with great satisfaction an inclination on the part of some thinkers to reintroduce the term ' substance ' into psychology.   We remember the position of fundamental importance which this term occupied in the metaphysics of the Schoolmen in its well-accredited sense of something permanently self-identical, that which subsists in itself (*id quod per se stat*) ; and although it has been subjected to persistent attacks from the days of Locke, Hume, Berkeley,

---

[1] See e.g. Brett's *History of Psychology, Ancient and Patristic*, especially chap. viii., ' The Neo-Platonic Idea of Man,' and chap. x., ' The Doctrine of S. Augustine.'

in the eighteenth century down to our own time,
when we find it dismissed with scarcely any comment
as an outworn expression of a discredited philosophy,
we are by no means convinced that the attacks upon
it have been altogether just, and in some cases have
been due to a mistaken idea of its meaning. Christo-
logists need not be over eager to abandon a term
which, though rent to tatters and covered with con-
tempt by eighteenth-century and nineteenth-century
philosophers, may yet come to its own again in the
hands of twentieth-century psychologists. This is
a point, however, which we shall not press, because
we believe it to be quite possible to translate the ideas
of Leontius of Byzantium into terms of modern
thought, and still to retain his Christology, which need
not be bound up with the acceptance or rejection of
the term substance.

The questions we have to ask of modern psychology
are mainly these :

(1) To state whether the soul is spiritual or
material.

(2) To define its relations with the body, its origin
and future destiny.

(3) To define human personality.

At the outset we are met by a difficulty, in that
psychologists are divided amongst themselves as to
whether the discussion of these ultimate questions
is strictly within the purview of the science of psychology, or whether they must not be left to philosophy
and theology.

(a) Some regard the task of psychology to be
simply the registration of the phenomena of sensations,
perceptions, thoughts, volitions, emotions, and the
like, which may be classified, analysed, and possibly

132

reduced to the smallest number of fundamental activities. Here psychology halts, and is content with the humble task of description; leaving to metaphysics the further and more ultimate questions which inevitably present themselves as the result of the data described and analysed.

(*b*) Others claim for psychology a much larger scope, and include within its province not only a generalisation of facts, but the further enquiry into the inner nature and constitution of the root and subject of these phenomena. Not only must psychology describe and classify the operations of the mind or soul (ψυχή, πνεῦμα)—the Ego, Self, or Spirit—it must also pass on to the consideration of the nature and constitution of the soul itself. Whence is it? What is it?

The difference between these rival claims as to the scope of psychology is really, as Dr. Aveling points out, the difference between psychology with and without a soul.[1] For our purpose we accept that wider interpretation of the scope of psychology which is ably advocated, e.g., by Dr. Maher, who devotes the Second Book of his learned work to the subject of Rational Psychology, which he distinguishes from Empirical or Phenomenal Psychology, assigning to the former the investigation of the results presented by the latter. In this distinction Dr. Maher is following Sir W. Hamilton, who described the results deduced from the phenomena presented by empirical or experimental psychology as inferential psychology, or the ontology of the mind. It is the task of this

---

[1] See an article under this title in *The Quest*, April 1915, vol. vi. No. 3, and compare Wm. McDougall's treatment in *Body and Mind*, chap. viii.

last to attempt an answer as to the nature and constitution of the soul, basing its conclusions both upon observation and inference.

> The aim of Rational, Metaphysical, or Philosophical Psychology [Dr. Maher tells us] is to penetrate to the source of the phenomena of consciousness. It endeavours to ascertain the inner constitution of the subject of our psychical states, and to discover the relations subsisting between this subject and the body. In a word, Philosophical Psychology seeks to learn what may be gathered by the light of reason regarding the nature, origin, and destiny of the human soul. —*Psychology*, 7th edition.

Nothing could be better for our purpose than to ask of Rational Psychology what it can tell us on these points, and we shall then be in a position to see how far our modern knowledge of human nature helps us in the consideration of the Christological problem. We must follow Dr. Maher very closely and attempt to summarise his results, with which may be compared Wm. McDougall's fine treatment in the work mentioned above, *Body and Mind.*

(A.) THE SOUL.

What conclusion does he reach as to the nature of the soul ?

He seeks to establish the following propositions :

(*a*) The Substantiality of the Human Mind or Soul.

(*b*) Its persisting indivisible *identity* through life.

(*c*) The Simplicity of the Soul.

(*d*) The Spirituality of the Soul.

We have then these four propositions :

The soul is shown to be a substantial principle having a persisting indivisible identity through life : it is in its nature simple and spiritual.

Each of these propositions, taken by itself, [we are told] may afford but little positive information ; and even when they have been all combined, the synthetic concept of the nature of the soul thus reached will still necesssarily be very imperfect and inadequate ; nevertheless, it will constitute knowledge real and valid, so far as it goes.

And surely this conclusion is of great significance for our enquiry, if it can successfully withstand the attacks from every side which are aimed against it, and hold its own in the face of the rival theories by which it is challenged. We must not press Dr. Maher's conclusions beyond the point to which they take us. But what does he give us as the result of this analysis of human nature ? If the soul is a simple, spiritual, substantial principle ; if the most distinctive factor within man is an Ego, which, in the ultimate analysis, transcends completely the material organism of which it is the central principle, and knows itself as in some sense capable of leading an existence independent of the body ; then we may say that an analysis of the human yields us at its very central and basic point, in the very central subject of human personality itself—the Ego —something which at the very least may be named immaterial, incorporeal, and in this sense spiritual. Whether from other considerations we may enrich this ' spirituality of the soul ' with a much fuller content, and claim for it the possession of something infinitely more than the attribute of incorporeality, is a question for theology, and carries us beyond the realm of the science of psychology ; but this conclusion at least seems legitimate as the result of our enquiry : that an analysis of human nature in the light of modern psychology yields us, in its most central and distinctive principle—the soul—an element which transcends the material and opens out into the spiritual. Is it here that we are to look for a point of contact between the human and the Divine? Is it thus at the very centre of man's being, and in that which is most distinctive of man, that we find something which justifies the theological hypothesis of an essential affinity between the human and the Divine? If there is such an affinity, we shall expect to find it in that which is highest in man.

In that which is the most distinctive factor of man's constitution, modern psychology reveals to us the presence of something—an incorporeal, immaterial, or spiritual soul—which may well prove to be the meeting-place at the very centre of man's being—between the human and the Divine.

The importance of this conclusion cannot be over-emphasised. Lest, however, it be urged that Dr. Maher is influenced in any way by ' dogmatic prejudice ' in arriving at the conclusion he reaches, we may consider the verdict of Wm. McDougall, who certainly cannot be accused of approaching the subject with anything but an open mind so far as the desire to support religious doctrines is concerned. No reader of *Body and Mind* can accuse the author of unfairness in his presentation of the case of his opponents. Anyone reading chapters vii.–x. cannot but be impressed with the weight of arguments which seems at first sight to incline wholly towards the rejection of animism; the conclusions therefore reached in chapters xiv.–xvi. are not those of one who in any sense can be accused of having under-estimated the force of the arguments on the other side, and the constructive work in chapters xvii.–

xxiv. comes as a welcome relief to anyone who still clings to the hypothesis of the soul. We can take fresh courage when so impartial and unprejudiced an advocate as Wm. McDougall combats so successfully the adverse verdict of science, and champions to-day the ' Animistic ' as against the ' Mechanistic ' dogma in the consideration of the psycho-physical problem. What, then, are the conclusions reached by McDougall ? He deduces overwhelmingly strong reasons for accepting, as the best working hypothesis of the psycho-physical relation, Animism as against Parallelism. He rejects Wm. James' 'transmission theory ' and the existence in the universe of ' a lot of diffuse mind-stuff, unable of itself to get into consistent personal form, or to take permanent possession of an organism, and yet always craving to do so.'

As regards the soul, McDougall indicates what negative assertions may be made with some confidence :

We can say that the soul has not the essential attributes of matter, namely, extension (or the attribute of occupying space) and ponderability or mass ; for if it had these attributes it would be subject to the laws of mechanism ; and it is just because we have found that mental and vital processes cannot be completely described and explained in terms of mechanism that we are compelled to believe in the co-operation of some non-mechanical teleological factor, and to adopt the hypothesis of the soul.

He rejects the description of the soul as a ' substance,' in the old scholastic sense of a core or substratum underlying and distinct from all the attributes of a thing. On the analogy, however, of a material thing or being as a sum, not only of ' permanent possibilities of sensation,' but also of enduring possibilities or capacities of definite kinds of action and reaction upon other material things, so we may describe a soul as ' a sum of enduring capacities for thoughts, feelings, and efforts of determinate kinds.' Instead of the word ' substance ' as the name for any such sum of enduring capacities, McDougall proposes the word ' thing ' or ' being.' He then goes on to describe the soul in positive terms as follows :

We may then describe a soul as a being that possesses, or is, the sum of definite capacities for psychical activity and psycho-physical interaction, of which the most funda-mental are (1) the capacity of producing, in response to certain physical stimuli (the sensory processes of the brain), the whole range of sensation qualities in their whole range of intensities ; (2) the capacity of responding to certain sensation-complexes with the production of meanings, as, for example, spatial meanings ; (3) the capacity of respond-ing to these sensations and these meanings with feeling and conation or effort, under the spur of which further meanings may be brought to consciousness in accordance with the laws of reproduction of similars and of reasoning ; (4) the capacity of reacting upon the brain-processes to modify their course in a way which we cannot clearly define, but which we may provisionally conceive as a process of guidance by which streams of nervous energy may be concentrated in a way that antagonizes the tendency of all physical energy to dissipation and degradation. These are the fundamental capacities of conscious activity that we may assign to the soul, and we may say that in the laws or uniformities that we can discover in these processes we may discern the laws or the nature of the soul ; and the view that the soul is this sum of psychical capacities we may express by saying that the soul is a psychic being.

Moreover, our author, whilst criticising the Cartesian description of the soul as a thinking being, prefers rather to describe it as ' a being capable of being stimulated to conscious activities through the agency of the body or brain with which it stands in relations of reciprocal influence.'

Further, we must maintain [he says] that the soul is in some sense a unitary being or entity distinct from all others ; for we found that prominent among the facts which compel us to accept the animistic hypothesis are the facts of psychical individuality, the fact that consciousness, as known to us, occurs only as individual coherent streams of personal consciousness, and all the facts summed up in the phrase, ' the unity of consciousness.' We found that these facts remain absolutely unintelligible, unless we postulate some ground of this unity and coherence and separateness of individual streams of consciousness, some ground other than the bodily organisation.

These capacities and functions, then, are, according to McDougall, ' the minimum that can be attributed to the soul.' But there remains the problem of ' Memory,' so ably dealt with in chapter xxiv., and this carries us still further forward in the task of defining the soul. If memory is, in part at least, immaterially conditioned, this hypothesis of the dual conditions of memory makes it possible for us to believe that the soul,

if it survives the dissolution of the body, carries with it some large part of that which has been gained by intellectual and moral effort ; and although the acceptance of the view we have suggested as to the essential part played by the body in conditioning the sensory content of consciousness, would make it impossible to suppose that the surviving soul could enjoy the exercise of thought of the kind with which alone we are familiar, yet it is not inconceivable that it might find conditions that would stimulate it to imageless thought (possibly conditions of direct or telepathic communication with other minds), or might find under other conditions (possibly in association with some other bodily organism) a sphere for the application and actualisation of the capacities developed in it during its life in the body.

Wm. McDougall finally suggests the probability of the soul being operative in the guidance of bodily

growth, either directly or by means of a general
control exercised by it over some system of subordinate
psychic agents. He concludes his brilliant work
with a few pregnant thoughts concerning the hypothesis of the soul's part in heredity, and its place in
the scheme of organic evolution.

(B.) Its Relations with the Body.

But can we carry our investigation still further?
Can we define more closely the relations of this
spiritual soul to the body? Here again modern
psychological research can help us much.

We find the following rival theories :

I. *Materialism.*—This teaches that ' thought is
a secretion of the brain ' (Cabanis). ' There subsists
the same relation between thought and the brain
as between bile and the liver ' (Vogt).

' Thought is a motion in matter,' a ' phosphores-
cence ' of the brain (Moleschott).

Thought, spirit, soul, are not material, not a substance,
but the effect of the conjoined action of many materials
endowed with force or qualities. . . . In the same manner
as the steam-engine produces motion, so does the organic
complication of force-endowed materials produce in the
animal body effects so interwoven as to become a unit, which
is then by us called spirit, soul, thought. The sum of these
effects is nothing material ; it can be perceived by our senses
as little as any other simple force, such as magnetism,
electricity, &c., merely by its manifestations.—Büchner.

These quotations, cited in Dr. Maher's work, give
us a fair conception of the materialistic hypothesis
which seeks to reduce the mind to matter, and to
show the absolute dependence of mental life on

140

bodily condition ; a dependence which it claims is more and more conclusively demonstrated with every advance made in physiology and pathology.

II. *Idealism.*—The counter-hypothesis is that of idealism, which seeks to read all matter in terms of mind ; postulating that matter is dependent for its very existence upon a perceiving mind, and that the most primary data for consciousness are mental and not material phenomena.

This theory [says Dr. Maher] overcomes all difficulties as to the relations between body and mind, or the possibility of inter-action between them by boldly denying the reality of any material substance existing in itself without the mind. It holds that our consciousness of mental states is *immediate* and *primary*, whilst our assurance as to the reality of matter is at best *mediate* and *secondary*. . . .

It assumes that matter could not act upon mind ; and finally concludes that the most philosophical course is to deny all extra-mental reality to matter, and to look upon the seemingly independent material world as an illusory creation or emanation of mind itself.

III. *Monism.*—But the most serious assault which at present is being directed against the doctrine of the spiritual soul and future life is, according to Dr. Maher, Monism, which he thus describes :

In its best-known form this hypothesis, for it is essentially a *metaphysical* conception, has been styled the *Double-Aspect Theory*, and the *Identity-hypothesis*, because of its maintaining that mental states and the concomitant nerve-changes are simply different ' aspects ' of one and the same being. It has been called the New Spinozism, from its affinity to the metaphysical theory of the father of modern Pantheism ; and it has also been termed the doctrine of *Psycho-physical parallelism* from its denial of all inter-action between the psychical and the physical processes which take place in the living being. . . ,

141

Marked by important differences in the hands of its various exponents, Monism, in all its forms, adheres to the cardinal tenet that *Mind and Body are not two distinct realities but merely two ' aspects,' ' sides,' or ' phases ' of one being, and that there is no real interaction between mental and bodily states*.

The difficulties presented by the doctrine of Parallelism—which practically rules out all religious conceptions and hopes—and the rival doctrine of Animism—with which he believes the future of religion is intimately bound up—are dealt with in Wm. McDougall's *Body and Mind*, and he sums up in favour of animism, as the best working hypothesis of the psycho-physical relation. Now from a review of these rival theories, it may be legitimate perhaps to venture upon a suggestion.

May we assume that Materialism, Idealism, and Monism are all attempts to secure the recognition of different aspects of the truth, and to this extent that each is relatively correct ? Their results taken together would suggest :

(1) That mind *does* to a certain extent depend upon matter.

(2) That mind *is* to a certain degree independent of matter.

(3) That consequently there is a *relative* interaction and interdependence between mental and bodily states, but that this is not *absolute*.

IV. Although the attempt of Materialism to define the soul purely in terms of matter, and the attempt of Idealism to read all matter in terms of mind, have both failed, yet both theories have been of great value in helping us to realise how close and intimate a relationship exists between mental activities and the bodily conditions and movements which accompany them. The exaggerated emphasis upon the difference between ' soul ' and ' body,' as a reaction from the materialistic hypothesis, has led to a tendency to divorce the two, and to regard them as distinct and even antagonistic ' substances ' having nothing in common ; capable even of subsisting in themselves as distinct and independent entities, or of combining into a union resulting in man—an individual being composed of two ' substances ' : body and soul, united.

This false dualism has in its turn given rise to theories which have attempted to overcome it either by the identification of matter with mind, or a pantheistic attempt to merge both in a higher reality. From these false theories we learn the lesson of the profound interdependence of ' body ' on ' soul,' and relatively, though not absolutely, of ' soul ' on ' body.' All the data of experimental psychology impress more and more upon us their intimate union, and consequent action and reaction the one on the other within that unity. Moreover, the verdict of human experience yields us neither body nor soul as two distinct ' substances ' or ' things in themselves.' We only know them in man, from whose bodily and mental activities we can deduce their existence, and something of their nature. The result of this analysis gives us the ' soul ' as inseparably bound up with the body while life lasts, and yet possessing an element which entitles us to claim for it spirituality and ' substance,' in the sense that although in its union with the body in man it receives its subsistence only in virtue of this union, yet it is capable of subsistence in itself independently of the body, and exhibits certain qualities of a transcendental character. We can, of course, form no conception of what the soul is in itself, i.e. as an absolute substance. This transcends our experience, but at the same time we deduce its 'substance' from its activities, which are objects for experience. Of the mind apart from the body, or of the body apart from the mind, we know nothing. Our knowledge of them is our knowledge of their indissoluble union, and of their distinction only within that unity.

V. That consequently the real starting-point for any discussion of the relations between body and soul, mind and matter, is not a false dualism which sets the one over against the other as imaginary, distinct entities ; but from the thought of their essential and indissoluble unity within an individual person : a unity which nevertheless does not destroy their difference, but within which each reaches its completion, in their mutual subsistence, the one in the other.

We have to realise that the spirit strikes its roots deep down within the body, which is the vehicle of its self-manifestation, the instrument through which it functions. We have to banish from our thoughts the older Eastern conception of the body as a prison-house in which the ' soul ' is temporarily confined, and the consequent belief that the soul's perfect realisation of itself comes only with its complete emancipation from the fetters of sense and the material environment in which it has been stifled. On the contrary we have to face the hypothesis that although existence for a soul without a body and independent of a body is conceivable, yet it is not normal. The disintegration of body and soul at death leaves both in some sense incomplete. Indeed, it is doubtful whether we are justified in calling a disembodied spirit ' man ' in the sense in which we use the term of a living being. ' Man ' without a body is ' man ' whose completeness has to this extent been impaired. In this sense other considerations force us to believe that the divorce between ' body ' and ' soul ' at the change we call death is not normal, nor anything but temporary, and is never meant to be permanent. Some such thought as this underlies the Christian teaching of the resurrection of the body in contrast to the immortality of the soul. We look for the redemption of the whole man, and not simply of one part of him, even though that part be the highest. So close and intimate is the union of ' body ' and soul,' so indissolubly are they united, so indispensable to man's normal life is the ' body ' as an integral factor in the growth and development of his personality, that it is difficult to think of the severance between ' body ' and ' soul ' as anything but abnormal, and as leaving the man anything but incomplete.

VI. The importance of this for Christology would seem to be :

(a) The interesting parallel it presents. Exactly the same false dualism supposed to exist between ' body ' and ' soul,' ' mind ' and ' matter,' as two distinct ' substances,' having nothing in common, and even capable, in some sense, of independent subsistence, is found also in the past to have been applied to the Christological question of the ' Two Natures ' in Christ.

Just as to-day our starting-point for an investigation of the relation of ' soul ' to ' body ' must be from our experience of their indissoluble union and interdependence within the unity of an individual life,

in virtue of the fact that they have a common element
which alone makes such a unity possible, and is the
condition of their action and reaction the one upon
the other within that unity, which nevertheless does
not obliterate their difference : so also in the case of
Christology ; the starting-point for an investigation
of the relation between the human and the Divine
natures must be the historical fact supplied by New
Testament data of their indissoluble union within the
Person of Christ, in virtue of the fact revealed by the
Incarnation of their possession of a common element
in the essential affinity between them ; which fact alone
makes such a union conceivable, and which, because it
is affinity and not identity, secures that the difference
between the two is not obliterated by their union.

(*b*) The warning it gives of the danger in Christology of any attempt to disintegrate the human nature
of Christ in the interests of any particular theory.
The impossibility of conceiving of human nature
without both ' body ' and ' soul ' in most intimate
union and interdependence, makes it all-important
for Christology to preserve at whatever cost the unity
of the human nature of Christ, if it is to retain in any
sense its reality and completeness.   No theory which
disintegrates *His* human ' Body ' and ' Soul,' sub-
stituting for the latter an alien element or principle,
e.g. the Logos, can be sound except upon one condition :
namely, that the latter, in taking the place of the
former, is capable of performing for the human body
every function which would naturally have been
performed by a human soul, and of existing in such
a relationship to the human body as would have
existed in the case of a human soul.   This condition
can only be fulfilled if there is such an essential affinity

between the Logos and the human soul as to make such an exchange possible without in any sense detracting from the reality and completeness of the human nature thus formed within the unity of Christ's Person. This again presupposes that the Logos is not alien from human nature.

Apollinarianism, we venture to think, could never have been advocated if the indissoluble union of body and soul in human nature had been fully realised, and this heresy really resulted from a false dualism which regarded ' body ' and ' soul ' as in some sense separate and distinct ' substances.' Origen's doctrine of the ' pre-existence ' of the soul suggests such a conception, since this theory inevitably regards the ' soul ' as a nature complete in itself, and having no need for subsistence in a ' body ' in order to reach its completeness. We have tried to show, however, that there was one line of thought within the circle of Apollinarian teaching which did fulfil this condition to which we have referred. If Apollinaris held that human nature was in a sense incomplete, and only reached its completion by the advent of the Logos, Who, far from being alien to human nature, was Himself its archetype; then in a dim way we can conceive how His Incarnation was possible. Further, the doctrine of the En-hypostasia has, as its foundation, this same condition fulfilled; since the presupposition of that doctrine, as we have tried to show, is the existence of such an affinity between the human and the Divine as to make the advent of the latter into the former not the advent of some alien element, but the advent of something which by its very constitution and nature could coalesce with the human, and by its union with, and its subsistence in, the human give to the latter a

completeness and perfection which it could receive in
no other way.

But if we are to ground such a conception in the
very constitution of human nature itself, we shall have
to go deeper down into the depths of the human and
show conclusively that *it is imperfect and incomplete
in itself.*

Does modern psychology suggest this? If we are
to go a step further in our analysis of the spiritual
'soul,' we must go a step deeper and examine modern
conceptions of human personality.

(C.) Human Personality

(*a*) *Definition of the term.*—Hitherto we have used
the word ' soul' in the sense of the subject of our
mental life, the ultimate principle by which we feel,
think, and will. We now wish to centre our thoughts
more upon the developed mind's consciousness of
itself by which it enters upon the possession of its
' personality,' and comes to know itself as a self-
conscious being.

The Ego [says Dr. Maher] does not *create* but *discovers*
itself. In Jouffroy's felicitous phrase, it ' breaks its shell,'
and finds that it is *a Personal Agent with an existence and
individuality of its own,* standing henceforward alone in
opposition to the universe. . . .
After the realisation of its personality has been attained
in fully developed self-consciousness, we must still carefully
distinguish between the mind's immediate *perception* of
itself in its operations, and the *abstract quasi-objective notion*
of his own *personality* habitually possessed by every human
being. The *former* is an act of concrete apprehension, in
which I cognize myself as real *cause* or *subject* of my operations
or states. *The abstract notion of my personality,* on the
other hand, is a conception of a highly complex character.

148

It is an intellectual abstraction formed out of the concrete perception of self combined with remembered experiences of my past life.   It is commonly viewed by me in a quasi-objective manner.   It includes the *self*, but accentuates the *states* of self.   It gathers into itself the history of my past life—the actions of my childhood, boyhood, youth, and later years.   Interwoven with them all is the image of my bodily organism ;   and clustering around are a fringe of recollections of my dispositions, habits, and character, of my hopes and regrets, of my resolutions and failures, along with a dim consciousness of my position in the minds of other ' selves.'   Under the form of a representation of this composite sort, bound together by the thread of memory, each of us ordinarily conceives his complete abiding *personality*. This idea is necessarily undergoing constant modification ; and it is in comparing the present form of the representation with the past, whilst adverting to considerable alterations in my character, bodily appearance, and the like, that I sometimes say : ' I am completely changed ; ' ' I am quite another person,' though I am, of course, convinced that it is the same ' I ' who am changed in accidental qualities. It is because this complex notion of my personality is an abstraction from my remembered experiences that a perversion of imagination and a rupture of memory can sometimes induce the so-called ' illusions or alterations of personality.'

This distinction which Dr. Maher draws between the immediate apprehension of self as present in man's mental activities, and the habitual representation of himself in the form of a complex conception, elaborated by intellectual abstraction, is of great help when we come to the consideration of ' human personality ' and endeavour to question it as to its constitution.   We all of us have this quasi-objective view of ourselves by which we distinguish our own individuality in contrast to other persons.   What we have to do is to attempt an analysis of it and to see what results it yields.

149

(b) Analysis of Human Personality.—Dr. Illing-worth, in his able treatise on *Personality, Human and Divine,* gives us in Lecture II an analysis of the conception of human personality, and finds the constituent elements to be three :

Self-consciousness, the power of self-determination, and desires which irresistibly impel us into communion with other persons—or, in other words, reason, will, and love. These are three perfectly distinct and distinguishable functions, but they are united . . . by being the functions of one and the self-same subject, and gain a peculiar character from this very fact. They are the thoughts of a being that wills and loves, the will of a being that loves and thinks, the love of a being that thinks and wills; and each attribute may be said to express the whole being, therefore, in terms of that attribute.

But he goes on to remind us that personality is not an inanimate or abstract thing, but that it lives and grows: it is essentially alive, and can only be known as living.

Personality, then, lives and grows, but, in so doing, re-tains its identity ; the character in which it issues, however versatile or complex, being never a disconnected aggregate, but always an organic whole. Its unity may seem to vanish in the variety of experiences through which it goes, yet only to reappear, enlarged, enriched, developed, or impoverished and degraded, as the case may be, but self-identical.

Dr. Illingworth goes on to adduce arguments for his further conclusion that we are spiritual beings, and that the witness of our consciousness to its own spirituality never has been and never can be explained away by materialism. He concludes his lecture by emphasising a point which is of immense importance, and as we think fully justified by the verdict of our own experience, when we attempt to analyse the abstract quasi-objective notion of our own personality :

150

namely, the sense we have (*a*) that this personality is the one thing we know best, but (*b*) that it is also the most mysterious thing we know.

There are ' abysmal deeps of personality ' which startle us at times by the vastness of the vistas which they half disclose. We are dimly aware of undeveloped capabilities within us—capabilities of energy, intelligence, and love—which we cannot conceive ultimately frustrated and function-less; germs without a future, seeds without a fruit; and which, therefore, irresistibly point to immortality as the sole condition in which a personal being can find scope.

We have, then, these outstanding facts given as the result of self-analysis of ' personality.'

(1) Its constitution : self-consciousness, self-determination, love.

(2) The essential and abiding unity of all these attributes as constituent elements of our individuality.

(3) The clear consciousness of growth, development, resulting in character. The clear conviction that we are alive and in process of becoming.

(4) The clear sense of incompleteness, finitude, imperfection, limitation.

(5) The perception of undeveloped powers, capacities, and hidden depths of personality, which forbid us to set any limits to our powers of a higher becoming.

The conclusion to which we seem forced to come is that personality is not the starting-point, but the goal of our development. We are ever in process of becoming, and the business of life is the development of personality.

In no sense therefore is it possible to speak of a perfect human personality, since at every step in this never-ending process of becoming we are

151

conscious of larger vistas opening out in front of us ; an ever-present reminder that we have not yet reached the limits of our capabilities and the consequent inevitable query as to whether in this world we ever can.

(c) *The Principle and Condition of Growth of Human Personality.*—It is when we pass on to consider what is the principle, and what are the conditions of growth of human personality, that we find another most important factor which is also given as the result of an analysis of the quasi-objective view of ourselves which for the purposes of this enquiry we have named ' personality.'

This factor is the sense of dependence.

If individuality is the first note suggested by our modern use of the word ' personality,' which is defined as ' limited individuality,' yet this claim to independence yields on deeper analysis to a more fundamental feature of personality which is summed up in the word ' dependence.'

And this characteristic has led at least one writer to challenge boldly the current philosophical idea that personality is ' limited individuality,' and to claim for the word a much wider content than is assigned to it by modern psychology.

The Rev. W. Richmond, in his work entitled *An Essay on Personality as a Philosophical Principle*, is not content to take the definition of the term as suggested, for example, by Professor Ward in his article ' Psychology ' in the *Encyclopædia Britannica.*

Prof. Ward defines ' personality ' as ' the concept which every intelligent being more or less distinctly forms of himself, as a person M or N, having such and such a character, tastes, and convictions, and such and such a history, and such and such an aim in life.'

This is the modern idea of the word person, as is shown, e.g., by current language when we speak of ' personal sympathy,' ' personal antipathy,' ' personal affection,' ' personal religion.'

' All these emotions,' says Mr. Richmond, ' are eminently personal in the sense that they are eminently individual. They intensify the sense of individual life. They are keen, vivid, emphatically accented moments of individual existence.' But he goes on to show that a deeper analysis reveals them to be only possible in relation to a person other than the self which experiences them.

And the purpose of Mr. Richmond's essay is to define personality in broad contrast with current modern philosophical utterances on the subject in which it is assumed to be essentially individual, essentially limited. The true definition of personality in the individual is, according to Mr. Richmond, ' the capacity for society, fellowship, communion.'

We do not propose to follow the arguments by which this view is upheld, but we draw attention to it as showing that the note of ' dependence,' even if we do not assign to it the primary place in our analysis of ' personality,' is nevertheless an essential element, and plays an all-important part in the development of personality. Undoubtedly the inward ' self ' is ever in process of becoming, and this growth goes on continually and is in no way permanently arrested by the fact of the body reaching its maturity and being ever in process of decay. It is one of the most striking features of the 'spirit' that it can triumph over bodily infirmities, and that, e.g., intellectual moral and spiritual growth can continue right up to the point where the advent of death renders it no longer possible for the spirit to function through the material body from which it is wrenched. All growth is a mystery, and the conditions upon which it depends are to a large extent beyond our immediate apprehension, but we are learning more and more to-day the enormous influence of ' environment ' as an integral factor in the process of growth. The new philosophy of food bids us remember that *what we eat, we are*. *We grow by that upon which we feed whether physically, mentally, morally, or spiritually.* The finite Ego grows by contact with the non-Ego. This is not to admit that the Ego only comes to self-consciousness by contrast with the non-Ego ; because ' personality ' includes something besides its contrast with its object. We can have a certain knowledge of ourselves prior to our consciousness of self derived from the contrast presented to us by the external world. We believe in our internal world as something in itself, and we do not admit that all our knowledge comes from contrast with the data given from outside which reach us through the avenues of the senses. If we were not self-conscious, no amount of knowledge poured upon us from without would generate self-consciousness in ourselves. The self-consciousness is there, prior to its more vivid realisation, as the result of the reaction of the Ego upon the non-Ego. The most that we can admit in this connection is that a *latent* self-consciousness can be developed by reaction from the external world, and indeed may never emerge without the aid of an external stimulus,

154

but this is not to say that the latter creates the self-consciousness.

But in the consideration of the growth and development of the Ego the part played by external stimuli is all-important and decisive. The stimulus of the non-Ego is an essential element in the growth of a finite personality, which only realises its capacities in the endeavour to respond to the calls made upon it by the environment in which it finds itself placed. And this environment includes ' persons ' as well as ' things.' Further this environment reveals more vividly than ever the limitations of our personality ; limitations as to time, place, thought, and action, &c. All this reveals the ' dependence ' of finite personality upon environment, using the latter term in the widest possible sense. Hence the importance of ' fellowship,' ' communion,' for the development of finite personality. The command ' Know thyself ' can only be obeyed in virtue of the fact that man is a social animal. An independent or self-centred existence is, in the degree in which it is possible to be realised, a stunted growth. Nature teaches us the simple lesson that nothing isolated can grow. We have only to read biography to realise how true are the words of Bishop Creighton, who says in one of his letters :

Life is a sum of relationships. There is no independent or self-centred existence. I am what I am in relation to others, and I know myself by seeing myself reflected in my influence on others—my power of touching their lives, and weaving their lives and mine into some connected and satisfactory scheme which contains them all and points to some developments.

Environment supplies the food, whether persons

or things, upon the assimilation of which the growth of finite personality depends. If we have established this point, we have only to consider for a moment the needs revealed by human nature to see that these are not only material for the body, but embrace also that which can satisfy the higher life whether mental, moral, or above all spiritual. Man needs physical, mental, moral, and spiritual food for the development of his many-sided and complex personality. An analysis of human personality reveals this, and nothing less than this, for the development of the ' self.' In this sense again what we eat we are, we become that upon which we feed. The mind needs its own special ' food ' for its growth and development. The same thing is not less true of the spirit. It needs spiritual food for its growth and development.

No analysis of human personality which left out the religious needs of the deepest self within man would be adequate. It is a commonplace of religious literature to assert that such needs are felt by man, and the absence of them in individuals marks the latter as abnormal. The normal man as a spiritual being has needs which can only be supplied from spiritual sources.

A glance at, for example, W. James' *Varieties of Religious Experience*, justifies the assertion that however we may explain the phenomenon of religious experience, the fact of it cannot be gainsaid. However we may differ in our theories as to its origin and meaning, we have to recognise it as a definitely established fact of religious psychology. An examination of the data supplied by religious experience furnishes us with a mass of evidence to establish the fact that human personality testifies to its own consciousness of growth as the result of definite stimuli from outside. No fact of religious experience is more definite than this. One of the clearest facts established by religious psychology is the testimony of the Ego to its own self-consciousness of an ' influence' outside itself playing upon the very roots of its being ; a definite sense of someone whose felt presence in the inmost recesses of the soul has been the condition of the soul's own growth. In this sense the soul's inward religious development has been conditioned by its reception from without of ' spiritual' food. And thus for the spiritual as well as for the material part of us the law holds good that we grow by that upon which we feed. No analysis, therefore, of human personality can be considered adequate which fails to do full justice to this testimony from religious experience, that within the self are definite, if unfathomable, spiritual needs ; and that these needs, equally with others in the bodily or the mental spheres, are met by and developed through contact with outside influences, both from the material and the spiritual worlds.

This is, of course, to postulate that the ' environment ' necessary for man's true development embraces the invisible as well as the visible world. It is to assert definitely that the invisible world, and especially God, is as real a factor of man's environment as the visible world and especially other human persons. It is to deny that the visible is a complete environment sufficient for the development of man's complex personality. It is to maintain that man's environment embraces two worlds : the visible and the invisible, both of which are capable of supplying stimuli. If the question be asked : what proof, if

any, is there that man thus receives stimuli from the
invisible as well as from the visible worlds ; the answer
is an appeal to the data of religious psychology,
embodying as these do definite records of the experiences of direct Divine action upon the soul, e.g.
experiences of 'irruptions' from the invisible world,
the felt consciousness of communion with the Unseen
God, the definite sense of calm, peace, assurance, and
the gift of grace to help in a time of need, the joy of
forgiveness, the triumph over temptation ; in short
the whole phenomena of the spiritual life, which
constitute for the religious consciousness of man
definite evidence of contact with God, and the reception from the invisible world of 'gifts' from on high.
Whether such religious experience necessitates the
further conclusion that man possesses a higher 'sense'
or faculty by which he is able to perceive the presence
of such phenomena, and through which God is able
to find access to the human spirit, is a question we
may leave unanswered. We know that the material
world reveals itself to us through the organs of sense
or in sense-perception. The testimony of the religious consciousness confirms its reception of phenomena from the immaterial, invisible world. Through
what channel or channels such phenomena reach us
matters but little, so long as we recognise the fact that
they are received and minister to man's spiritual
growth. Our religious feelings, thoughts, and experiences are real contents of our consciousness, and as
such offer definite data for a philosophy of religion.
Our analysis of human personality thus leaves us
with a clear conception of man as a being to whose
power of a higher becoming no limit can be set, the
development of whose capacities is vitally bound up

with the sum of relationships by which he finds himself surrounded, and whose deepest needs demand for their satisfaction an environment which embraces not only the visible, but also the invisible world, not only finite ' persons ' and ' things,' but also the infinite and invisible God. *If human personality is imperfect, and only the advent of the Divine into it can secure its true development towards perfection, we have here surely another key to the doctrine of the Enhypostasia.*

Human personality is imperfect. What is necessary to its perfection ? The answer is God. But before we consider the relations of human personality with God, we must see what we can learn from Revelation as to the nature of God Himself.

This brings us to the second part of our task, the attempt to analyse the Divine Nature.

159

4.

THE ANALYSIS OF DIVINE NATURE

(*a*) GOD IS LOVE.
(*b*) GOD IS PERFECT PERSONALITY.
(*c*) THE TRANSCENDENCE AND IMMANENCE
OF GOD.

(A.)

GOD is Love.—We need not spend much time in the consideration of this central conception of Christian Theism. The simple statement in St. John's Epistle is the summing up in a sentence of a flood of revelation concerning the very being and nature of God, whose essence is shown to be Love by the Incarnation and work of Christ. Upon this foundation is built up the doctrine of the Atonement. The Incarnation is revealed as a movement of Divine compassion which finds expression in an act of infinite condescension, by which God Himself comes forth ' to seek and to save that which was lost.' ' God so loved the world that He *gave.*' It is of the essence of love to give in self-sacrifice, and the analogy of imperfect human love is here a help in our efforts to realise something of the depth of meaning contained in this mighty impulse to sacrifice on the part of One ' Who for us men and for our salvation came down from Heaven and was Incarnate. . . .'

If the Heart of God thus revealed is a heart of mercy and compassion, redemptive love and consequent suffering are not alien to Him, and the doctrine of His impassibility, as we have seen, will have to be modified. The lesson revealed by the Incarnation and the Cross is the lesson of a Suffering God, and nothing less than this can constitute the foundation-stone of the atoning work of Christ. Moreover, in every attempt to conceive of the relation of the Divine to the human, whether in the Person of Christ Himself or in our relationship to God, full weight must be given to this simple and yet unfathomable statement : ' God is Love, and he that abideth in love abideth in God, and God abideth in him.'

No *a priori* arguments as to what is or is not possible for God to do can for a moment be allowed to overrule the plain facts of what He has done, and is doing, in virtue of His love for mankind, and in virtue of the further fundamental fact that the deepest thing we know of Him is that He is Love. No *a priori* arguments as to the conditions of an Incarnation can stand in the way of the revelation in time and space of Love Incarnate in the Person of Jesus Christ. This fact must condition our every utterance upon the mystery of the Incarnation.

Further, that God is Love is a revelation which not only yields us the basis for a Trinitarian doctrine, but leaves us with the thought of the Self-Imparting God going out towards His Creation, and yet, because it is His Creation, remaining within Himself all the time ; so that we, His creatures, have our being entirely within the circle of Himself. Thus in love, human and Divine, we have a meeting-place between God and man which constitutes the basis of a relation-ship between them.

A study of the history of Christology shows that over and over again a false idea of God has vitiated attempts to interpret the Person of Christ.   Moreover, the key to His Person lies in His work.   There can be no doubt but that what kept Athanasius firm in his Christology all through the Arian controversy was his grip upon the reality of redemption through Jesus Christ.   From what Christ had done for men, and was doing in men, Athanasius deduced who Christ was.   So to-day we believe that the more the doctrine of a Suffering God is taken as a key to the interpretation of the doctrine of the Atonement, the clearer will be the realisation that ' God was in Christ, reconciling the world unto Himself ' ; and the clearer, consequently, will be the realisation of the essential Divinity and humanity of the God-Man. Here perhaps, if anywhere, lies the value of the Ritschlian Christology, which bids us approach the Person of Christ through His work, and to seek to apprehend His Deity through our experience of His Person and work in the Christ of history, and in the Christ of our own spiritual experience.   Personal experience in Christ, which comes to us as members of a redeemed humanity, privileged to partake of the benefits of His redemptive suffering, is the value-judgment by which we come to realise Who He is, as the perfect revelation of God.   Ritschl tells us that the ethical estimate of Christ according to His vocation carries with it the religious recognition of Him as Revealer of God.

Whilst we are free to admit that having read and re-read Ritschl's *Justification and Reconciliation*, his standpoint has never appealed to us ; we do see, however, its strong emphasis upon the work of Christ in history and personal experience as a key to our apprehension of His Person, and consequently the need

for membership of His Body in order that any man
may be fully qualified to pronounce upon the question
as to Who Christ was. We have said this much at
this point with reference to Ritschlian Christology,
because we do not propose to deal with it any more
fully in our later treatment of some modern Christological theories in Part III of this work.

But to return to our main point from this digres-
sion, if God is Love, then Saviourhood is grounded
in His very Being; and if the means of man's salvation lie along the road of redemptive suffering and
the Calvary sacrifice, the Gospel picture of Jesus
walking with steadfast face along that road, answers
once and for all the question as to whether God
can suffer.

(B.) *God is Perfect Personality.*—The doctrine of
a personal God is a thing which is taken for granted
both in Old and New Testament. The belief may
be anthropomorphic in its origin, but this is no
objection to its truth. It bears witness to the fact
that man was made in the image of God, and that
God must be so like man as to be capable of inter-
course with him. Because man is a person, God
cannot be less ; and the Christian revelation of the
character of God implies His Personality in which
His character can inhere. But more fundamental
from this point of view is the revelation that God
is Spirit, and that God is Love. These two facts
are a sufficient basis upon which to found the
personality of God. But what do we mean when we
speak of God as *perfect* personality ? Here we are
helped by the philosophy of Hermann Lotze, and
it is to him that we shall appeal for an answer to
our question. We believe that in Lotze's treatment

of personality, human and Divine, we shall find a very helpful contribution in our endeavour to re-state the doctrine of the Enhypostasia in terms of modern thought. One of the outstanding features of Lotze's philosophy is his identification of the conception of infinite substance with the religious conception of the living God, and his definition of the all-one substance as the absolutely Good and the All-personality. This is the conclusion of his great work, *The Microcosmus*, in the closing paragraphs of which he tells us that—

the true reality that is and ought to be, is not matter and is still less Idea, but is the living personal Spirit of God and the world of personal spirits which He has created. They only are the place in which Good and good things exist; to them alone does there appear an extended material world, by the forms and movements of which the thought of the cosmic whole makes itself intelligible through intuition to every finite mind.

We would draw particular attention to the chapter on the Personality of God, in which Lotze endeavours to elucidate this notion of the One Being, which is the indispensable pre-supposition of all intelligibility in finite things. In the effort to establish this proposition, he passes from metaphysics to theology, and lifts us at once from the meta-physical postulate of the Infinite to the religious thought of God.

' The longing of the soul,' he tells us, ' to apprehend as reality the Highest Good which it is able to feel, cannot be satisfied by or even consider any form of the existence of that Good except Personality.'

So he subjects the attempts to find more satisfying forms of existence for this Highest Good in ideas of an Eternal World-Order (Fichte), of an Infinite Substance (Schelling), a Self-developing Idea (Hegel), to a searching criticism, and decides in favour of the supposed commoner idea of a Personal God.

He examines the common objections urged against the personality of God from the point of view of our knowledge of human personality. An Ego, it is urged, is not thinkable without the contrast of a Non-Ego, or Not-Self; hence personal existence cannot be asserted of God, without bringing even Him down to that state of limitation; of being conditioned by something not Himself, which is repugnant to Him.

It is true that human personality is limited and conditioned, but none of these limitations is applicable to the Perfect Eternal Infinite Being. Lotze proves that although human personality is dependent upon the Non-Ego for the stimuli necessary to its development, yet it possesses at least a latent self-consciousness prior to its fuller development in contrast with the external world. He will not allow that all our knowledge comes from contrast with the Non-Ego, and he shows that no amount of external stimuli could *generate* within us self-consciousness. The self-consciousness is there prior to the reaction with the Non-Ego, by which it is more vividly realised.

It may be that only the being who in thought contrasts with himself a Non-Ego from which he also distinguishes himself, can say I to himself, but yet in order that in thus distinguishing he should not mistake and confound himself with the Non-Ego, this discriminating thought of his must be guided by a certainty of self which is immediately experienced, by a self-existence which is earlier than the discriminative relation by which it becomes Ego as opposed to the Non-Ego. . . .

We admit that the Ego *is thinkable* only in relation to the

Non-Ego, but we add that it *may be experienced* previous to and out of every such relation, and that to this is due the possibility of its subsequently becoming thinkable in that relation.

Now although it be admitted that, for a finite being, stimuli from without are necessary as incitements of its action, yet this does not apply to the Infinite Being, whom Lotze shows is not so dependent upon external stimuli; nor does He need the contrast of an external world because of His self-sufficingness.

The Infinite Being, not bound by any obligation to agree in any way with something not itself, will, with perfect self-sufficingness, possess in its own nature the causes of every step forward in the development of its life.

Lotze proves conclusively a point to which attention has already been drawn, viz., the limitations and imperfections of finite personality, not the least significant of which is this very need of external stimuli for its development, and its inability ever to rise to complete self-consciousness.

In point of fact [he says] we have little ground for speaking of the personality of finite beings; it is an ideal, which, like all that is ideal, belongs unconditionally only to the Infinite, but like all that is good appertains to us only conditionally, and hence imperfectly.

Lotze gathers up the results of his investigation in the following propositions :

(1) Selfhood, the essence of all personality, does not depend upon any opposition that either has happened or is happening of the Ego to a Non-Ego, but it consists in an immediate self-existence which constitutes the basis of the possibility of that contrast wherever it appears. Self-consciousness is the elucidation of this self-existence which is brought about by means of knowledge, and even this is by no means necessarily bound up with the distinction of the Ego from the Non-Ego which is substantially opposed to it.

166

(2) In the nature of the finite mind as such is to be found the reason why the development of its personal consciousness can take place only through the influences of that cosmic whole which the finite being itself is not, that is, through stimulation coming from the Non-Ego, not because it needs the contrast with something *alien* in order to have self-existence, but because in this respect, as in every other, it does not contain in itself the conditions of its existence. We do not find this limitation in the being of the Infinite; hence for it alone is there possible a self-existence, which needs neither to be initiated nor to be continuously developed by something not itself, but which maintains itself within itself with spontaneous action that is eternal and had no beginning.

(3) Perfect Personality is in God only, to all finite minds there is allotted but a pale copy thereof; the finiteness of the finite is not a producing condition of this Personality, but a limit and a hindrance of its development.

In this conception of God as Perfect Personality lies another key to the reinterpretation of the doctrine of the Enhypostasia.

(C.) *The Transcendence and Immanence of God.*— Both these conceptions are equally necessary and equally vital in the Christian conception of God. By holding these two truths with equal force, Christian Theism is able to steer a middle course between Pantheism and Deism. The doctrine of the Divine Transcendence preserves the truth of God's superiority in contrast to all His creation, and secures that the line of demarcation between the Creator and the creature is never obliterated, even when the intimacy of the relationship between the two presses most forcibly upon the human mind and inclines it to a pantheistic conclusion. The doctrine of God as the Perfect Personality, with its insistence upon His eternal self-sufficingness, is here helpful as giving us one certain mark of His Transcendence. Our knowledge of Him as Creator in contrast to the universe, and our knowledge of His Perfection in contrast to our imperfection in moral character and spiritual life, are other marks by which we can be helped to grasp something of what we mean by the Transcendent God. But more than this, His Transcendence means that our finite minds can never embrace Him in all His Fulness of Being. There must ever remain in Him heights and depths beyond our power of apprehension; and our knowledge of Him is limited both by His Revelation of Himself to us, and by our capacity to receive that Revelation. Moreover, His Transcendence involves the further thought that He is not exhausted by His creation, but is more than adequate to it, and excels it in every conceivable way. This conception alone will save us from pantheism when we pass on to consider God in His relationship to the universe. His Divine Immanence is only conceivable because of His Transcendence. Otherwise we have a God shut up within His universe and One whose Being is limited by the fact that it is co-extensive with it. But the Christian conceives of God as first transcendent over all, and secondly present in and with all created things.

The analogy of our own relation to the work of our hands helps us to understand, to a certain extent, how God can be transcendent and yet immanent; but a better analogy perhaps is our relation to matter. In our study of the relationship between body and soul, spirit and matter, we have seen that whilst we only know spirit as immanent in, and functioning through matter, yet we have reason to believe that it possesses a relative independence and transcends matter. Some such analogy, if not pressed too far, may help us when

we try to conceive of the relationship between the
Divine Spirit and His creation. He is immanent in
it, He functions through it, but this is only possible
because He is transcendent above it, and, as the
Absolute, is not conditioned by it, nor in any sense
dependent upon it. This saves us from the pantheistic error of identifying Him with any part of it
or of thinking any part of it to be absorbed by Him.
Rather must we think of His Immanence as a relationship between Himself and His creation, which
secures its separation from Him even in the midst
of its closest identity with Him. We are to think
of God as abiding in and with His creation, which He
sustains and inspires. ' From Him, and through Him,
and unto Him, are all things.' His Immanence involves a network of relationships between Himself and
all creation, whereby the latter is upheld, sustained,
pervaded through and through by Him, intimately
related to Him, and yet never identified with Him.
And this network of relationships includes finite
spirits. His Immanence in creation necessitates His
Immanence in man, created in His own image. This
relationship between the Infinite Spirit and His
finite created spirits, between the Personal God and
the sons of men, constitutes the highest form of
communion existing between God and His universe
that we know ; and the reason is, because it differs
from all other relationships between the Creator and
the creation, inasmuch as man is conscious of it
and capable of responding to it. ' In Him we live
and move and have our being ' reveals not only His
Immanence, but our consciousness of it. It is the
ground not only of man's relationship to God, but
of his preservation in that relationship of his own

identity, and freedom to respond or no to the appeal
for communion which comes from the Creator.   And
the climax of God's Immanence in man was the Incarnation itself, which revealed in its fulness the great
truth of God as a Self-imparting God.   The name
Immanuel, ' God with us,' given to the Incarnate
Christ, was the guarantee that the Immanence of
God in man had reached a climax, and had opened up
for man the possibility of a new relationship between
himself and God, mediated through Christ.   But this
thought must be safeguarded when we view the Incarnation in itself, apart from its relation to us.   We
must ever remember that it revealed God's Transcendence as well as His Immanence.   It was the
advent into time and space of One Who lives eternally
in a Transcendent sphere above and beyond the limitations of our finite and temporal life, and Who pre-
existed before the Incarnation.   Moreover, because it
was the advent of a pre-existent Ego, the Incarnation
is marked as distinct, not in degree but in kind, from
the highest conceivable form of inspiration of the
human by the Divine, or of Immanence of the Divine
in the human, such as we know in the case of man in
his relationship to his Maker.   It is difficult to find
a word by which to mark this differentiation.   Perhaps we shall best express our meaning if we say that
the union between the Divine and the human in the
Person of Christ was ontological and essential, a
point upon which Cyril of Alexandria was continually
insisting.   Incarnation is not intensified immanence,
as the following study of the relationship between
the human and the Divine in us will show.

Two

5.

HUMAN AND DIVINE IN THEIR
RELATIONSHIP

(*a*) RELIGIOUS EXPERIENCE, MYSTICISM, ECSTASY,
     INSPIRATION AND REVELATION, PROPHECY.
(*b*) COMMUNION WITH GOD IN CHRIST.
     GRACE.
     GRACE AND FREE-WILL.
(*c*) SUMMARY.

WE have now attempted to analyse Human Nature and Divine Nature. We have endeavoured to penetrate into the depths of both, and it only remains to consider the relations between them as these are revealed in man's communion with God. We shall then be in a position to gather up the results of our study and to apply these to the Christological problem. So we pass to a consideration of human personality in its relations with God. We have already covered this ground to a certain extent, but we wish to emphasise one or two points gained from a study of the data supplied by religious experience in general, and more particularly the distinctively Christian experience in Christ.

(A.) *Religious Experience in General.*—If we read the record of religious experience preserved for us in the literature of Mysticism, we find in the phenomenon of prayer, which the religious consciousness reveals as a definite contact between the human and the Divine, a most certain guarantee of the soul's communion with God. Prayer is the most primary

171

and distinctive feature of the mystic life, and it would be easy to multiply passages from the writings of the mystics which reveal their consciousness of definite contact with God through its instrumentality.

Whatever the variety of religious experience may be, the content of it is relationship with God, and one of the points we wish to investigate is this : whether there is evidence supplied by the data of religious experience that the human spirit in its relationship with the Divine continues to retain its own identity in and through the experience, even though the desire may be for absorption of the human in the Divine. The peril of mysticism is that the intense longing for contact with the Divine may take the form of a passionate desire for absorption in or fusion with the Deity, a pure pantheism in which human personality is lost.

Mysticism.—One of the most distinctive features of the mystic experience is the strong sense of the transcendence of God, and this rescues the soul from its own longing for absorption, and preserves for it a continued consciousness of its own identity and finite character, even in the midst of the most intense realisation of the all-pervading Presence and indwelling power of the Most High. In the mystic experience, the definite sense of communion with God, the immediate feeling of the unity of the self with God, the vivid consciousness of the all-pervading Presence, are quite compatible with the retention of the human soul's consciousness of its own identity in and through the experience through which it passes. The most that can be said is that the consciousness of self is forgotten in the experience of the Presence of Another.

The tremendous concentration of every faculty upon one definite object, God, causes the soul's awareness of its own existence to recede far back into the dim background, and the attitude of 'passivity' adopted in the mystic state lends itself to this temporary recession into the background, of the soul's own awareness of its own distinctive individuality. But that this individuality is not lost can be abundantly proved by quotations from the lips of the mystics themselves. Another point, however, to be borne in mind is the well-known difficulty of reproducing these mystical states as data for the analysis of the religious psychologist. Professor James has given us four marks by which we may test any experience, and judge of our right to term it 'mystical.' These are—(1) Ineffability. The impossibility for the mystic to impart or transfer the experience to another. (2) Noetic quality. These mystical states are states of knowledge, but (3) Transiency marks them and makes it extremely difficult for memory to reproduce them or describe them. (4) Passivity. This last 'mark' is well illustrated in Ribet's definition of mysticism. 'It is,' he says, 'a supernatural drawing of the soul towards God in which the soul is passive; resulting in an inward illumination and caress : these supersede thought, surpass all human effort, and are able to have over the body an influence marvellous and irresistible.'

The following striking utterances of the mystics themselves prove that the soul, even when 'God-possessed,' still retains its own identity. The quotations are taken from Evelyn Underhill's work, *The Mystic Way*.

173

(*a*) A passage from Gerlac Petersen's *Fiery Soliloquy with God* (cap. 15):

Thou art in me, and I in Thee, glued together as one and the self-same thing, which shall never be lost nor broken.

(*b*) A passage from St. Catherine of Genoa (*Vitae Dottrina*, cap. 14):

My *me* is God, nor do I know my selfhood save in Him.

Ecstasy.—We must, however, pay special attention to the question of religious ecstasy. Here we approach a most difficult and perplexing phenomenon of religious experience, and one frequently met with in the literature of mysticism, both general and Christian.

We may fairly regard cases like that of the Pythia, for example, as abnormal in the history of prophecy. The state in this case was induced by tremendous play upon the emotions, and the resultant impression that the subject in this highly excited state was wholly possessed and overruled by the deity; so much so that she was compelled to utter ' oracles,' the very meaning of which she did not in the least grasp, must be discounted to this extent. Whether such states are involuntary or self-induced, they can scarcely be regarded as anything but abnormal and pathological. It is legitimate to draw a distinction between such phenomena and the ecstasy experienced by some of the finest of the mystics, e.g. St. Paul, Plotinus, St. Teresa. The experience of being ' caught up,' ' bathed in,' or ' embraced by,' the Divine is admittedly one of rare occurrence in the lives of those who both by temperament and spiritual training have rendered themselves liable to such a religious ecstasy. But the most that can be said of such rare phenomena of the religious life is that the intensity of the spiritual experience, the vividness of the soul's consciousness of the presence of the Divine, is so great, that for the time the human faculties *seem to them* to be suspended, and the human personality swallowed up or lost in the Divine. But this is no proof that this has really taken place. The experience takes place upon a spiritual plane so exalted and so far above the level of the normal spiritual life as to make it practically impossible to analyse it. St. Paul cannot tell us definitely whether it was ' in the body ' or ' out of the body.' The note of ' ineffability ' is very pronounced, and it would be fatal to build upon such data a theory of the final destiny of the human soul as being absorption into the Divine. The whole weight of evidence gathered from other considerations in the study of the relations between the human and the Divine is against such a conclusion; and in view of the little we know definitely concerning the phenomenon of religious ecstasy, we cannot regard it as a proved exception to all the rules which we believe govern the action of the Divine Spirit upon the human in their relationship.

That the human is illuminated, heightened, intensified, rendered more truly human, but never absorbed by the Divine, is abundantly proved by a consideration of inspiration, revelation, and prophecy. The following brief study of all these subjects in the light of modern research confirms the point we wish to make. In no case can it be shown that the Divine fails to respect the human in their relationship.

Inspiration and Revelation. — Without entering into any detailed treatment of the vexed question

of inspiration, we venture to assert that the old
mechanical view has in our own day practically
ceased to exercise any real influence upon our
thoughts. The doctrine of ' verbal inspiration,' with
reference to the Bible, has broken down in the face
of an increasing recognition of the human element
in all inspiration, and not least in its particular
manifestation in and through the written Word.
We find it practically impossible to regard the
' inspired ' writers of Holy Scripture as simply the
' pens ' used by the Divine Spirit to record at His
dictation. We no longer think of the Bible as in
this sense a Divinely dictated book. Neither do
we regard ' inspired ' men as those whose human
faculties have become entirely suspended as the
result of the inflowing or inbreathing of the Spirit
into them. We realise that all inspiration is imparted
to, without impairing, any human faculties. If we
distinguish for a moment Inspiration from Revelation,
and regard the latter as the product resulting from
the Divine action functioning through the human
medium, we may say that the history of revelation
proves conclusively that the human element has
been preserved intact throughout the whole course
of its contact with the Divine, as exhibited in the
phenomenon of revelation itself. That the fruit of
inspiration in revelation is mediated through, and
to this extent conditioned by, the human, is an
hypothesis forced upon us by any study of the subject of revelation, and not least by the phenomenon
of its progressive character, which clearly indicates
that it has been in every age conditioned by man's
power of receptivity.

Prophecy.—So also with reference to prophecy,

There is nothing in modern thought which forbids us to believe that in every age man has been used by the Divine Being as a receptacle of revelation, and an organ through which His message could be conveyed to men. Further, a study of the history of prophecy forbids us to confine it to any one nation, and yet at the same time it is clear that the Divine Being exercised a power of selection and picked out ' chosen vessels ' as the media for His messages. The fullest and richest exhibition of prophecy is found within the ' prophetic period ' of the history of God's own chosen people. Without attempting to discuss the subject of Old Testament prophets and prophecy, it will suffice if we take the testimony of the prophets themselves, and the witness of their own self-consciousness to the relation of the Divine to the human in the phenomenon of prophecy of which they were the subjects. So far as we can gather from their own witness, these men of God continued to possess all their human faculties, even though not in a normal state (as in the case of deeply stirred emotions in extreme spiritual exaltation), and yet at the same time they were conscious of Divine influence : in some cases so vividly realised and distinctly felt as to enable them clearly to distinguish the Divine activity, and even the Divine voice from their own thoughts. Again, the impartation of the Divine message was in some cases perceived and received as a spiritual intuition when they were in a state of rapt devotion and communion with God. But in no case did the impartation from without from the Divine destroy the human self-consciousness of the man who thus became the channel of a Divine communication.

Not less true is this of the New Testament cases of inspiration as the result of the advent of the Holy Spirit into the lives of the Christians ; even though the human consciousness testified to the reality of His *abiding* and *continuous Presence,* as a permanent Dweller within the human heart. Even when the Divine permanently abides within the human, the latter is not passive. The human will is still exercised, the human consciousness of self-identity in the Presence of Another is still maintained. So much so that St. Paul, for example, remains quite clear as to the distinction between his own thoughts and those which he believed he had received from above. He warns his readers of this distinction between his own ideas, opinions, counsels ; and the ' commands ' of God given through him to others. Moreover, the compulsion exercised by the Divine upon the human will is not irresistible, but rather of the nature of moral suasion. The injunction that the spirits of the prophets are to be subject to the prophets is only explicable on the assumption that they could be. The Divine Spirit may control and direct, but it is always with the willing consent of the human, and the co-operation of the Divine and human wills working in harmony. The whole impression we gain from a study of inspiration and prophecy is that of the human faculties quickened, enlightened, intensified by the advent of the Divine ; but not suppressed, and if controlled and overruled, yet only by the consent of the human will.

(B.) *Communion with God in Christ.*—When we come to consider more closely the distinctively Christian experience in Christ from the ' coming of the Holy Ghost ' at Pentecost onwards, the data supplied by the New Testament and the history of Christian experience afford overwhelming evidence of the Christian belief in every age, that God was invading human individual lives in a *new way and through new channels*, and that His Divine influence upon the souls of men was being mediated through Christ. The classical example is the religious experience of St. Paul, but what is there revealed of his own consciousness of his own identity, even in his human spirit's awareness of the inflowing of a new life and the indwelling and energising of a Divine Spirit within it, is not less true of the experience of the humblest follower of Christ.

> I live, and yet no longer I, but Christ liveth in me.

Such a passage as this is crucial in any effort to define the relationship between human personality and God.

We have here the human and the Divine in most intimate relationship and most vital union. And the result is not the consciousness on the part of the human Ego of any loss of any element distinctively human, nor the absorption of the human by the Divine ; but, if anything, a heightened realisation on the part of the human of all that is most distinctively itself, as the result of its union and communion with something which is not itself. Paul was never more truly Paul than when his life was hid with Christ in God. The saint is never more conscious of self-realisation than when his whole personality has lost itself in the consciousness of the presence and all-pervading influence of God upon it.

Grace.—In connection with this distinctive experience in Christ, which has for its goal the recreation of a new humanity to be conformed to the image of Him Who

was Himself ' the image of the invisible God,' we
have to consider more closely the process by which
this is accomplished. How are sinful men thus to
become purified, invigorated, and transformed ? The
answer is by Divine Grace. We must therefore
examine all that is summed up in Christian experience by this term. We have to remember at the
outset that the richness of content, which the word
itself came to have in the theology of St. Paul,
and which it now possesses in Christian thought, is
itself due to Christian experience in Christ. For the
Christian, the word connotes not only a Divine attribute, the redemptive mercy of God towards sinners,
but the *results* of this disposition of God in Christ
towards men. When we speak of the Grace of God
in Christ, we think not only of the Giver, but of His
Gifts ; not only of His Grace, but of all the blessings
which flow from it to us. If its origin is the goodness,
compassion, long-suffering, love, mercy, and patience
of Almighty God in His relations with sinful men, its
results in Christian experience are the sum total of
blessings which the human soul receives in its communion with God in Christ. And if we are to select
from amongst these blessings one which is most distinctive of all Christian experience, and that which
differentiates Christianity from all other religions,
it must be the gift of power ; the power of the Holy
Ghost as a dynamic sin-conquering force in Christian
experience. No reader of the history of the early
Church can fail to be struck with this outstanding
feature of Christianity as it was felt and experienced
in the lives of those who set out to turn the world
upside down. And if any one of them had been
cross-questioned as to the source of this power, their

answer would have been the substance of St. Paul's triumphant cry : ' I can do all things through Christ which strengtheneth me.' ' I am not ashamed of the Gospel, for it is the power of God unto salvation to everyone that believeth.' Hence the old-fashioned definition of Grace as ' the power of God working in the soul of man ' is true to Christian experience, and substantiated by the verdict of Christian history. Now when we consider Grace as the sum-total of blessings imparted to the Christian in Christ from God, through the operation of the Holy Spirit, we find that this is nothing less than *the Self-emptying of God into man, and this process is mediated through Christ.* ' The Grace of God was given you in Christ Jesus,' says St. Paul, and his experience was that this Grace was an outflowing of the Divine into the human, as the direct outcome of the work of Christ, culminating in the Calvary sacrifice, and the benefits available for men as the result, and conveyed to men in Christ. Nothing is more certain than that the theology of St. Paul is rooted and grounded in his own personal, spiritual experience in Christ. His great doctrines of Justification by Faith, and Sanctification in Christ, are based upon his own self-consciousness of his own death unto sin, and new birth unto righteousness; his own knowledge that he owed his all to Christ, and that Christ had made him, and was continuing to make him, a new creature. And we shall not understand St. Paul's theology until we have frankly faced the conclusion to which he himself was driven to come; namely, that, as the result of his new life in Christ, there was flowing into him a stream of new life and power which had as its purpose nothing less than the refashioning of his whole personality into the veritable

likeness of Christ Himself.   This Divine Self-emptying
and Self-impartation on the part of God in Christ, had
nothing less than this for its object.   When St. Paul
speaks of growth in Grace, and in the knowledge of
the Lord Jesus Christ, he has in mind no less high a
goal than this as the purpose of God in Christ ; that
men, made originally in His image, may be transformed into His likeness.   St. Paul's language therefore in, for example, the Galatian Epistle, where he
says, 'My little children, of whom I am again in travail
until Christ be formed in you,' is not to be dismissed
as a mere rhetorical utterance, but is the expression
of a great truth which the Apostle was ever seeking to
bring home to his converts, viz. that the goal of the
Christian life was nothing less glorious than the perfection of the Christ-life in each one, not only their
birth into Him, but their growth and development
into His fulness, their transformation into His likeness.   A passage like 2 Corinthians iii. 18 indicates
St. Paul's clear grasp of the truth that the result of
such a life in Christ as he and others were striving to
live, could only be such an enrichment of the human
by the Divine, as to enable the former to attain to that
perfect reflexion of the latter, which was the very
purpose of its creation and the predestined goal of
its development.   'But we all, with unveiled face reflecting as a mirror the glory of the Lord, are transformed into the same image from glory to glory, even
as from the Lord the Spirit.'   The purpose of Divine
Grace then was, and is, man's full salvation ; which is
not simply a negative freedom from sin, but a positive
growth in holiness, and the development of the whole
human personality by its relationship with the Divine
into something so glorious, so transfigured, so perfectly

human, as to be called the likeness of the Divine. St. Paul would have agreed that we can place no limit to man's capacity for a higher becoming, but he would have grounded such a belief in the fact that the revelation of God in Christ revealed Him as One Who Himself was ' full of grace and truth,' and that as a consequence of His work of salvation we in Him are capable of receiving ' of His fulness and grace for grace.'

Now although our consideration of Grace and its influence upon human life reveals it to be all-powerful in the growth and development of man's highest life, yet, throughout all its operations, it can never be said so to dominate and transform the human as to change its essential character into something entirely different. Even though Grace makes us most God-like, yet likeness and identity are two different things ; and when, for example, St. Athanasius sums up the purpose of the Incarnation in the famous sentence :

αὐτὸς γὰρ ἐνηνθρώπησεν ἵνα ἡμεῖς θεοποιηθῶμεν.

he does not mean to imply that man's resultant growth into the Divine likeness involves his absorption into the pleroma of the Godhead in any pantheistic sense. Even though, as we have seen, Christian experience testifies to the reception of what we can only describe as the very life of the Divine into the human ; and even though we receive of His fulness, poured into the human from on high, as life-giving power, yet in all such experience the testimony of Christian self-consciousness would suggest rather a heightening, an intensification of the human powers and faculties, than any transformation, still less annihilation, of the human in its relationship with the Divine.

Grace and Free-Will.—We need not seek to penetrate into the deeper and more mysterious aspects of
Divine Grace in relation to the problem of human free-
will before reaching a definite conclusion on this point;
because, even if the evidence were sufficient to prove
the irresistible character of Divine Grace in its contact with human free-will, this would not involve the
destruction of the human faculty by the advent of
the Divine, but only the suspension of the exercise
of its functions. No wholly satisfactory solution
of this mysterious problem will ever be reached.
Augustine and Pelagius each saw *too* clearly one side
of the truth, and hence bore their witness in opposite camps. Both could appeal to Scripture and to
Christian experience as in their favour, because the
testimony from either source is inconclusive. The
problem has its parallel, of course, in the history
of the doctrine of the Two Natures in Christ. An
undue emphasis upon human free-will obscures the
equally vital truth of Divine Grace; whereas an
undue exaltation of the power of Divine Grace leaves
no room for the equally vital truth of human freedom.
The human mind is faced with the task of holding
both truths as complementary, and only seemingly
mutually destructive when considered from the point
of view of logical consistency; but the dualism and
antagonism are hardly felt in Christian experience.
Even if a man's experience of Divine Grace is of
such a kind as to lead him to describe it as pre-
venient, co-operative, indispensable, and irresistible,
yet, against his own personal consciousness, he has
to set the Christian teaching as to perseverance,
endeavour, and all those exhortations to fashion his
own life after the pattern of Christ's example, which

imply as their necessary presupposition human freedom, human will, and human activity, without the presence of which such exhortations would be meaningless. If Christianity had to choose between Pelagianism and Augustinianism, there is no doubt but that the Christian life in Christ would be decisive in favour of the latter. The dictum of Julian of Eclanum—' Homo libero arbitrio emancipatus a deo '—is flatly contradicted by Christian experience with its keen sense of dependence upon God as the very basis of the spiritual life. The deepest analysis of human nature reveals its need for something more than Christ's example if it is to be redeemed. It has more than once been pointed out that an imperfect anthropology inevitably leads to an imperfect Christology, and in this sense the connection between Pelagianism and Nestorianism is very significant. ' The Nestorian Christ was the fitting Saviour of the Pelagian man.' But the admission that the human needs the Divine for its restoration, completion, and perfection, is not only a necessary foundation for a doctrine of the Incarnation, but it is also essential for an understanding of the relation of the Divine to the human, whether in us or in the Person of Christ.

His character as the head of a new humanity, the source and fountain of man's true life, is inexplicable upon the basis of the Pelagian assumptions, so concisely put by Dr. Bright in two sentences: (a) 'We need no special supernatural Grace, and that, because we have no inborn disease of sin.' (b) ' Thou madest us men, but it is we who have made ourselves righteous.'

We conclude, then, that in the phenomenon of Christian experience in Christ, with all that is implied by the word 'Grace' in this connection, we have nothing less than the attempt on the part of the Divine to become incarnate in His Body the Church, and to reproduce Himself in men transformed through His indwelling Spirit into 'new creatures,' destined to grow up into the perfection of His likeness. And, further, such a purpose is being carried out as the direct result of the Incarnation, life, and work of Jesus Christ. The mystical union between Christ and the Christian, which for him is his consciousness of the indwelling of the presence of God in the inmost recesses of his soul, gives us as clear and definite a view of the relationship between human personality and God as is possible to obtain from the data of religious experience. And if our analysis of human personality revealed it as dependent for its growth and development upon a network of relationships within the environment by which it is surrounded; the highest of these relationships is that which the human spirit is found capable of forming with God, Whom it believes to be the source of its spiritual strength, the food for its spiritual growth and development. Its full realisation is dependent upon communion with God, and in Him alone is the satisfaction of all those needs which the sense of incompleteness, finitude, imperfection, and limitation reveal to it. *The conclusion is that without God human personality is incomplete, and that He alone can supply it with that which alone can help it to its full realisation.*

If, then, the goal of human personality in its effort to full realisation is God, the union of the soul with God, the communion of the soul with God; there must be an affinity between man and God which is the cause of the soul's aspiration towards

186

Him and His drawing of the soul towards Himself.
This is one of the cardinal doctrines of religion as
well as the most definite belief of the mystics.   Upon
this ' potential likeness to God in every man ' is built
up the Mystic Way by which man seeks to grow up
Godwards.   Thus Macarius of Egypt says, ' We can
only behold that which we are.'   There must be some
Divine quality in man which is the justification for
the ' Scala Perfectionis ' with its three stages—the
Purgative, the Illuminative, and the Unitive.   This
last, which culminates in the union of the soul with
God, would be impossible if it were not for the fact
that we are created in the Divine image ; since only
the Godlike can know God.   The teaching of both Old
and New Testaments on this point is conclusive.
Man is a spirit, created by God in His own image,
having the breath of life breathed into his nostrils.
Sin has blurred and marred this image, and the coming
of the Second Adam who is ' the image of the invisible
God ' was for the very purpose of recreating fallen
humanity by a process of regeneration or the ' new
birth.'   Hence the purpose of the new life in Christ
is that we may be conformed by God to the image
of His Son, through the operation in us of His Holy
Spirit.

The claim put forward for Christianity that in
it is found the highest and best form of mystical
experience, and that Christ Himself was the true
and perfect Mystic, has been put forward with persuasive power by Evelyn Underhill in *The Mystic
Way*.   But this claim would rest upon a very much
stronger basis if it can be shown that in the varieties
of religious experience the Christian communion
with God in Christ is *different*, if not in kind, at any

rate in degree, from all other mystical experiences, and that this distinctively Christian experience dates from the coming of the Holy Ghost. We have only to examine the contents of the Gospel as preached by St. Paul, ' the prince of all true Christian mystics,' to see that from the very first Christianity claimed to be, and, still more, *was experienced to be*, a new Gospel of Power opening up a new and living Way of access for the soul to God. And this Way was Christ. The whole content of the Pauline Gospel, which is the record of his own spiritual experience ' in Christ,' is concerned with the proclamation to men of this new fact in spiritual history. The Incarnation meant the advent of the Divine into the stream of man's earthly life ; the invasion of the Divine into the sphere of the human in the Person of the God-Man. And the proof of it was confirmed by the distinctively Christian experience in Christ of the advent of the Spirit into the depths of human personality. The work of Christ *for* us is followed by the work of Christ *in* us. The union of God with man in the Incarnation is followed by the union of the soul with Christ.

Without attempting to indicate the distinctive characteristics of Christian Mysticism as found more especially in the writings of the two great mystical thinkers St. Paul and St. John, we can point to the New Testament teaching generally, and claim for it this much at least, that we have there depicted a new life, a new religious experience ; and that this is associated, in the minds of those who felt it, with the personality of Christ, Who for them was a living and abiding reality in their midst, and through Whom they had access to God by a new and living Way.

The record of religious experience ' in Christ '

contained in the New Testament is more than amply sufficient to establish the fact that Pentecost meant for Christians a changed relationship between the soul and God ; a new relation between the human spirit and the Divine Spirit. If the Old Testament Scriptures afford ample evidence of the advent of the Divine Spirit upon men, yet, in every case this was fro n without, as an external force, and not necessarily of a permanent character ; but Pentecost revealed the Spirit as dwelling and *abiding within* man's human personality. The difference is remarkable, and one fact alone will account for it, viz. the Incarnation. The union of the Divine and the human in the One Christ made possible an extension of the Incarnation, whereby the Divine Spirit might come to dwell within a human personality. The flood of a new spiritual life begins to pour into the new humanity in Christ ; the new Creation, the Church which is His Body. The new relationship between the human and the Divine, consummated first in His own Person, is now made possible between Himself and His brethren, who are thus enabled to share His life. The human personality thus linked with the Divine Spirit, as the result of this new relationship, grows and develops in virtue of the union. ' They were all filled with the Holy Ghost.' The new birth is followed by the religious experience of ' a new life hid with Christ in God ' and the consequent inflowing of the Divine into the human. Such a union between the human and the Divine is a phenomenon which dates from Pentecost, which is therefore distinctively Christian and was first made possible by the Incarnation.

(C.) *Summary.*—We have now examined human

189

nature in the light of modern psychology. We have also considered the light shed upon the Divine Nature by revelation. We have further studied the relationship between the human and the Divine, as revealed in religious experience. We must now apply the results thus obtained to the Christological problem.

(1) Can we venture to penetrate deeper into the mystery of the relationship between the human and the Divine in the Person of Christ from our knowledge of this relationship as it is revealed in the Christian life in Christ ?

An affirmative answer is justified by the fact that the same Jesus Christ Who was Incarnate in His own Person as the Son of Man is now imparting Himself to us in His character as the Head of a new humanity, which receives its life and is becoming what it is only in virtue of its living and vital union with Him. Whatever of the Divine is in us as the result of this union is *His* Divinity. The relationship of it to our human nature therefore should surely guide us in our effort to understand its relationship to His own human nature which was incorporated by Him into the unity of His Person.

(2) But there are important and vital differences between Him and us which must never be lost sight of when we endeavour to argue from the analogy of the relationship between the human and the Divine in us to their relationship in His Person. We have to remember that in all the examination of the relationship between the human and the Divine in man which we have been conducting, our starting-point has been a finite, imperfect, limited, and sinful human personality, into which the Divine comes as a life-giving, sin-conquering, and sanctifying power.

Obviously the analogy between His perfect sinless human nature and ours in these respects breaks down. Further, in the case of man the advent of the Divine Life into the human in no wise changes its essentially human character. The ' God-possessed ' man, even on the highest spiritual plane of religious ecstasy, is none the less man, no matter how great a flood of Divine Power and Divine Life descends upon him. We have found no record of any man having become other than a man as the result of his union with God. On the contrary, whilst we have not been able to set any limit to a man's capacity for receptivity from the Divine, the result is always the human imperfect being becoming more truly human. There is a growth and development of human personality in a ' God-atmosphere ' which is a necessary environment for the satisfaction of its deepest needs ; but, whilst we can set no limit to man's power of a higher becoming through union with the Divine, the highest goal he can ever hope to reach is his transformation into the likeness of God, *not* his ever becoming a part of God or the Image Himself. The line of demarcation separating man from God, the creature from the Creator, in this sense, is never obliterated. This is decisive against the Monophysite hypothesis in whatever form it may be advocated, since, if human and Divine are never confused in us, neither were they in the Person of Christ.

(3) Moreover, applying these considerations to the Christological problem, we have also here the death-blow to all Adoptianist theories whether ancient or modern. No man, however Divinely endowed or inspired, can ever become anything but man. When we consider the Person of the God-Man we have the

union of Perfect God with Perfect Man; not the union of an imperfect human personality with even the fullest measure of Divine Life.

He was Divine first and human afterwards. He was eternally the image of the invisible God. We can only hope to become, at the highest, fashioned anew into His likeness. The difference is vital. He *is* the image, we can never become anything beyond a likeness to it; and likeness is not, and never can be, identity.

(4) Therefore the starting-point for a consideration of the relationship between the human and the Divine in His Person is *not*, as in our case, an imperfect human being into whom the Divine flows from above; but is a Perfect Divine Personality entering into, taking up into Himself, our human nature. The difference, we believe, is crucial and vital for a sound Christology, and a failure clearly to perceive this difference is the foundation of much recent Christological speculation based upon psychological data supplied from an analysis of imperfect human personality. It is not simply a difference in the standpoint from which we view the relationship between the human and the Divine in His Person, i.e. as to whether we begin from the Alexandrian or the Antiochene theological point of view. The difference is more vital than this. We believe that the tremendous emphasis upon the manhood and truly human life of Christ in our own day, due to the influence of the Liberal school, has made theologians reluctant to face the New Testament portrait of the God-Man, Who, however truly human His earthly life may have been, was none the less God Incarnate; and, as such, presents us with a unique phenomenon in the history

of psychology, viz. a unique consciousness, a unique and sinless personality. If we allow ourselves to dwell exclusively upon the truly human life of the God-Man we are inevitably tempted to read into that life traits and characteristics which we know to be normal in our own lives, and which we infer therefore from our *a priori* psychological presuppositions must have existed in His life. The analogy is pressed beyond anything justified by the differences between Him and ourselves. The consequence is that whilst our faith would accept Him as the sinless Son of God, our psychology bids us reduce Him to our own level, and endow Him with a ' human personality ' such as we are conscious of possessing but such as He never had. His personality, human and Divine, was and is unique.

(5) If modern psychology bids us speak in terms of ' consciousness ' and ' personality,' we cannot be too careful in applying these terms to the problem of the Person of Christ.

We must be quite clear in our own minds that His ' consciousness ' was different from ours. We have no knowledge of a perfectly pure and sinless consciousness. Moreover, His ' personality ' was different from ours. We have no knowledge of an Ego which, because it was eternal, may conceivably have given Him in His Incarnate state a knowledge of Himself as He existed prior to His advent in the Flesh.

(6) These considerations force further questions upon us. Are we to regard the Incarnation as God becoming Incarnate in the Person of Christ in order to achieve the redemption of mankind ; or is He simply the man Jesus, whose human consciousness

opened up an avenue through which God might exercise a maximum of control in human life ? Is it a case of the Divine Logos Himself becoming Incarnate, or the human personality of Jesus receiving of the Divine beyond measure ? Is it true that 'in Him dwelt all the fulness of the Godhead bodily,' or are we simply to regard Him as one in whom the Spirit dwelt ὡς ἐν οὐδένι ἄλλῳ ?

These issues were clear enough to those whose task it was to formulate the ancient Christology. We fear, however, that in our own time they have once more become obscured, by reason of the attempts which are being made to restate the Christological problem with the aid of data supplied from psychological research, and to read into the Gospel portrait of the God-Man, traits and features which we know to exist in a purely human consciousness, and which it is therefore presumed must have been possessed by Him. If we are to speak of ' Two Consciousnesses ' instead of ' Two Natures,' are we to begin with His purely human consciousness, and to regard His Divine Consciousness as something added to this and having an undefined relationship to it ? Or had we not better frankly face the fact of an Incarnation which resulted in the advent into our finite world of a unique consciousness, human and Divine, which must for ever transcend and baffle any psychological analysis of it ?

(7) Our starting-point is to be a unique consciousness human and Divine in the Person of the God-Man. Yet it is to be *a single consciousness*. We may call it Divine or human, or, strictly speaking, both at once. The dualism of ' Two Consciousnesses ' is open to just as severe a criticism as is urged against the ' Two

Natures' doctrine.   Modern theologians are seeking to overcome this dualism and wish to speak of a single consciousness, human and Divine, at one and the same time.[1]

What other theory than the doctrine of the Enhypostasia can meet this difficulty ?   If we are to have neither a duplex personality nor an impersonal manhood, what solution other than the Enhypostasia can give us a *single consciousness human and Divine* indissolubly united in the unity of the One Person ?

It will help us now to reinterpret the doctrine of the Enhypostasia in terms of modern thought if we clear the ground still further by an examination of one or two theories put forward recently to meet the difficulties we are considering.

[1] See Dr. Mackintosh's criticism quoted at length in the earlier part of this thesis.

PART THREE

SOME MODERN ATTEMPTS AT CHRISTO-LOGICAL RECONSTRUCTION

WE have seen that Psychology has played a prominent part in recent Christological speculation.

In our analysis of human nature we purposely refrained from reference to certain phenomena of a more or less pathological character, to which nevertheless appeal has been made in attempts to solve the Christological problem. We refer to the abnormal cases of 'multiple personality,' 'altered personality,' 'double consciousness,' and other like phenomena of memory and self-consciousness which have occupied the attention of the Psychical Research Society for some time past, and which F. W. H. Myers treats at some length in his great work *Human Personality and its Survival of Bodily Death*, and in his earlier papers on the *Subliminal Consciousness*.[1] It is true that we have not explained such phenomena when we have labelled them abnormal or pathological, but the evidence, so far adduced, though it may suggest the *possibility* of the normal human consciousness becoming disintegrated and split up into seemingly dissociated sections, does not prove it, and the phenomena may quite conceivably be explained upon an entirely different hypothesis. The supposed rupture of the unity of the psychic life may be due to a dislocation of memory which results in these

---

[1] *Proceedings of S.P.R.*, vol. vii.

illusions, or alterations of personality, whilst all the time the unity of consciousness and the real identity of person in both conditions is being preserved. Memory is essential to personal identity, and the 'alternating personality' may be a pure illusion self-induced, and due *not* to a disintegration of the Self but to temporary perturbations of memory.[1] Without, however, attempting to grapple with the complexities of what are admitted to be very obscure phenomena of mental pathology, we are on sound ground when we refuse to look to such phenomena for an 'explanation' of the duplex consciousness of the God-Man, and to apply the uncertain conclusions and surmises of such a subject to the problem of Christology.[2] To speak of the man Jesus as the 'alternative personality' of the Second Person of the Trinity, or as 'a dissociated section of the Divine consciousness' maintaining itself in its full Divinity by His side, is to use language which, even if justified by the *certain* results of investigation into the obscure regions of our own distracted nature, can scarcely be regarded as valid or satisfactory when applied to the Person of Christ.

(2) The most cautious and reverent use of the results of modern psychological investigation will be found in Dr. Sanday's very interesting speculations in his recent book, *Christologies : Ancient and Modern*, supplemented by his lectures on *The Problem of Personality in Christ and in Ourselves*.

Dr. Sanday points us to the relations of the

[1] See Podmore, *Studies in Psychical Research*, chap. xii., on Secondary Consciousness.

[2] See D. A. Murray, *Christian Faith and the New Psychology*, and compare the treatment of this subject in Oswald Dykes' series of papers in the *Expository Times*.

subconscious and subliminal self to the whole self. The ' larger self ' is made up of the conscious part of experience and that other part which is subconscious or unconscious. This latter part is the more important of the two. Dr. Sanday quotes passages from Myers' work, and also from Wm. James and other psychologists, to show the importance of this ' subliminal ' self and the part played by it as a well-accredited psychological entity. We are asked to see in the relationship between the ' subliminal ' and ' supraliminal ' self in man a possible key to the relationship between the Divine and the human in the Person of Christ. Dr. Sanday tentatively suggests two propositions :

(1) 'That the proper seat or *locus* of all divine indwelling, or divine action upon the human soul, is the subliminal consciousness.'

(2) 'That the same, or a corresponding, subliminal consciousness is the proper seat or locus of the Deity of the incarnate Christ.'

This is an attempt to locate the sphere of influence of the Divine in us, and to argue from the analogy of the relationship of the human to the Divine in us to the relationship between them in the Person of Christ. Now in our review of the relation of the human to the Divine in man we did not attempt to locate the Divine indwelling, nor to indicate any particular part of man to which we might point as the sphere in him of the Divine Presence or action. Dr. Sanday thinks, however, that if we can so locate the Divine in us, we shall have the key to the problem which presents itself to us when we strive to conceive of the relation between the human and the Divine in Christ. Where is the Divine in us to be located ? Dr. Sanday thinks

in the ' subliminal ' self, where it is found working
at the roots of our being far beneath the surface of
our normal life, whilst the results of this working
are seen in their effects as these make themselves
felt from time to time in our consciousness. We see
the result and infer the cause.

Instead of the word ' proper ' seat in the above
definition, Dr. Sanday would almost write ' primary.'

I do not of course mean [he says] to deny that this divine
element makes itself felt, and at times directly felt, in consciousness. But it seems *to come up* (as it were) unto consciousness, as if from some lower and deeper sphere.

Again he tells us that—

It does not seem too much to say that these lower regions
are the proper sphere within which the Spirit of God acts
upon the soul of man. In this fact—as far as it is a fact—
I seemed to see the key to the nature of the union between
the human and the divine in Christ.

Dr. Sanday brings many weighty considerations
to the support of his propositions. He points us to
the data of religious experience which we have been
considering, and shows that whilst the action of man
in seeking communion with God is a conscious act,
of the Divine response man is not directly conscious.
Answers to prayer do not come directly or consciously,
but we perceive the effects and argue back to the
cause ; some subtle Divine movement and secret
working upon our ' subliminal ' self deep down beneath the ' threshold ' of consciousness, the presence
and action of which is only known when its effect
is experienced in the ' fruit ' of the Spirit.

Dr. Sanday recognises that in certain exceptional
natures these secret workings come nearer to the
surface than they do with others ; for example, in

the prophets and latter-day saints whose experiences were so vivid as to rise up into consciousness to a degree that we cannot parallel from ourselves.

There are doubtless many degrees of communion; and the measure that we should apply to these degrees is the extent to which they enter into consciousness. But in ordinary experiences the communion that I speak of is usually sub- or unconscious; and even in exceptional experience, it begins in the sub- or unconscious region and gradually expands upwards and outwards.

So the conclusion is that the ' subliminal self ' is the medium of Divine inspiration and Divine indwelling.

And that which was true of the servants—the prophets and holy men of old—was true also of the Son. Even with Him, in His incarnate nature, Divine inspiration and Divine indwelling was not essentially different in the modes and region of its working.

Dr. Sanday's theory has been criticised from many points of view, and his conclusions have not met with any wide acceptance. We may here indicate one or two reasons for our reluctance to confine the working of the Divine in us to any one region of our complex being, or to regard the ' subliminal self ' as the medium of Divine inspiration or indwelling. Rather do we prefer to believe that the *whole* human spirit is the proper locus of the Divine indwelling, and to think of the Divine immanence in us as pervading our *whole nature*; and only to the extent to which this is effected can we be said to be truly human.

(*a*) In the first place can we speak of ' locating ' an influence or still more a Divine presence ? Spirit, whether human or Divine, has no local habitation, neither can we confine it to any particular organ of the body. Dr. D'Arcy's keen criticism of Dr. Sanday's attempt to think of personality as in space is surely sound (see the correspondence in the *Hibbert Journal*). Consciousness has no place, no locus ; and Dr. Sanday's argument that because the language of psychologists is spacial and material (e.g. the *field* of consciousness, the *margin*, the *centre*, the *sub*-liminal, the *threshold*, &c.) therefore we can speak of our personalities as divided up into different strata, with boundary lines dividing the consciousness into ' upper ' and ' lower,' is not conclusive. This demonstrates rather the inability of language to convey to the mind what is, in the ultimate analysis, something of which we can form no conception. Our senses cannot perceive ' spirit,' and therefore no mental image we try to form of it, or no language we use to describe it, will be adequate, and if psychologists make use of spacial and material terms to describe an immaterial thing they must not be taken literally. The most that we can do is to describe the ' effects ' of spirit, not ' spirit ' itself, whether human or Divine, and the ' effects ' we may speak of as ' influence,' ' inspiration,' ' indwelling.' A thing may be said to be ' in a place ' when it exerts action or is effected by action in that place. In this sense the soul's presence may be located where its influence is felt, and the Divine Spirit spoken of as having a locus.

So we may conceive of the Divine Spirit as permeating and pervading man's whole being in the sense of influencing and giving vitality to every part, but not in the sense of being locally attached to any particular organ or residing in any particular locus such as the ' subliminal self,' wherever that may be.

We are reminded of the attempts on the part of earlier thinkers to locate the ' spirit ' of man in some particular organ. The ancients thought of it as seated in the liver, and so connected with that organ those higher emotions which they ascribed to the ' spirit,' e.g., courage. Others located ' spirit ' in the heart of man, and indeed a glance at modern language is sufficient to show this. Even to-day we speak of the coward as ' white-livered,' ' chicken-hearted,' and the brave man as ' lion-hearted.' Biblical language recalls the ' humble and contrite in heart,' and the reminder that ' out of the *heart* of men evil thoughts proceed, fornications, thefts, murders,' and so on. The attempt in our own time to locate the spirit in the brain and to find the seat of man's personality in the pineal gland is interesting, because it was due partly to man's ignorance of the precise function of this particular gland. But this attempt has failed, and every other attempt to locate the ' spirit ' of man in any member or organ or region, whether ' subliminal ' or otherwise, of his complex being is doomed to failure. We may well believe that the cult of the ' subliminal self,' which is much in vogue to-day, is due to a certain extent to our ignorance of what it is. Hence it is a convenient ' explanation ' of all psychological difficulties, which are regarded as solved once they are referred to the subliminal region.

(*b*) Mr. Myers, in his papers on the Subliminal Consciousness, claimed for it a very wide scope.

I suggest, then, that the stream of consciousness in which we habitually live is not the only consciousness in connection with our organism. I accord no primacy to my ordinary waking self, except that, among many potential selves, this one has shown itself the fittest to meet the needs of common life.

There is in each one of us an abiding psychical entity far more extensive than he knows,—an individuality which can never express itself completely through any corporeal manifestation. All this unexpressed psychical action is conscious, all is included in an actual or potential memory below the threshold of habitual consciousness. This subliminal consciousness may embrace a far wider range both of physiological and of psychical activity than is open to the supraliminal consciousness. The spectrum of consciousness in the subliminal self stretches indefinitely in either direction, extending on the one side to physiological processes which have long dropped out of human knowledge, on the other to certain supernormal faculties (telepathy, clairvoyance, prevision), of which only stray hints have reached us in our present stage of evolution. Conformably with this view, a stream of consciousness flows on within us, at a level beneath the threshold of ordinary waking life ; sleep is no longer to be conceived as the mere abeyance of waking activities, but as a phase of personality with characteristics definitely its own ; crystal vision, the hypnotic trance, and allied states open a door into this hidden life ; and the improvisations of genius are manifestations of subliminal activity intruding upon the primary consciousness.

Whilst the facts Myers adduced call still for an adequate explanation, his own psychical theory goes beyond the facts, and involves assumptions and conjectural interpretations which have not yet been substantiated.[1]

The theories which are being put forward regarding the character of this supposed ' subliminal self ' have gone far beyond the point justified by the actual data supplied by psychological investigation. We may quote an interesting passage on this point from the article ' Identity ' in the *Encyclopædia of Religion and Ethics*. The writer is striving to establish his

[1] *Vide* Podmore, *Studies in Psychical Research*, pp. 409-10.

contention that personal identity is primarily identity
of form, not of content or matter, and in this connection he criticises the theory of the ' subliminal self.'

It is, of course [he writes], a fact capable of establishment by careful observation . . . that mental ' states ' do
not arise and vanish instantaneously ; they have a period
of ' marginal ' existence which may exist both before and
after their occupation of the ' centre ' of attentive consciousness. But the doctrine of the ' subliminal self ' extends
this conception of the ' margin ' surrounding the ' focus '
of consciousness beyond the limits within which its validity
can be submitted to experimental tests. The ' subliminal '
is thought of as a region in which mental contents of all
kinds still persist as actual, though unconscious, when they
have disappeared from even the ' margin ' of consciousness,
and from which they can be evoked again in the processes
of recall. As a symbol for the truth that the actual condition of consciousness may be largely determined by
experiences which are no longer present to consciousness,
there can be no objection to the use of such a notion ; but
when the attempt is made to regard the symbol as an explanation—for instance, to explain recollection by the supposed
persistence of a percept or idea ' below the threshold,' or
to convert a mental tendency into an actual conjunction of
' subliminal ' states—and, most of all, when personal identity
is supposed to rest upon such an actually unchanging body
of ' subliminal ' mental contents, it should be clear that we
are dealing with the Humian fallacy in a new dress. An
identity which is really one of form and law is being illegiti-
mately converted into one of material constituents. If
we are right in holding that personal identity requires no
notion of an unchanging ' substrate,' the theories which may
be formed of the character of the supposed ' subliminal '
self will have no bearing upon the problem of identity. In
fact, the very problem to be solved, in what the identity of
a person consists, obviously breaks out again when we ask
what is meant by the unity and self-identity of the supposed
' subliminal ' personality itself.

The above considerations should bid us pause

before we seek to use so uncertain and indefinite a concept as that of the 'subliminal' self as the basis upon which to build up either a theory of the relation of the Divine to the human in us or in the Person of Christ.

But the most interesting feature of Dr. Sanday's theory from our point of view is that it represents a brilliant attempt to overcome the dualism presented by the 'Two Natures' doctrine and the 'Two Consciousnesses' suggested by certain modified forms of Kenotic Christology.   Dr. Sanday is feeling his way towards a single consciousness, human and Divine, as the only secure basis for a unity of Person in the One Christ.   So he seeks refuge in psychological analysis, and secures for the God-Man a unity of Person by combining the two consciousnesses within the unity of that 'larger self' which is composed of the conscious and the subliminal.   If we think of the Divine Consciousness in the Person of Christ as resident in the subliminal and fully open to the Divine inflowing, whilst the human consciousness is supraliminal and receives from the Divine as this 'swims up' from below the threshold ; we have here a real attempt to secure for the God-Man a *single consciousness* even if we are compelled to think of it as in some sense divided into two strata.[1]

Apart from the question as to whether such a relationship between the two strata of the single consciousness gives us any safeguard from a Monophysite mixture, or confusion of the human and the Divine in the Person of Christ, we have still such a

---

[1] Compare Myers' treatment of the *strata* of consciousness in his article on the subject of the 'Subliminal Consciousness.' *Proceedings of the S.P.R.*, vol. vii. p. 305 ff.

division between the two as is fatal to that picture of perfect harmony in the life of the God-Man presented to us by the Gospel narratives ; and above all, is it true that the New Testament data supply us with a purely human consciousness invaded from time to time or even continuously by a Divine consciousness ?

As one acute critic says :

Is there any suggestion in the narrative of a movement on the part of Jesus, to and fro, between the subconscious and the conscious spheres ? Is not the deepest note of His character the continuousness of His conscious fellowship with God as of the Son with the Father ? Is there a hint anywhere of a shutting off of His Divine consciousness during the greater part of His human experience ? There is certainly no indication of the shock which a *merely* human consciousness would receive if it were suddenly invaded by a Divine consciousness. Is not the dualism of two consciousnesses as fatal to the harmony of the life and character of Christ as that of the ' Two Natures ' ever was ? Or, at least, are not the two consciousnesses really coincident, the Divine being the root of the human, the human being penetrated, formed, and inspired by the Divine ?—T. B. Kilpatrick, article ' Incarnation,' *D.C.G.*

We conclude, then, that whilst there is much of an interesting and even fascinating character in Dr. Sanday's speculations, their foundation upon the basis of the supposed existence of the ' subliminal ' self in the sense in which he advocates it, makes it difficult, if not impossible, for us to accept his attempt at a reconstruction of Christology on these lines. And, moreover, our investigation of the relationship between the human and the Divine in us, has shown how unsafe it is to use this as an analogy when we try to conceive of the relation between the human and the Divine in the Person of Christ. The differences between Him and us *quâ* Personality are so great as to convince us that a starting-point for a sound Christology is not to be found so much in our resemblance to Him as men in whom His Spirit dwells, as in His difference from us as One Who was Son of God in a generic sense in His own right, and Son of Man in a unique sense in virtue of His sinless and perfect manhood.

(3) *Kenotic Theories.*—The starting-point of the Kenotic Christology is the great truth of the Divine Condescension, the reality of the Divine Self-sacrifice, the result of which is shown in the humiliation of the Son of God. We have a clear recognition that the motive of the Incarnation was a movement of Divine compassion springing from the love of God for mankind. It is of the essence of love to give, and whatever the cost, to pay it. Hence if the Incarnation involved a self-limitation on the part of the Divine, no *a priori* objections to such an act can be allowed to outweigh the historical fact that ' God so loved the world that He *gave.*'

The second great truth for which the Kenotic Christology contends is the reality of Christ's manhood. The problem therefore is to determine what limitations the Divine must undergo in order that He may live a truly human life as a man amongst men. What were the conditions of our Lord's life on earth ? It is assumed that where Divinity is incompatible with a truly human life there the Divine must give way to the human in the Incarnate life. This is the *principle* of the Incarnation. The *method* is some form of Divine depotentiation or self-limitation.

The most thorough-going and consistent form of

Kenoticism was that advocated by Gess, who thought that it was essential for the Divine Logos to cease from the exercise of His functions as the Second Person of the Trinity, and to deprive Himself even of His consciousness as the Logos in order that He might be able to submit to the process of a human birth in time and space.

By a supreme act of will He deprived Himself even of His self-consciousness as Logos. He entered into that night of unconsciousness in which our life begins.

Other forms of the Kenotic Christology are less drastic. Thomasius and some later writers, notably Dr. Fairbairn, draw a division or distinction between the so-called physical attributes of Deity— omnipotence, omniscience, omnipresence—and the ethical attributes—truth, love, &c. It is considered possible for the Logos to surrender, or to refrain from the exercise of, or to exercise to a limited degree, these physical attributes, the retention or exercise of which in their fulness would be incompatible with His Incarnate life as the Son of Man. A very cautious and clear statement of this type of Kenotic theory is found in Dr. Fairbairn's work, *Christ in Modern Theology*.

Besides the theories of Gess and Thomasius, which give us two leading types of Kenotic theology, we have the later and far more valuable contributions of the British Kenotic theologians who have presented this form of Christology with such a wealth of illustration, thoroughness of treatment, and reverent restraint as to commend it to a wide circle of thoughtful men : and indeed we may say that the work of men like Bruce, Gore, Fairbairn, D. W.

Forrest, W. L. Walker, P. T. Forsyth, and others, constitutes a solid and distinctive contribution to theological thought, and justifies the claim that the British School are pre-eminent in the field of Kenotic Christology.

The earlier forms of the Kenotic theories in the past met with very strenuous opposition, and were attacked from many points of view. The more modified and cautious forms in which the theory is put forward by later theologians escape some of the difficulties. We have never attached much importance to the exegetical controversy, because the justification for some form of Kenotic Christology rests upon a much firmer basis than the exegesis of certain isolated texts[1] upon which elaborate theories have been built. Gifford's criticism of the exegetical basis of Kenoticism is very severe as the result of his examination of the famous passage in Philippians, but the edge of it can be turned if the doctrine of the Kenosis is shown to be based, not so much upon Biblical and historical foundations of an insecure character, as upon the outstanding fact of the Incarnation itself, which must have involved a Kenosis, whatever theory we may choose to hold as to its method. As Dr. Mackintosh says :

We are faced by a Divine self-reduction which entailed obedience, temptation, and death. So that religion has a vast stake in the *Kenosis* as a fact, whatever the difficulties as to its method may be. No human life of God is possible without a prior self-adjustment of deity. The Son must empty Himself in order that from within mankind He may declare the Father's name, offer the great sacrifice, triumph over death ; and the reality with which, to reach this end, He laid aside the form and privilege of deity is the measure of

[1] 2 Cor. viii. 9 ; Phil. ii. 5-11.

that love which had throbbed in the Divine heart from all eternity.

But whilst we fully recognise that God in Christ is God stooping down and becoming poor for our sakes, yet we must not go beyond what is revealed in the New Testament as to the extent of this ' poverty.' There is much force in Hall's criticism [1] that any Christological theory which involves the surrender on the part of the God-Man of any Divine attribute essential to the validity and perfection of His Divine work as Saviour stands self-condemned.   If the strong point of the Kenotic Christology is its clear recognition of the Incarnation as the advent of God to man, and the Divinity of the pre-existent Logos is never questioned, the subsequent self-depotentiation, self-extinction, or even self-limitation may be conceived of as so great that the resultant Incarnate Christ is at best a perfect man and nothing more.   A Christology which begins from the Alexandrian standpoint and ends with a purely human Christ such as rationalism asks us to accept, will not commend itself to men who feel and know that their salvation is bound up with the reality of the work of Christ as the Divine Son of God as well as the human Son of Man.

Dr. Martensen in his *Christian Dogmatics* revives the older idea of the Logos as functioning through two centres of personal activity, and in some sense leading a kind of double life as the eternal pre-existent Logos upholding all creation, and, as the Incarnate Logos, performing His mediatorial work within the limits of His manhood.

It must be allowed [says Dr. Martensen], that the Son of

[1] F. J. Hall, *The Kenotic Theory*.   Compare H. C. Powell, *The Principle of the Incarnation*.

213

God leads in the economy of the Father a twofold existence ; that He lives a double life in His world-creating and in His world-completing activity. As the pure *Logos of Deity*, He works through the kingdom of nature by His all-pervading presence, creates the presuppositions and conditions of the revelation of His all-completing love. As the *Christ*, He works through the kingdom of Grace, of Redemption, and Perfection, and points back to His pre-existence. . . . We are to see in Christ, not the naked God, but *the fulness of deity framed in the ring of humanity ;* not the attributes of the divine nature in their unbounded infinitude, but the divine attributes embodied in the attributes of human nature (*communicatio idiomatum*). Instead of the omnipresence we have that blessed presence, concerning which the God-Man testifies, ' He that seeth Me seeth the Father ' : in the place of omniscience comes the divinely human wisdom which reveals to babes the mysteries of the kingdom of heaven ; in the place of the world-creating omnipotence enters the world-vanquishing and world-completing power, the infinite power and fulness of love and holiness in virtue of which the God-Man was able to testify ' all power is given to Me in heaven and on earth.' [1]

This gives us the picture of the Son of God leading a twofold existence ; in one sphere of His activities exercising the Divine attributes of omnipotence, omniscience, and omnipresence without restraint, in the other sphere exercising these Divine powers to a limited degree. Just as we have found Dr. Sanday appealing to modern psychology in support of a Christological theory, so also, in the case of some modern forms of Kenoticism, appeal is made to the same source for help in the effort to conceive of a Being living a double life from two non-communicating centres. If in the One Christ there was a double centre of consciousness, then it was possible for Him to know Himself as the Divine Son in all His glory upholding the universe by His omnipotent power,

[1] *Op. cit.*, p. 267.   (E. T.)

and at the same time to be conscious of Himself as man in all the limitations and weaknesses of a truly human life. But the theory of ' Two Consciousnesses ' is met by the formidable danger that it almost necessarily involves a duplex personality. To escape this difficulty resort is made to yet another theory of a self-consciousness composite in character, partly human, partly Divine. This gives us one self-consciousness belonging to neither nature by itself, but proper to both in virtue of the fact that it is the centre of a Divine-human personality.

Evidently, then, modern thought, as reflected in all these conflicting theories, is beset by the same difficulties as confronted the earlier thinkers, who had to seek some outlet from Nestorianism on the one hand with its dual personality, and Eutychianism on the other hand with its composite Divine-human personality. Escape from these difficulties is not gained when we have taken refuge in modern psychology and talked of ' Two Consciousnesses ' instead of 'Two Natures,' or sought a solution in the conception of a composite Divine-human personality. It is becoming more and more clear that, in the absence of any *proof* that in the Person of Christ there were two streams of consciousness co-existing in the same personality, it is idle to speculate as to how such a thing could be, even though psychology offers to help us over the difficulties.

In what direction, then, are we to seek for a solution ? Ancient Christology came to rest in the doctrine of the Enhypostasia. Modern Christology is seeking an outlet from the same difficulties which beset ancient Christology, and is satisfied with neither a duplex nor a complex personality. The more the New Testament is appealed to, the clearer is its emphasis upon the unity of Christ's Person. What is the secret of this unity ? Is it a *single* if unique consciousness, and if so, what theory so unites the ' Two Natures ' in the One Person as to give a single unique consciousness as the centre of both ?

Before we consider the claims of the doctrine of the Enhypostasia, we must examine one other theory, which seeks to construct a modern Christology upon the basis of a single Divine self-consciousness in the God-Man.   This theory is propounded in Dr. Weston's work, *The One Christ*.   A single Divine self-consciousness conditioned in and by manhood, God in manhood becoming conscious of Himself only so far and in the measure in which such knowledge can be mediated by His manhood ; this, so far as we can gather, is what Dr. Weston wishes us to accept as the key to a study of the New Testament portrait of Jesus Christ.   With this we may compare the earlier treatment of the same subject on similar lines by Dr. Moberly in his great work, *Atonement and Personality* (chapters iv. and v.).

Dr. Weston clearly grasps how vital it is for a sound Christology to have as a starting-point this conception of a single consciousness of the Christ, but he is careful to warn us in a footnote that ' the process may be dual, since two natures are His *media* of knowledge ; but the self-knowledge of the Incarnate, through His manhood, is a single know-ledge of Himself as God-in-manhood.   And any know-ledge independent of His manhood is outside the Incarnation.' [1]

[1] Note, p. 174.   New edition.

Although Dr. Weston submits the various Kenotic theories to a searching criticism, he ends by himself advocating a very cautious and carefully safe-guarded form of Kenotic Christology, in which the Incarnation is viewed as an act of immeasurable self-sacrifice and an act of supreme Divine power whereby the life of the Logos is so ordered that—

within a certain sphere He wills to have no consciousness of Himself that is not mediated for Him by His human soul. It is a supreme exhibition of divine love and power ; it allows for the gradual development of the consciousness of the Incarnate in the measure of the growth of His human soul ; while at the same time it secures the divine character of the consciousness itself.

We may quote from Dr. Weston's summary : [1]

To sum up then, the Logos, in His state of Divine Glory, possesses a true consciousness of Himself as God the Son, omnipotent and omniscient. In virtue of His omniscient wisdom, by His omnipotent power, He ever imposes upon Himself a law of self-restraint, so framed that, in the Incarnate State, His exercise of His own proper powers is at every moment to be adapted to the measure of the capacity of His ever-growing manhood. As living under this law, within the conditions of manhood, He knows Himself not as God the Son exercising full divine power through a free and unlimited Divine Nature, but as God the Son limited and conditioned in manhood ; and unable to act or speak or think outside the limits imposed upon Him by His manhood. So living and so conforming to the law of self-restraint, He is the centre of the new relationships with His Father and His creatures that make up the life of the Incarnation ; the existence of these relationships depending upon the indwelling of all creatures by the unlimited Logos in virtue of His omnipresence, and upon the reality of the limited self-consciousness of the Logos as Incarnate.

Thus in His eternal relationships the Logos is found performing an act of immeasurable self-sacrifice, in which the

[1] Pp. 179-180. New edition.

Father who sends Him into the world is seen to share; and within the special relationships of the Incarnation the Logos in manhood is found offering at every moment an act of consummate obedience to the original law of self-restraint. The initial act of self-sacrifice belongs to the eternal relations, being based upon His self-consciousness as omnipotent Logos; the continuous act of obedience is the expression in terms of humanity of the primary act of self-sacrifice, and is based upon His limited self-consciousness as Logos in manhood. The latter alone has to do with the life of the Incarnate; and it alone concerns us in our estimate of the self-consciousness of the Christ. In fact, self-sacrifice in God is only intelligible to us after it has been translated into the terms of human thought.

There is much of a helpful and illuminating character in Dr. Weston's work, and he elaborates his theory in a way which cannot but impress those who are prepared to accept his main assumption that the self-limitation of the Word of God was an act consummated *prior* to the Incarnation; an act of will in the sphere of His Divine activities, and which He made as the unlimited Word of the Father. By an initial act of will the Logos determined to enter upon manhood, and to face to the uttermost all the consequences of that act. His self-restraint is thus not due to a series of acts within the sphere of His Incarnation. Moreover, apparently, we must not conceive of the God-Man as ever in His Incarnate state acting as God unlimited. All the activities of the unlimited Logos are confined to the sphere of His eternal, universal relations, and when He acts in the sphere of the Incarnate state, His Divine powers are always conditioned by, and mediated through, His manhood. But can we grant these assumptions?

The question that presents itself to our mind is

whether the evidence derived from the self-revelation
of Jesus Christ does not contain data which make it
hard to believe that, in His Incarnate state, His self-
consciousness of His Deity was *wholly* conditioned by,
and mediated through, the manhood He had assumed ;
and, further, whether His Divine powers were
circumscribed within this same limit ? We think,
for example, of His miracles. Do not the Gospel
narratives reveal Him as doing things which transcend
manhood's capacities ? We think of His Divine
prerogatives, and find ourselves wondering whether
the claims of Christ do not inevitably suggest that
they are founded upon a self-consciousness transcendent in its character, and wider far than any
limitation which His manhood must have imposed
upon it had He allowed it to do so. Is not His
universal appeal—' Come unto Me, all ye that labour
and are heavy laden, and I will give you rest '—only
conceivable upon the hypothesis that, at the time
it was made, His self-consciousness of Himself as
God had so far transcended the limits of the power
of His manhood to mediate such a knowledge, that
He was able to know the fulness of His Divine nature
as the Eternal Unlimited Lord of Glory and Power,
Whose all-embracing love could receive a universe
of finite souls and minister to their every need ?
Does not such a self-consciousness transcend the
limitations which His manhood must inevitably
have placed upon it if He had been content to
allow it at that moment to do so ? Again, we think
of His testimony to His self-consciousness of sinless
perfection, and remind ourselves that we have no
knowledge of what a perfectly pure consciousness is,
and that when we try to conceive of it in Him we

are face to face with a unique phenomenon which transcends human experience. We contemplate His filial consciousness, which marks His relationship to God as unique ; differing not in degree but in kind from ours, and which was, moreover, the medium and channel through which has been conveyed to the world that insight into the very heart of God, which constitutes the claim of Christianity to be a complete and final revelation. Now this revelation to men of the very essence of God was only possible in virtue of the fact that He who conveyed it to men was Himself the Son, and *quâ* Son knew what no human consciousness could embrace, still less convey to men. If it be urged that we can set no limit to manhood's capacity for mediating such a Divine revelation, because we have no knowledge of the powers of a sinless manhood as a vehicle for the self-manifestation of God to men, we admit the point, but prefer to take refuge in the thought that, after all, sinless perfection is something differing not only in degree but in kind from anything human, and to this extent is as unique in the Person of Christ as was His filial consciousness. The uniqueness of His relationship to God as ' of one substance with the Father ' is the foundation for the finality and completeness of His revelation. The uniqueness of His sinless perfection is the foundation of His atoning work in redemption. Are we to believe that His work both as Revealer and Redeemer was conditioned by, and mediated through, the limitations of the manhood He assumed ? We hesitate to answer this question in the affirmative, in view of the above considerations. And our reluctance is still further strengthened when we allow ourselves to contemplate the conditions under which we imagine that a truly human life could have been lived. What is involved in the Gospel portrait of the earthly life of Jesus Christ? It means that 'In the midst of human history, which presents to us doubtless many bright spots, many great deeds, and many noble natures, but, at the same time, an uninterrupted chain of imperfect and sinful beings—in the midst of this history, whose purest light is never wholly undimmed, there is said to have appeared One who was altogether holy and undefiled, whose character was absolute truth, righteousness, and love, as He fully manifested by word and deed, in sufferings and in death.'

Now, is such a picture conceivable upon any other hypothesis than that at every moment of His earthly life He was transcendent above, and yet immanent in, the manhood He had assumed? Surely only so far as He was at every moment truly Divine could He have been at any moment truly human. Far from His transcendence destroying the possibility of His living a truly human life, it is the necessary presupposition without which the latter were an impossibility. Only because He was the unlimited Logos in His Incarnate state could He be the Ego of a perfect manhood in every conceivable relationship in which that manhood stood to those with whom He came into contact. We conclude, then, that whilst the fact of an Incarnation forces us to accept some form of Kenosis, and to believe that the unlimited Logos was circumscribed in some way as regards the exercise of His Divine powers and activities within the sphere of His Incarnate state, we are reluctant to go much further than this, and to define more closely the limitations under which the Eternal Son laboured during His earthly life. The Alexandrian and Cyrilline Christology leave us with the eternal, unlimited Logos as the subject of the manhood. Both, however, recognise some form of self-limitation on the part of the Logos in His Incarnate state, whereby the Divine nature is restrained, and the manhood thus allowed to act humanly. This leaves the door open, so to speak, for the Logos to exercise His Divine powers and prerogatives *to the full*, if and when He wills so to do. Dr. Weston invites us to close this door, and in this way not only to escape many difficulties, but to secure a much more consistent and comprehensible Christology. We should like to do so, but the risk seems too great.[1] If we turn away from this most enticing form of Kenotic Christology, what is the alternative ?

Let us see what can be said for the doctrine of the Enhypostasia.

[1] See further the fuller treatment of this question below, pp. 252–264.

THREE

2.

THE REINTERPRETATION OF THE DOCTRINE OF THE ENHYPOSTASIA IN TERMS OF MODERN THOUGHT

THE difficulties presented to modern thought by the ancient Christology centre round the dualism of the 'Two Natures' doctrine, and the 'Impersonal Manhood' of Christ.

We are told that the 'Two Natures' doctrine, in its traditional form, introduces into the life of Christ an incredible and thorough-going dualism totally out of keeping with the unity of Person, which is the first reality we touch in the New Testament portrait. We are asked to think in terms of personality, and to secure that the self-consciousness of Jesus be a single consciousness moving always as a spiritual unity. The modern mind will have nothing to do with 'Two Natures' thought of in the abstract, adjusted to each other, or combined in unspiritual modes.

Moreover, strong objection is taken to the word 'nature,' as suggesting the existence of a complex whole of attributes and qualities which can be thought of as real, apart from a unifying and focal Ego.

Hence the doctrine of the impersonal manhood of Christ is attacked as a meaningless abstraction. It is clearly perceived that some such doctrine is deducible from the Cyrilline Christology, which postulates the unlimited Divine Logos as the central Ego of the God-Man. The unreal character of an

223

impersonal humanity is keenly felt, whilst the alternative hypothesis of a duplex personality raises at once the Nestorian difficulty.

So we are bidden to throw over the old terms, which we are told belong to a discredited philosophy, and to think them out afresh in the light of modern psychology. We have tried to do so. We quite see the force of the objection to an ' impersonal manhood.' Personality is, and must be, central, and the whole complex of attributes and qualities briefly described as ' human nature ' can have no existence apart from, and except in, vital union and relationship with a unifying and focal Ego as its subject. If the Two Natures are to be preserved within the unity of the One Person, the single self-consciousness by which they are united must be of such a character and content as to be capable of being the subject of both at one and the same time.

(2) But Leontius of Byzantium put forward his doctrine of the Enhypostasia to meet precisely these difficulties. There was the Alexandrian theology, with its perversion in Eutychianism on the one hand, Antiochene theology, with its perversion in Nestorianism on the other ; and Chalcedonian theology embracing the truth for which both Alexandria and Antioch contended, and avoiding the errors alike of Eutychians and Nestorians. Leontius was faced with the task of reconciling the Chalcedonian Christology, with its clear insistence upon the reality and completeness of Christ's manhood, with Cyrilline Christology ; which, in postulating the Divine Logos as the centre of personality in the God-Man, necessarily implied that in some sense or other the manhood of Christ was impersonal.

Could an impersonal manhood be in any sense complete when it lacked that element which is most distinctive and central in man? Did not Cyril's Christology so reduce the manhood of Christ as to make it appear a mere series of attributes, or an unsubstantial accident of the Godhead in the One Christ? Such charges could only be met by securing for the manhood of Christ, within the unity of His Person, a relative independence and a personality of its own. Could this be done without stumbling into the Nestorian error? Leontius thought that it could, and offered the doctrine of the Enhypostasia as the only way of safety amidst these pitfalls. By it he secured the Cyrilline position that the Ego of the God-Man was the Divine unlimited Logos. By it he also secured that the manhood of Christ should not lack its most distinctive characteristic. It received its personality from the Logos. It had no independent personality of its own, but neither was it a mere series of attributes. It had no existence prior to the Incarnation, but became hypostatic, and received its subsistence, and consequently its completeness, when the Divine Logos became its Ego. The manhood of Christ in the Christology of Leontius was thus more than a mere accident of the Godhead, and yet less than an independent individual person. As John of Damascus put it later, in words which seem to convey to our minds a perfectly intelligent conception :

He took on Himself the elements of our compound nature, and these not as having an independent existence or as being originally an individual, and in this way assumed by Him, but as existing in His own subsistence.

In this theory the basis of the union between

the human and the Divine is found in the fact that
the Divine Logos is the subject of both, whilst the
difference between the two is safeguarded in that
the Incarnate Christ possessed Two Natures.

(3) We have seen that even though we speak
in terms of ' consciousness ' rather than ' nature,'
modern thought is still baffled by the dualism which
is so strongly objected to in the Chalcedonian
Definition. The hypothesis of a double Self is
repugnant to the modern mind. If we are to think
in terms of ' personality ' instead of ' substance,'
then the whole trend of modern thought in the field
of Christology is to secure that the self-consciousness
of Jesus be a single consciousness moving always as
a spiritual unity. This, and this alone, it is felt,
will safeguard the reality of the Gospel portrait,
which from first to last presents us with the *One*
Christ. We have examined theories which are
attempts to secure this single consciousness, and
have given reasons for our inability to regard them
as fully satisfying all the conditions of the problem.
Now the doctrine of the Enhypostasia, as we interpret
it, secures that the self-consciousness of the God-
Man is a single-consciousness which is not purely
human, nor merely human, but truly human, and
this because, and only because, it is at the same time
truly Divine. Therefore it, and it alone, could be
the subject of both Natures, and be the basis of their
union within the Person of Christ.

(4) The basis of the doctrine is the fact that the
Divine Logos, prior to the Incarnation, already
possessed everything needful to enable Him to live
a truly human life. It is the same conception
which we have seen was so strong a point in the

Apollinarian Christology, namely, that there is in God a human element. His advent, therefore, in the flesh brought to the human nature He assumed, not an alien element such as would render a truly human life for the God-Man an impossibility, but just that which alone could make the life of Christ in every stage of its growth and development a truly and perfectly human life. The Divine Logos was capable of being the Ego, not only of His Divine but also of His human Nature ; because His Personality in virtue of its Divinity already embraced all that is most distinctive of a truly human personality. The human and the Divine are not two contradictory, but two complementary terms, and the less is contained in the greater. His Divine self-consciousness was, in virtue of its Divinity, a truly human self-consciousness. His Ego was Divine—it was also human ; therefore it could be the subject of both natures. The foregoing considerations are sufficient to show that we are not, by this doctrine of the Enhypostasia, seeking to revive the Monophysite heresy in a new and subtle form.

(5) Human nature as we know it is never complete, never perfect. Herein lies the fatal error of those who, thinking to secure the reality and completeness of Christ's manhood, speak of His self-consciousness as purely human. Had it been so it could not have been either perfect or complete. Had Christ exhibited a purely human consciousness, He would by that very fact have revealed His imperfect manhood. If we are to judge of what a perfect manhood is we must go outside human experience, for we have no knowledge of it in ourselves. None among the sons of men has ever yet been a perfect man. If we wish to know a perfect

man we must look to the Christ, Who was perfect
man because, and only because, He was something
more. And the something more is that which
alone can make our human personality complete;
that without which it must ever be merely, but not
truly, human. He was perfect man because He was
perfect God. He, and He alone, could live a truly
human life, because at every moment of His earthly
career He was also the Divine Son of God. He was
never more truly human than when ' in Him dwelt
all the fulness of the Godhead bodily.' If the Incarnation was to be a revelation of man, not in his
incompleteness and imperfection, but as he ought
to be, it had to be the revelation of One Who was
not merely human, nor possessed of a merely or
purely human consciousness. This would have revealed His incompleteness. What was wanted was
a revelation of One Who was Divine, and therefore perfectly and completely human, even if infinitely more than this. The human Ego in man
is incomplete. The manhood of Christ, if it had
possessed a human Ego only, would have been
incomplete. Hence the Logos as its Ego was the
sole condition which could secure its completeness.
We may not speak of Christ's manhood as being
real and complete except on one supposition, namely,
that its personality was Divine. Though it might
be purely human, it could not be truly or completely
human without the Divine element.

Therefore the doctrine of the Enhypostasia is the
only one which can secure for the manhood of Christ
that reality and completeness which the Church
believes He possessed when she speaks of Him as
τέλειος ἄνθρωπος.

(6) This view is still further confirmed by ouꞌ consideration of personality, human and Divine.

Not only is the doctrine of the Enhypostasia rooted and grounded in the belief that there is an essential affinity between the human and the Divine —whereby He Who was the Divine image could be that image within manhood, in virtue of the fact that man himself was created in the image of God— but deeper still, the Incarnation was a revelation in time and space of a unique personality. Our analysis of human personality revealed it as ever incomplete, ever growing and developing, ever in a process of becoming, and we found it impossible to set any limits to its powers of a higher becoming if and when it was receiving from the Divine and living in a 'God-atmosphere.' Our examination of religious experience confirmed the fact that man was never more truly man than when his personality was united to God, and when, as the result of the union between the soul and God, the Divine was pouring itself into the human. Paul was never more truly Paul than when his life was hid with Christ in God.

We further found that God is Perfect Personality. We have striven to do full justice to Lotze's contention that ' complete personality can be in God only, while to man can belong but a weak and a faint copy thereof.'[1] Now, is it inconceivable that He Who is Perfect Personality could become personal in the flesh and live a truly human life ? If He possesses in a perfect degree that which is most distinctive of manhood, i.e., personality, is it inconceivable that His Ego, infinite in its Divinity, could nevertheless be the Ego also of the manhood He assumed ? Is it

[1] *Outlines of Philosophy of Religion*, p. 72.

inconceivable that His self-consciousness should be a
single Divine unique consciousness, giving Him a
knowledge of Himself as the Divine unlimited Logos
in virtue of its infinite extension, eternal character,
and all-embracing fulness, and yet at the same time
giving Him a knowledge of Himself as the human
Son of man circumscribed by the limitations inherent
in a finite existence ?   In endeavouring to conceive
of such a single unique consciousness, we are helped
by Dr. Iverach's reminder, that ' The conception of a
perfect self-consciousness consists in the fact that it
is in possession of itself, and *can set the bounds of its
own experience.*   Self-knowledge, self-reverence, self-
control—in these, and not in finitude or infinitude,
lies the conception of a perfect selfhood.' [1]

(7) The doctrine of the Enhypostasia secures that
such a consciousness would be at once Divine and
human at every stage of His growth from babyhood,
through boyhood up to manhood.   It would be a
single consciousness, unique in its Divine character,
eternal, unlimited, and therefore capable of giving
Him a knowledge of the fact that He issued forth
from God and came into time and space, and would
leave the world and return whence He came.   It
would mediate for Him His knowledge of His filial
relationship with the Eternal Father, Whose Son He
knew Himself to be.   It would secure for Him an
unbroken communion with God, in its fulness transcending our finite comprehension, but the effects of
which were seen in His superhuman powers and
activities, of the source of which He Himself is never
in any doubt.   It would be the source of His work
as the revealer of God to men, and Himself that

---

[1] Art. ' Consciousness,' *Enc. of Religion and Ethics.*

revelation incarnate. Moreover, it was a sinless self-consciousness, perfectly pure, perfectly holy, the source therefore of His perfect insight into men, and the ground of His claim to forgive sins. These elements in His single-consciousness would result from its eternal, unlimited, and sinless character.

(8) But at the same time it was a truly human consciousness, limited to the degree in which such a consciousness would have to be limited in order that the Son of God might conform to all the laws which govern our existence as finite individuals. It would mediate His self-knowledge as a man among men. It would grow and develop along perfectly normal lines within the limits of an earthly life and by contrast with that environment of persons and things which surrounded it. The growth of this single consciousness, viewed from the point of view of its truly human character, would not be a miraculous growth in any sense as failing in any point to conform to the laws which govern the growth of our personalities as finite limited beings in a finite world ; except in so far and to the degree in which a truly human consciousness is capable of transcending the limitations which we experience in our life as the result of sin and its consequences in our physical, mental, moral, and spiritual life. Jesus would live a truly human life as a man among men, and the verity of His human experience would never be in question, and yet it would be the experience of One Who at any and every moment of it was the Son of God. Hence there would be no need to draw any distinction between His Godhead and manhood relative to the conditions or experiences through which He passed in the days of His flesh.

(9) We need not assign one set of experiences to His human nature and another to His Divine, nor deny that the Divine could experience all that we know Jesus Christ did experience during His earthly life. The Incarnation, if it means anything, means God living a truly human life under all the conditions and limitations of a finite and creaturely existence. His humiliation was the humiliation of the Son of God, His Passion and Calvary sacrifice, the suffering of God Incarnate, and infinite therefore in its efficacy. We need never pause to question as to which ' nature ' we ought to assign any particular experiences He underwent, or any particular act He performed in the days of His flesh. The doctrine of the En-hypostasia rules out all Docetic unreality from the life and work of the God-Man.

(10) Again, we have not to conceive of two distinct personalities, one human and one Divine, the former gradually becoming more and more interpenetrated through and through by the latter, and Jesus Christ becoming more and more Divine with every stage and development of His earthly life. All theories of gradual or progressive Incarnation are rendered unnecessary by the doctrine of the Enhypostasia. Nor are we compelled to speculate as to how two distinct personalities or two separate streams of consciousness could ever become fused into a single personality or a single consciousness. There is no question of a fusion of the human and the Divine in the sphere of the consciousness whilst preserving a distinction in the sphere of the natures. We have a single and complete personality, a single and complete consciousness as the starting-point, not the goal of our Christological theory.

(11) The doctrine of the Enhypostasia secures that the particular is contained in the universal. The Divine Ego contains the human, and yet is not exhausted by that fact. The single unique Divine self-consciousness of the Incarnate Christ is the universal, revealed in and through the particular, embracing the latter and yet not limited by its range. Of the Incarnate Christ we may say that the form of His consciousness was human, but its content was Divine. Its range, viewed from one standpoint, was unlimited — viewed from another standpoint, was limited and yet none the less *self*-limited. It was the subject of both natures. If two natures were His media of knowledge, who is to set a limit to what He could or could not know ? Who is to say that any knowledge independent of His manhood was outside the Incarnation ? Is not this to view the Godhead as giving way to the manhood to such an extent as to make the Christ in His Incarnate state the possessor of one nature only ? The doctrine of the Enhypostasia secures for the Christ in His Incarnate state a range of consciousness passing out beyond the limits of a finite mind. The same self-consciousness could mediate two sets of knowledge—all that He knew as God, all that He came to know as the result of His earthly experiences in the days of His flesh. No critical reconstruction of the Gospel-portrait of the Christ has ever yet succeeded in proving that there were no elements in His self-consciousness of a superhuman character. A sound Christology must account for these elements. The doctrine of the Enhypostasia does so ; and points to them as the natural revealings of a unique Divine self-consciousness opening out into the Infinite, the natural product of a superhuman

233

personality transcendent above the limitations of our finite and circumscribed existence. We have no need to believe that He ceased to be God when He became Man, nor to think that because He condescended to live under the conditions and limitations of a finite existence that therefore He must necessarily have ceased to live and move and have His Being in that larger and vaster universe native to His Personality as the Divine Son of God.

(12) The outstanding difficulty will be the question as to how the particular can perfectly embody its own universal. How could the particular man, Christ Jesus, be nevertheless the Universal Man, the Second Adam, the archetype and representative man, belonging not to any one age, but claimed as the ideal of every age? The same difficulty, viewed from another standpoint, is this : How a single, unique, Divine self-consciousness could be at once unlimited and yet limited? The doctrine of the Enhypostasia allows for both these facts, but does not explain them. Our answer to both these questions is an appeal to the Gospel-portrait for confirmation of the fact that it was so. We point to the Incarnate Christ as One Who lived a truly human and finite existence, whilst at the same time transcending these limitations at will. If it be urged that logically the particular cannot fully embody its own universal, we can only point to the Gospel data and say that the Person of Christ is the bankruptcy of logic.

If we be asked what Christological theory will cover the above astounding facts, we plead for a consideration of the doctrine of the Enhypostasia, which, whilst it does not solve the problem, at least suggests how such a thing is conceivable. It is possible to escape these difficulties by denying that there is any evidence in the Gospels for the fact that the Divine Logos continued to remain unlimited when He became Man. We shall therefore appeal finally to the Gospels, and if we can prove from a study of Christ's Personality *quâ* His manhood that in Him the particular did embody its own universal, that He was at once both *a* man and *the* Man ; and if, further, from a study of His Personality *quâ* His Godhead, we can prove that His self-consciousness was at once limited and finite, and yet unlimited and infinite in its range, then we can fairly claim that the doctrine of the Enhypostasia covers the facts revealed by a study of the Gospel-portrait of Jesus Christ.

3.

THE THEORY CONFIRMED BY AN APPEAL TO THE CHRIST OF HISTORY AND THE CHRIST OF EXPERIENCE

IT may thus add considerably to the strength of our case if, finally, we test the doctrine of the Enhypostasia by an appeal to the New Testament portrait of Jesus Christ, and that general impression of His Personality which we gain from a study of His place in history. Is this theory consistent with what we know of the Christ of history and the Christ of experience ? This is the ultimate test. Does the hypothesis fit the facts ?

(1) Now at the outset, although we shall approach the Gospel narratives from the point of view of a believing Christian, it is satisfactory to note that all the efforts of rationalism and Liberal criticism have not yet succeeded in reducing the Christ of history within the categories of a purely human type of personality. The one-sided criticism of the Liberal school has in our own time brought its own nemesis. A tremendous reaction has set in which threatens to go to the opposite extreme in its emphasis upon the transcendental and superhuman elements in the Gospel portrait of Christ. The Modernists are turning against the Liberals. The Eschatological movement under the leadership of Johannes Weiss and Schweitzer threatens to make it impossible hereafter for Liberal criticism to come to rest in a purely humanitarian view of the Person of Christ. The Eschatologists are

236

seeking to do full justice to the self-witness of Christ and the transcendental character of His claims. Although the attempt to explain His Person wholly in terms of Apocalyptic is doomed to failure, yet the value of the Eschatological movement lies in the fact that the believing Christian may approach the Synoptic records now, and trust the evidence they give of the unique Personality of Jesus Christ, without fear that in so doing he is hopelessly ' unscientific ' and lacking in critical discernment.   It is delightful to find at last a recognition of the fact that there is no essential difference between the Christology of the Synoptics and that found in the Fourth Gospel. At the most it is a difference in degree and not in kind.   As one writer reminds us :—

Eschatology certainly emphasises the fact, which is coming to be recognised more and more from other points of view, that even the Synoptists do not set before us a merely Human Teacher or Prophet, and that Christology is not a late and mistaken development.   It ascribes to Jesus Himself the claim to be more than man.—C. W. Emmet, *The Eschatological Question in the Gospels*, p. 73.

Thus, if the value of Liberal criticism has won for us the reality and completeness of the humanity of Christ and emphasised all those elements in His life which we associate with His human nature, the Eschatological reading of the New Testament records has drawn attention once more to the equally clear indications of His Divinity, and emphasised all those transcendental elements in His life which we associate with His Divine nature.

We need not spend time, therefore, in striving to prove that the Gospel portrait presents us with a Two-Natured Christ.   What we have to enquire is whether this portrait forces us to conclude that the Incarnate Christ was *wholly* limited by the manhood He had assumed or whether He is revealed as the Unlimited Logos also.

(2) We shall appeal to the facts recorded in all four Gospels, and especially to the self-witness of the Christ, because the character of His self-consciousness is one of the foundation-stones of the doctrine of the Enhypostasia as we interpret it. But before doing this we must face a preliminary objection which may be raised, viz., our right to use the Fourth Gospel in this enquiry.

If it be urged that we have no right to use the Fourth Gospel in this way as substantiating the claims of Jesus, or as a witness to His own self-consciousness, because no final agreement has yet been reached with reference to the whole problem of the relation of the Fourth Gospel to the Synoptic narratives, nor with regard to its right to be considered as of any weight from the historical point of view, we venture to submit in defence the query as to whether the present position of critical opinion upon the Johannine problem does not justify our adopting a more conservative attitude than was possible, say, even ten years ago ? Whatever may be thought now of Watkins' Bampton Lectures for 1890— *Modern Criticism considered in its Relation to the Fourth Gospel*—the tendency of this same criticism seems to be more and more towards the conclusion he reached. Dr. Westcott's work has never yet been conclusively discredited by the negative school, and the attitude adopted by Dr. Sanday in his *Criticism of the Fourth Gospel* is one still possible, at any rate for English scholars, who in the absence of conclusive proof to the contrary may continue to believe in the authenticity and historical character of the Fourth Gospel, and to use it, though with care and caution, in the field of Christology. We are bold then to claim to avail ourselves of the evidence afforded by the Fourth Gospel as of real historical value, and we do this the more readily when we find, for example, that Dr. E. A. Abbott, in the very latest part of his monumental work, *The Diatessarica*, is discovering that the Fourth Gospel, in spite of its poetic nature, is closer to history than he supposed, and that the writer,

mystic though he was, and poet though he was, believed himself to be an historian, too, and used every particle that he could find of misunderstood tradition in the oldest of the Gospels, in order to bring out what he conceived to be the historical truth, while at the same time tingeing it with a spiritual and symbolical interpretation.—'The Fourfold Gospel,' Section I., Introduction, p. 27.

Whilst allowing, therefore, for the truth hidden in Weisse's statement that 'It is not so much a picture of Christ that John sets forth, as a conception of Christ; his Christ does not speak *in* His own Person, but *of* His own Person,' we shall none the less treat John's statements in the way in which he himself, we may well believe, intended that they should be treated : as the words not only of a mystic, poet, and even historian, but of an eye-witness, and of one whose subsequent life in Christ confirmed for him, at any rate, the truth of what he records.

We fully recognise, of course, that any use of the Fourth Gospel has to be made with caution, in that the style of the discourses are due to the author, and we can never be quite sure whether the

239

words of Jesus are literally those He spake or whether the author has not given us their substance in his own words. Passages can be adduced which seem to prove that in the discourses the words of the Master pass over insensibly into the words of the author, but if we recognise quite clearly that the whole Gospel itself may be a fulfilment of the Master's own promise that His disciples, under the guidance of His Holy Spirit, should be led into all the truth, and be enabled to grasp the fuller import and deeper meaning of much which passed their comprehension as they listened to His teaching when He spake to them in the days of His flesh ; then, whether the Fourth Gospel contains the words of Christ literally, or after they have passed through the human medium of an inspired Apostle's mind, matters little in comparison of the outstanding conviction of their truth as this is abundantly confirmed in Christian experience. 'The Words of the Word' (as Stier so aptly describes them) bear the truth of their origin in themselves, and their authority lies in their own intrinsic worth. It is true that we shall find Him saying things about Himself in the Fourth Gospel which are not so clearly substantiated by parallels in the Synoptic Gospels, but so long as there is no irreconcilable contradiction between the self-witness of Jesus in the first three Gospels, and that contained in the fourth, and if what is contained in the fourth can be seen to be a natural deduction from, or even a developed form of what is contained in the other three, there is no reason why we should be refused permission to use it as equally authoritative for Christology. The remarkable fact about the authors of all four Gospels is, that whilst they write with a

full knowledge of Jesus as the Lord of Glory, the
risen and ascended Christ of God, nevertheless they
are faithful in their witness to the record of His
earthly life ; and if they let us see quite plainly the
reality of His manhood, they are equally faithful to
what they knew when they let us see also His Godhead
flashing forth at times in miracles and in His own
self-witness.   If there is a more marked emphasis
upon this last fact in the Fourth Gospel, the writer
is none the less faithful in his record of the truly
human character of the God-Man.   If St. John's
work is an ' inspired meditation,' the product of
long years spent upon his knees in communion with
his risen Master, this is not to say that the Apostle's
resultant profounder grip upon the supreme religious
significance of the Christ he had known, destroys in
consequence the historical value of the picture he
gives us.   If it is true to say that whilst the Synoptists
give us mainly the picture of Jesus in His varied
relationships to men, St. John dwells more upon the
relationship of Christ to God, this is but two sides
of one great truth, and Christology must take account
of both in the interpretation of His character.   *Jesus
looking outwards towards men* is one side of the
picture which the Synoptists reveal, but this is quite
incomprehensible by itself and except in conjunction
with the other side upon which St. John lays most
stress—*Jesus looking inwards towards God*.   The
one reveals His Personality in its truly human
character, the other in the transcendent nature of
its constitution as fully Divine.   We claim then the
right to make use of this ' Spiritual ' Gospel equally
with the Synoptic narratives, as of real historical
value in the interpretation of the Person of Christ,

both from the impression He made upon others, and from His own self-witness.

(3) We have become so used to the psychological reading of the New Testament data that it comes almost as a shock to be told that ' we possess no psychology of the Messiah.' It is refreshing to learn that after all our natural impressions from a reading of the Markan narrative are probably correct, and that there is no record there of the ' development ' of Christ's Messianic consciousness, nor are we bound to believe that He became gradually more and more conscious of His Divinity and of His filial relationship to God. Schweitzer almost over-emphasises the revolution which thorough-going Eschatology is bringing about with reference to the way we read the Markan text. Thus in *The Quest of the Historical Jesus* Schweitzer tells us that—

In order to find in Mark the Life of Jesus of which it is in search, modern theology is obliged to read between the lines a whole host of things, and those often the most important, and then to foist them upon the text by means of psychological conjecture. It is determined to find evidence in Mark of a development of Jesus, a development of the disciples, and a development of the outer circumstances ; and professes in so doing to be only reproducing the views and indications of the Evangelist. In reality, however, there is not a word of all this in the Evangelist, and when his interpreters are asked what are the hints and indications on which they base their assertions they have nothing to offer save *argumenta e silentio*. Mark knows nothing of any development in Jesus, he knows nothing of any pæda-gogic considerations which are supposed to have determined the conduct of Jesus towards the disciples and the people ; he knows nothing of any conflict in the mind of Jesus between a spiritual and a popular, political Messianic ideal ; he does not know, either, that in this respect there was any difference between the view of Jesus and that of the people (p. 330).

And again :

The psychological explanation of motive, and the psychological connexion of the events and actions which such critics have proposed to find in Mark, simply do not exist. That being so, nothing is to be made out of his account by the application of *a priori* psychology. A vast quantity of treasures of scholarship and erudition, of art and artifice, which the Marcan hypothesis has gathered into its storehouse in the two generations of its existence to aid it in constructing its life of Jesus has become worthless, and can be of no further service to true historical research.   Theology has been simplified. . . . Thorough-going scepticism and thorough-going eschatology, between them, are compelling theology to read the Marcan text again with simplicity of mind (p. 331).

Hence when Beyschlag tells us that ' the probability is that He came gradually to think of Himself as the deliverer promised by the prophets,' or when we are told that the Cross was an afterthought in His Plan which He decided to adopt when every other method had failed ; we can take refuge in another hypothesis which has at least equal claims to be heard, and ask ourselves whether we may not look for the ' development ' not so much in the self-consciousness of Jesus as in the minds of His followers.   We are not bound to believe that as His ministry proceeded His thoughts became clearer and the meaning and end of it grew plainer to His mind.   We know how the deeper meaning of His teaching only gradually unfolded itself to the minds of His disciples as they looked back upon it in the fuller light of the Resurrection and their new experience ' in Christ ' subsequent to Pentecost. So we may well believe that it was not *His* mind which became more and more illumined with the thought of the Kingdom, nor that it was *His* ideas about it which grew and even altered ; it is equally permissible

to assume that He knew its nature and His purpose
from the outset of His public ministry, and deliber-
ately set Himself to instruct the minds of His followers
in its principles and truly spiritual character.   Hence
the changed and spiritualised conception of the
Kingdom was a thing which took place not within
His consciousness but in *theirs* as the result of His
teaching.   And how slow they were to understand is
clear to anyone who will read the Gospel narratives
with the aid of a book like Latham's *Pastor Pasto-
rum*, or Bruce's *Training of the Twelve*. So also
the deepening of the realisation of His Divinity may
well be looked for not in His self-consciousness but in
the minds of the disciples who came to Him because
they believed that He was the Messiah, but stayed
with Him because they discovered that He was the
Son of God.

(4) According to the doctrine of the Enhypostasia,
the Personality of Jesus Christ being, at the least,
truly human, we may expect to find in the Gospel
narratives the record of the truly human life of the
Incarnate Son of God.   And the Gospel portrait is
certainly this, even though it is at the same time, as
we hope to show, something more than this. We
can accept without any reserve the Lucan statement
that ' Jesus increased in wisdom and stature and in
favour with God and man ' ; we need have no hesitation in giving full weight to that beautiful picture of
the Christ made perfect through suffering which the
writer of the Epistle to the Hebrews presents. The
Gospels depict the earthly life of the Incarnate Son of
God as normal in the sense that He underwent a
growth and development in body and mind, being
subject to temptation up to and beyond anything

experienced by sinful man before or since His time, inasmuch as He, and He alone, resisted unto the uttermost.   We can believe that He learned from experience, and qualified for His work as our perfect High Priest in the school of suffering.   At the same time we can give full weight to the thought of the τελείωσις of Christ as applied to His manhood, and remind ourselves that at any and every moment of His earthly life, from babyhood, through boyhood, to manhood, He could be described as ' perfect ' only because He was Divine, and the life He lived amongst men was what it was in virtue of the fact that it was the life of the Incarnate Son of God.   This is a thought which we may well believe was never far remote from the minds of those who wrote these Gospel records, and if it did not prevent them from ascribing to Jesus all that varied human experience and that ' perfection through suffering ' by which alone He became qualified to be the Captain of our Salvation in virtue of His perfect sympathy, we can only account for the beautiful picture they give us, on the assumption of its truth, and their realisation that, far from a truly human life being incompatible with that which the Son of God might be expected to live, on the contrary, His having lived it was a revelation of that perfect and complete harmony which could and did exist between the human and the Divine Natures in His Person.   Modern Kenotic theories have so obsessed our minds with the thought of the limitations imposed upon the Divine Personality by His Incarnation within the dimensions of our finite human existence, that we have failed to do justice to the equally striking fact, recorded for us in the Gospel story, of the wonderful growth and expansion of that truly human nature

of Christ, as the result of His being its subject.   The
simple fact that His human life, at every stage of its
growth and development, and in every relationship in
which it was placed, was able to be what it was, is in
itself a witness to the possibilities opened up before
us of an indefinite extension and expansion of our
powers and capacities if the same Divine Spirit dwells
in us and has full possession of our lives.   Whilst His
Godhead was limited by His manhood, His manhood
was wonderfully enriched and developed by its union
with His Godhead.   The Gospels faithfully record
both these sides of the one truth.   They present us
with the picture of One Who is circumscribed and
limited ; hungry, tired, thirsty, weak and faint at
times, experiencing the weakness of a human body
in its failure to respond to the calls of the Spirit.
Yet at the same time we see how His Personality so
expressed itself in and through the medium of His
body as His vehicle of manifestation, that the very
body itself became transfigured, glorified, spiritualised
to an extent and degree which amazed those whose
privilege it was to behold Him praying, or to meet
Him returning from the Mount of Transfiguration.
And if His Personality could so change His human
body, what shall we say of the equally amazing expansion of His human powers and faculties of mind and
spirit, which made men wonder Who He was, even in
the days of His flesh ?

The Gospels, then, reveal the Christ as having lived
a truly human life, perfect at every stage of its growth
and development.   Our Christology enables us to
accept this picture with the fullest possible frankness.
Every limitation which the Son of Man can be shown
to have lived under, every detail of a circumscribed

existence to which Kenotic Christology has drawn our attention, including, of course, the fact of Christ's human knowledge being limited, upon which Gore laid such stress in the famous Bampton Lectures, and later in the dissertation on *The Consciousness of Our Lord*, we can accept without hesitation. All that is involved in the Christ's possession, not simply of intelligence, but of intelligence moulded by a certain training and education as a Jew, and which was circumscribed within the limits of the scientific knowledge and mental equipment of the age in which He lived, we can accept as the necessary conditions essential to His human life, if that is to be described in any sense as an historical reality, and if we are to regard Him as a Man Who lived at a particular time and in a particular environment.

But when we have said this, we have drawn attention to but half the truth contained in the Gospel portrait. To admit that the Christ had a mind moulded by the environment of a Jew's life in Palestine in the first century is not to deny the equally vital truth revealed in the Gospels, that His whole earthly life was so truly human as to be capable of transcending its historical setting, if we may so put it, and of revealing itself as absolute, archetypal, universal ; incapable therefore of being identified with, or confined to, any particular age, but recognised to be for all time. This is a point more and more impressed upon us as we study His character. We express the truth by the statement that He reveals Himself not only as a man, an individual, a particular concrete human being, a distinct individuality, but also as Man, the Universal. This, logically, may be a contradiction, but it is none the less the whole truth revealed

247

in the Gospel narratives. Anyone reading the Gospels
is certain that Jesus Christ was a man, but we dare
not stop here if we are to do full justice to His
character.

We shall not have studied Jesus Christ for long as
an historical Person, in the setting of the time and
place in which He lived, in the revelation of His
character in and through His words and deeds, His
acts and habits, His limitations, in His self-revelation and self-witness to His own Personality and aims,
before it will begin to dawn upon us that in this individual Person, in this historical setting in which the
Gospels reveal Him, we are studying One Who belongs
not to the first century only but to all time, One Who,
though leading a particular life at a particular time, is
nevertheless, and in spite of these limitations, revealing the universal life, the perfect type of human life
for every age and for all men. It may be urged that
the wider conception of the Christ not only as a man
but as The Man, is derived exclusively from a consideration of the part His manhood has played in history.
The truth is rather that His place in history is but the
confirmation of the Gospel portrait of His wonderful
character, as this shines forth in the pages of those
who have sought to convey to their fellow Christians
something of the impression left upon them by their
fellowship with Him in the days when He moved
about amongst them on the shores of the Lake of
Galilee or in the streets of Jerusalem. If history
accords Him a place as the ethical Head of humanity,
this is nothing more than He Himself claimed to be
when He revealed Himself as perfect Man and bade
men follow Him.

Attention has often been drawn to the universality

and completeness of Christ's humanity as this is
proved by His acceptance among all the diverse races
of men to whom He has been preached. He alone has
proved capable of supplying the deepest needs of
human nature, and He still remains to-day the ideal
character, the goal of humanity's highest, noblest,
and purest aspiration. The claim of Christianity to
be the universal religion implies this. The Christ is
held to be God's mode of revealing to the whole world
the goal of humanity, and hence the Christ must be
preached to all men and in Him alone is salvation to
be found. But will it be denied that this is what He
was and what He knew Himself to be as He moved
amongst them in the first century ? Christ's place
in history is but the confirmation of His own claims,
and the verdict of twenty centuries of Christian
experience does but echo that of His disciples who
saw Him face to face and shared the amazement
of the multitudes at the gracious words which fell
from His lips.

The thought of the Christ as not only a man
but the Universal Man, the Second Adam, the Head
and Fountain Source of a new humanity, a new type
created in His image, is familiar enough to those of
us who have been at all influenced by the theological
writings of Dr. Du Bose. He is never tired of
insisting upon the universality of Christ's humanity,
not only in its exemplary and representative, but
also in its causal and creative sense—Christ our
Life—Christ not only the Divine truth of every man,
but the higher and Diviner self of every man ; the
eternally true ' I ' of every finite self ; personally
and creatively present in the Christian, making Himself the man's higher personality and life. Here

249

the attention is concentrated upon the Christ of experience, the risen and glorified Lord in His post-Ascension activities working in the hearts of men in and through the Holy Ghost. And it is because the Christ is in every age and to every race proving Himself to be the Second Adam, the Universal life of all men, that we are forced in seeking to interpret Him, to pass beyond the particular to the universal and to see in Him not only a man, but Man. No individual human being, however perfect, could be, so it is felt, all that the Christ is to all men. ' He who alone stands in this universal relation to humanity cannot be merely a member of it.' [1]

The universality of Our Lord's humanity [Dr. Du Bose tells us] is only explicable upon the fact that His Personality is a divine one. It is only God in it that can make it applicable to all or the truth of all. . . . The concrete universal of humanity which may be found in Jesus Christ belongs to it not as humanity but as God in humanity. It is God in it which makes that particular humanity of our Lord, His holiness, His righteousness, His life, valid and available for all ; so that every man may find himself in Christ, and in Christ find himself. But, to go further—may we not say, that the only true realism or idealism, the doctrine that the ideal is the real, is to be found in the New Testament doctrine of Jesus Christ ? He is the eternal creative idea, the ideal principle, as of everything else so especially of man as the end and heir of all. In that sense He is humanity from before the foundation of the earth, the Man from Heaven, the Son of man, in whom in the end all humanity and all else in humanity is to come to itself and to be fulfilled. The eternal final cause is first cause as well as *finis* ; the divine ideal is the only certain and true real.—Du Bose, *The Gospel according to St. Paul*, pp. 297–8.

Now if we are right in claiming that this impression of the Christ as the Universal Man, which receives its

[1] Forrest, *Christ of History*, p. 66.

decisive confirmation from a study of His place in history, is none the less an impression which is left upon us by the revelation of His character in the Gospels, where He is shown at the same time to be an individual man, Jesus of Nazareth, we are faced by the fact that here we have the universal revealed in the particular, and more than this, the particular is revealed as the complete embodiment of its own universal. How can a particular individual person, Jesus of Nazareth, a Jew of Palestine, living in the first century, have been at the same time what twenty centuries of Christian experience prove Him to have been,—the Universal Man, belonging not to any age, nor to any particular country, but for all time revealed as THE MAN. What Christological theory will cover such a fact as this ?

The key to the Universality of Christ's manhood lies in its truly human character, and the key to its truly human character lies in the fact that it was truly Divine. It was the humanity of the Son of God Himself. If in the Person of Christ the humanity of God is revealed, this can only be that humanity which pre-existed, that human element which is in God. Christ's humanity is a revelation of God's nature.

If Christ's humanity were not the Humanity of Deity [says Dr. Moberly], it could not stand in that wide, inclusive, consummating relation in which it stands in fact to the humanity of all other men (p. 90).

The Incarnation, if it is a revelation of Deity in humanity, is none the less a revelation of humanity in Deity : only thus can it be also a revelation of man's true relationship to God. Our study of

251

Christ's manhood, then, as this is revealed in the Gospels and confirmed by His place in history, forces us to adopt some Christological hypothesis which will cover these facts : (*a*) that there is a human element in God ; (*b*) that the Personality of Christ's humanity is a Divine Personality ; (*c*) that it is an Unlimited and Universal Personality as well as a Limited and Particular Personality, so that, as the subject of His manhood, it may be capable of revealing that manhood not only as the manhood of a particular man, but the manhood of the archetypal man, the universal man.

Let us now return to the Gospels and study them from another point of view. Let us consider them not from the standpoint of Christ's Personality *quâ* man, but of His Personality *quâ* God.

(5) Our first impression from a reading of the narratives is that Jesus Christ was a man. He must therefore have possessed a truly human and limited self-consciousness. But is this all ?

This may be the first impression, but it is not the only one, nor the one which challenges our attention. We have not to read even the Markan record for very long before the words and deeds of this same Jesus of Nazareth inevitably suggest that we are reading the life of One Whose whole Personality forces us to answer other questions of far deeper import concerning Him. And if the Synoptic narratives give us this impression, it is abundantly confirmed by what we find in the Fourth Gospel. All the questions inevitably raised by what Jesus does and says in the Synoptic records are immediately answered in the Fourth Gospel. Who is He Who claims to supersede the Mosaic Law, to forgive sins, to be the Judge of quick and dead, to occupy the throne of men's hearts and, as King, to claim their allegiance ? What man is this that even the winds and the sea obey Him ? The writer of the Fourth Gospel answers all these questions in the words of Thomas—'My Lord and my God ! ' But do the Gospels give us any indication that the Incarnate Son of God retained in any sense *fully* the possession of His Divine prerogatives and powers, and at times exercised them even after He had descended into the stream of human life and voluntarily submitted Himself to its inevitable limitations ? The doctrine of the Enhypostasia gives us the *Unlimited* Divine Logos as the Ego of the manhood in the Incarnate Christ. His self-consciousness was not only truly human, but it was the self-consciousness of One Who was the Incarnate Deity. He did not cease to be God when He became Man, nor lose the consciousness of Himself as God transcendent when He became God in manhood.

Is there anything in the Gospel records to suggest that in the exercise of His Divine attributes from time to time during His earthly life He was not *wholly* limited by the powers and capacities of the manhood He had assumed ? Do these narratives reveal to us One Who was not only a truly human personality, but One Whose deeds and words at times marked Him as a transcendent Personality, unlimited in the range of His consciousness, revealing things which not even a perfectly human but finite mind could embrace, doing things beyond the capacity of a finite man, however perfect ? Have we reason to believe that He not only revealed Himself to be God in and through His manhood so that He was verily and indeed 'God in man made manifest,' God leading a truly human life; but, besides this, that He could and did transcend the limitations of His finite and circumscribed existence as perfect Man, and that what enabled Him to do so was the fact that His Personality, whilst truly human, was at the same time superhuman; whilst relative and particular *quâ* His manhood, at the same time absolute and universal *quâ* his Godhead?

We will first consider His teaching. The people from the very outset were deeply impressed, and hung upon the gracious words that fell from His lips. But if His teaching impressed them, the authority with which He spake astonished them. 'And they were astonished at His teaching: for He taught them as having authority, and not as the scribes.'[1] If the high ethical character of His words struck home to their hearts and consciences, there was also something about His Personality, in contrast to the scribes, which amazed them. And this impression made upon His hearers, both by what He said, and still more by the way in which He said it, is confirmed by His own astounding claims concerning His teaching, as He viewed it from His own standpoint. 'Heaven and earth shall pass away; but My words shall not pass away.' Nothing short of this is His claim concerning the words He uttered. We are quite prepared, therefore, for a passage of similar significance, which we find in the Fourth Gospel: 'If a man love Me, he will keep My word: and My Father will love him, and we will come unto him and make our abode with him. He that loveth Me not keepeth not My words: and the word which

[1] Mark i. 22.

ye hear is not Mine, but the Father's who sent Me.'[1]
It would be easy to multiply passages which reveal
the Christ's own estimate of His teaching in its
eternal and abiding significance, as of vital import
for the salvation of souls.

Who is this Who dares to say, 'He that re-
jecteth Me, and receiveth not My sayings, hath
one that judgeth him : the word that I spake, the
same shall judge him in the last day'?[2] And
again, 'The words that I have spoken unto you,
are spirit and are life.'[3] If the verdict of the officers
sent to take Him[4] holds true, as we believe it
does, of all He said—'Never man so spake'—we
find ourselves asking the same questions which those
who heard Him were forced to put : 'Lord, to
whom shall we go ? Thou hast the words of eternal
life.'[5]

The authoritative character and finality of His
teaching, confirmed by the impression made upon
those privileged to hear it, and by the verdict of
history, and considered in the light of the Christ's
own revealed consciousness of its eternal and abiding
significance for mankind, leads us to ask whether we
have not here the words of a transcendent, moral
personality. Is it native to a truly human, but
finite and limited personality, to have the power to
speak a final truth, to lay down an ultimate ethical
code, and to be conscious that the words so uttered
shall never pass away ? The tone of absolute authority with which the words were spoken—'Heaven
and earth shall pass away, but My words shall not
pass away '—forbids us to see in them merely a

---

[1] John xiv. 23, 24.   [2] John xii. 48.   [3] John vi. 63.
[4] John vii. 46.   [5] John vi. 68.

prophecy inspired by a limited and finite knowledge. They suggest rather the utterance of One Whose range of consciousness stretched out beyond the finite and embraced all time. As the verdict of Jesus Christ, ' the same yesterday, to-day and for ever,' they are explicable; as the authoritative pronouncement of a timeless Personality, we can understand them; but we find it hard to believe that they are the words of One Whose range of knowledge was limited. The absoluteness of the authority with which He spake suggests the presence of an Absolute Personality Who, though moving in time, had all eternity opened out before His vision.

And this note of absolute authority is not confined to His words and teaching. It is recorded of the Incarnate Christ that He set His claims over men's lives far above those most sacred ties of kinship and blood which bind us to one another in our earthly relationships.

'He that loveth father or mother more than Me is not worthy of Me; and he that loveth son and daughter more than Me is not worthy of Me. . . . He that findeth his life shall lose it; and he that loseth his life for My sake shall find it.'[1] This is to claim from men such an absolute self-renunciation, and such a place in their hearts as could be claimed by none save by Him Who knew Himself to stand in a relationship to them such as could only be occupied by God Himself.

And if He so regarded Himself as the centre of religious worship, receiving as His right from men an allegiance they are justified in paying to none save to God Almighty, this is a witness to His own self-

[1] Matt. x. 87, 89.

256

knowledge, not only as God-in-manhood, but God Absolute, God Transcendent, God above the limits of a finite existence, God in the universality of His relationships with all His finite creatures. Could such a knowledge of Himself as is here revealed be mediated through the manhood He had assumed, or does it not suggest that He possessed in His Incarnate state not only a limited knowledge of Himself as God-in-manhood, but also an unlimited knowledge of Himself as God transcendent ? The position accorded to Him in the Epistles of the New Testament, and in the history of the Christian Church, as risen and ascended Lord of Glory, is claimed by Him as the Incarnate Son, even in the days of His flesh, and the character of His Personality not merely in its historical, but in its absolute significance in the world's history, is a thing which is recognised by Himself in the days of His humiliation. From the point of view of Kenotic Christology this is a hard fact to account for—from the point of view of the doctrine of the Enhypostasia it is just what we should be led to expect.

The transcendent character of His self-consciousness is further shown in His claim to forgive sins,— a claim which His opponents rightly pointed out was tantamount to an assertion of His Divinity. The record in Mark ii. 1–12, of the healing of the man sick of the palsy, is remarkable for the fact not only of the physical miracle of healing, but for the spiritual miracle behind this, of which, to their minds, it was the proof.

That Jesus claimed the power to forgive sins is undoubted ;[1] but the full significance of this claim is

[1] Luke vii. 47, xxiii. 43 ; cf. Matt. xviii. 18 ; John xx. 23.

only realised when we consider it in connection with
His further astonishing revelation of Himself as the
Judge of quick and dead,[1] a prerogative and a function
belonging to God alone. We have here a claim of
extraordinary magnitude. What kind of a consciousness is this which is capable of mediating to the Incarnate Christ a knowledge of Himself as the arbiter
of human destinies ? Could God-in-manhood know
Himself as Judge of the world ? The claim is based
upon a knowledge nothing less than omniscient in its
range. We expect such a claim to be made by One
conscious of the absolute character of His Personality
in its relationship with all mankind. It implies a
knowledge of Himself as God in all the fulness of His
omnipotent power. If the conditions of His earthly
life prevented His having a knowledge of Himself
anything less than this, could He have made the
claim ? Again, we consider His own self-witness to
His vocation as the Saviour of men, One Who has
come to redeem and to heal. This consciousness of
His Saviourhood marks His unique relationship to mankind, not only as Judge, but as Deliverer. He is conscious of possessing in Himself what is needful to heal
the ills of all who come to Him in response to His own
loving invitation. It was not that current Messianic
expectations created the Messianic consciousness of
the Christ. The truth is rather that He used the
current Jewish Apocalyptic as a vehicle for the expression of His own unique conceptions of the Messianic
office He had come to fulfil. ' The contemporary
" Messianic hopes," ' says Schweitzer, ' can only explain the hopes of Jesus so far as they corresponded
thereto, not His view of His own Person, in which

[1] Matt. vii. 22 ; Luke xiii. 25 ; Matt. xxv. 31,

He is absolutely original.'[1]   If we study the summary
of His work as Prophet, Priest, and King, we see that
in the fulfilment of all the Old Testament prophecy
concerning the Messiah's work in this threefold capacity, Jesus Christ so enlarged, enriched, and transformed the current expectations as to make His
Messiahship a thing unique in itself, transcending any
conception of it which the minds of men in previous
ages had been able to form, and giving to it a new
content and meaning.   And we may rightly argue
back from what He did to what He was, from the
uniqueness of His Messiahship to the uniqueness of
His Personality, from the uniqueness of His Messianic
consciousness to the uniqueness of its constitution.

Alike as the Messiah, the Son of David, the Son of
man, the Saviour, the Redeemer, the Advocate and the
Judge, He stands revealed as One Whose Personality
contains elements of a transcendental character which
mark Him as a supernatural Being ; One Who cannot be fully interpreted as having possessed a purely
human, or even a truly human, consciousness only.
Something more than this is demanded to explain the
unique constitution of His consciousness, and the
presence in it of elements which are not native to
man.

And this impression is still further confirmed when
we contemplate His filial consciousness, which is the
basis of His Messianic claims and work.   We have only
to consider that gem of Johannine Christology which
no critical ingenuity has yet succeeded in eliminating
from the Matthean and Lucan narratives,[2] to realise
that Jesus Christ in the days of His flesh possessed a
knowledge of Himself in His relationship to God, so

[1] *The Quest*, p. 365, note,   [2] Matt. xi. 27 ; Luke x. 21, 22.

full, so complete, so perfect in its content, as to amount to an identity of essence. Harnack accepts the authenticity of this passage, and regards it as containing the most important and characteristic utterance of Jesus concerning His own thoughts about Himself in His relationship to God.

'All things have been delivered unto Me of My Father: and no one knoweth the Son, save the Father; neither doth any know the Father, save the Son, and he to whomsoever the Son willeth to reveal Him.' The passage implies not only a consciousness of a unique relationship to God, but the basis of it is His pre-existence with God, antecedent to His birth as a human being. This is the ground of the Father's full knowledge of the Son, and the Son's full knowledge of His Father, a mutual knowledge none save they can share. Here we have the source of the Son's authority as the revealer of God to men, the justification for the finality and absolute character of His revelation.

After such a passage as this, read as it must be with all those other passages in the Gospels which illustrate the use of the correlatives 'Father' and 'Son,' and which represent Christ as speaking of God as His Father in a unique sense, we are prepared for the Johannine prologue. The central constituent in the consciousness of Jesus is the complete and unclouded sense of this filial relationship, evidenced at once by perfect mutuality of knowledge and love between Himself and the Father, and perfect submission and response to the Father's will. The root-element in this consciousness is a sense of Sonship to the Father, deeper, clearer, more intimate, more all-embracing and all-absorbing than ever was vouch-

safed to a child of man.   He is Son in His own right.
His is a generic Sonship, or, if we prefer the word,
an ontological Sonship, the basis of which is unity of
being or essence.

We have here the picture of One Whose whole
mind and being lie open without flaw or impediment
to the stream of Divine love which pours in upon it,
and Who responds to that love with exquisite sensitive-
ness and with entire completeness.   If such an One
were, as we believe Him to have been, bone of our
bone, flesh of our flesh, He was none the less at the
same time, Very God of Very God.

Now, if the Incarnate Son of God had such a
knowledge as this of His unique relationship to the
Father, are we to say that the range of His consciousness was limited in any sense, or that He *only* knew
Himself as God to the degree and to the extent to
which such a knowledge could be mediated by the
manhood He had assumed ?   We seem to have here
something more than the revelation of God-in-manhood.   It is God-in-manhood conscious at the same
time of Himself as God in His Trinitarian relation
ship—God therefore above manhood, God stretching
out above and beyond the limits of His Incarnate
state, God transcending, whilst immanent in, the
manhood He had assumed. This conclusion is more
and more forced upon us as we allow the full import
of the Christ's self-witness to His own pre-existence
to sink into our minds.   We find in the Fourth Gospel
the following astounding declaration of the Christ's
own consciousness of His timeless and therefore
absolute Personality :

' Verily, verily, I say unto you, before Abraham
was, I am.'

Compare with this statement others of equal significance :

'He that hath seen Me hath seen the Father.' 'My Father worketh hitherto, and I work.' 'I came out from the Father, and am come into the world : again I leave the world and go unto the Father.' 'And now, O Father, glorify Thou Me with the glory which I had with Thee before the world was.'

None can have read Dr. Hort's treatment of that great passage in John xiv. 6—'I am the Way, and the Truth, and the Life'—without realising the transcendent nature and all-embracing fulness of the claim therein implied ; and we believe that we are on firm ground when we argue from this to the unique consciousness of the Person Who uttered these words, and point to them as showing His knowledge of Himself as the absolute Personality.

This is not to say that we are endeavouring to find the marks of His Godhead only in these transcendental elements of His self-consciousness. It is revealed none the less in any and every word and act of His truly human life. His whole character is a revelation of God-in-manhood. But it is more than this. There are elements in His self-consciousness which we can only describe by the word abnormal ; elements which are not natural to a perfect humanity, or even, be it said, to God-in-man. In His self-consciousness the human is all-Divine, but we hesitate to say that the Divine is all-human. We feel that we must add that the Divine is also superhuman. Only such a proposition will fully cover those elements to which we have drawn special attention in this investigation. We are aware that such a proposition will be strenuously denied by many who will feel that by advocating it we are doing a disservice both to the human and the Divine in the Person of Christ.[1]   We believe, on the contrary, that we are rescuing the great thought of the Divine Transcendence from the obscurity into which it is tending to fall, as the result of an over-emphasis in our own time upon the complementary truth of the Divine Immanence.   After all, Deity in humanity, however truly wonderful a revelation of both Deity and humanity this may be, is not all that is implied by Deity.   God is not exhausted in the Incarnation, neither was the Incarnate Son.   His Personality, whilst it found a perfect human self-expression in and through the manhood He had assumed, nevertheless needed something more than this for its fulness of self-manifestation, and the Gospels allow us to see in certain things He did and said that He was not *wholly* conditioned by humanity, and that He could and did transcend it.

We have not dwelt upon His miracles, because we have preferred to consider the outstanding miracle of Himself.   His Personality is the crucial miracle. If He were what He claimed to be, then what He did is what we might expect such an One to do.   Miracles are the natural accompaniment of such a Personality. Here again a reaction is setting in.   We have only to read the last two books on this question— Dr. Illingworth's Essay, *The Gospel Miracles*, and Dr. Headlam's Lectures, *The Miracles of the New Testament*—to realise how strong a case can be stated for the Christian standpoint.   If miracles may be defined as meaning ' the supremacy of the spiritual forces of the world to an extraordinarily marked degree

---

[1] See Moberly, *Atonement and Personality*, Lecture V.

263

over the mere material,'[1] they are but another sign of the Divine transcendence, and an indication of God's omnipotence and freedom. Nor can we draw a distinction between the miracles of healing and the ' cosmic ' miracles, and say that we will believe the former because we think that we see their possibility, but disbelieve the latter because they are outside our very limited human experience. Is this distinction between the two classes of miracles a recognition of just the point we are striving to make ? The miracles of healing are accepted because they were the work of God in-manhood, and therefore can conceivably be repeated by a God-indwelt man amongst us ; whereas the ' cosmic ' miracles are rejected because they could only have been performed by supernatural means, and therefore by a transcendent Personality. God's Spirit can work in us and in Nature. The order of Nature is the expression of God's will. If He is limited it is always a case of self-limitation, and to this extent implies the possibility of a higher freedom which can be exercised if He so wills. And if this is true of God Almighty, why not equally true of God Incarnate ? The Incarnation, even if it involved limitation, was none the less a voluntary act, an act of self-limitation, and to this extent the Incarnate Christ had it always within His power to transcend the limitations which He had imposed upon Himself, and that He did so is shown by the fact of miracles which reveal His Transcendence in and through His Immanence, within the manhood He had assumed.

These, then, are the data supplied by the Gospels, to which we point as proving that the Incarnate Christ possessed a Divine and unlimited self-consciousness.

[1] Headlam, p. 335.

Is this conclusion absolutely inconsistent with that reached in Section 4, where the fact of His being truly Man, and truly a man, forced us to conclude that He must have possessed a truly human and limited self-consciousness? We point in answer to the Gospels themselves, which give us the data from which we deduce both conclusions. However incredible or logically impossible such a phenomenon may appear, the fact remains that in the Person of Jesus Christ is revealed One Who was a particular man, and yet the Universal Man; One, moreover, Whose consciousness was at once limited and unlimited, finite and circumscribed yet infinite and uncircumscribed in its range, human and yet Divine, Divine and yet human. If we say that it is intellectually inconceivable and historically impossible, the facts reprove us. Faith can grasp it. The Gospels record it. Is there any hypothesis which will cover it? The doctrine of the Enhypostasia is the one which we venture to suggest. It is based upon grounds which make it at least conceivable to the human mind. It does not solve the problem, because the problem is ultimately insolvable by any finite mind. It postulates a logical impossibility—the particular cannot embody its own universal. But the Person of Christ is the bankruptcy of human logic. And it is better for us to face this last fact than to endeavour to gain intellectual consistency at the cost of explaining away or reducing the Christ within the categories of human finite reasoning. If we do so there will always be the danger of another generation rising up to rebuke us by confronting us with the Gospel-portrait. The Kenotic Christology in the past, in its eagerness to safeguard the reality of Christ's manhood, and to emphasise the fact that He was an historical Person with a truly human mind moulded by the environment of Palestine, limited by the scientific and historical horizon of the men of the age in which He lived, has tended, if anything, to make us shut our eyes to the equally patent fact that this is but half a truth. The reaction has come in the rise of the Eschatological School, which may yet rescue for us the other half of the truth. The value of the doctrine of the Enhypostasia, to our mind, lies here : that by it we are enabled to hold both halves of the truth in spite of the logical inconsistency involved, and to do full justice to all the data supplied by a study both of the Christ of history and the Christ of experience. The furthest point reached by the ancient Christology was the doctrine of the Enhypostasia as this was put forth by Leontius of Byzantium, and incorporated in the final formulation of Greek theology by John of Damascus. Since that time many and varied attempts have been made to go beyond this point. We know of none which have succeeded. Our intellectual pride may revolt against such a verdict. But can it be seriously questioned ? With all our modern knowledge we may realise perhaps better than the ancients the difficulties of the Christological problem. But a fuller realisation of the difficulties is not a solution. The Christ still baffles us. To us as to His followers of old, He puts the question : ' Whom say *ye* that I am ? ' The human intellect remains dumb, and cannot frame an adequate answer. Faith replies quite simply : ' My LORD and My GOD ! '

> The very God ! think, Abib ; dost thou think ?
> So the All-Great, were the All-Loving too—
> So, through the thunder comes a human voice
> Saying, ' O heart I made, a heart beats here.

Face, My hands fashioned, see it in Myself.
Thou hast no power nor may'st conceive of Mine,
But love I gave thee, with Myself to love,
And thou must love Me who have died for thee!'

The madman saith He said so: it is strange.

These, then, are some of the points we should urge
in favour of the doctrine of the Enhypostasia, and
we venture to think that at least we have established
its right to a more favourable consideration at the
hands of theological thinkers than it has yet received.
We do not claim that it solves all difficulties, far from
it.   It leaves us with little advance beyond the point
reached by the ancient Christology, except that we
are able to fill their ideas with a far richer content in
view of our wider and deeper appreciation of personality, human and Divine, and our clearer grasp consequently upon the essential factors in the Christological
problem.   If anything, our modern science and philosophy make it increasingly difficult for the human
mind to grasp the problem of Christ's Person.   We
recognise more clearly the fact of His Personality as
unique, differing in kind and degree from anything
within the range of normal human experience, and
yet of a type with ours in its truly human content.
Yet the more clearly the uniqueness of His Personality is perceived, the more difficult it is to understand, and the more it baffles any attempt to analyse it.
If the result of our modern investigation in psychology
is a tendency vastly to extend the range of human
consciousness, and to set no limit to the number or
the character of its possible relationships above and
below the ' threshold ' of our normal conscious life,
we are the more bold to plead for a reconsideration
of the doctrine of the Enhypostasia, when we come
to the study of the self-consciousness of One Whose

Personality to-day, after twenty centuries, is more central than ever in the whole history of mankind, and towers above us all, marking Him as unique among the sons of men.

What other hypothesis than the doctrine of the Enhypostasia is adequate to cover the revelation in the Person of Christ, of One Who was invading our human life from a range of consciousness infinite in its extension, and yet of a type with ours, capable therefore of acting in the place of a truly human consciousness such as a perfect manhood would naturally possess ?

Upon no other theory can we continue to speak of His having possessed ' Two Natures,' and yet as having had but a single consciousness. This is the only theory which suggests a way of escape from the pitfalls of Nestorianism and Monophysitism, the only passage open for us between the two alternatives of a duplex personality and an impersonal manhood ; unless we are content to halt amidst the absurdities and contradictions of a complex Divine-human personality.

It leaves us with a Christology little if anything advanced beyond the furthest point reached by the most acute and profound thinkers of the past. It involves, however, no break with the Christology of the New Testament, and the creeds and dogmatic utterances of the ancient Church. We have not to forsake the New Testament tradition of a Two-Natured Christ, nor to lose that impression of the unity of His Person, which is the first reality we touch when we come into close contact with the portrait of Jesus Christ as He lived in Palestine twenty centuries ago. By this theory we conserve the truth that God is Perfect Personality. We show that the true relationship between personality human and Divine is revealed in the Person of Christ.   We are also enabled to give due weight to the growing recognition in our own time of Christ's Personality as the creative factor in Christianity, and central in the whole history of mankind.   We are able to understand, dimly it may be, why He should be the MAN, the ideal goal of all our striving, and why we, as imperfect personalities, can find our consummation and completion only by receiving from Him that which He alone can give. We do full justice to that great truth enshrined in Apollinarian Christology—which partly accounts for the persistent recurrence of the latter in varying form ever since the time when it was put forward by the great Bishop of Laodicea, and formulated by his followers—viz. that the key to the right interpretation of Christ's manhood, not only in its particular and historical, but also in its universal and absolute significance, is to be found in the fact that there exists in God Himself a human element, and consequently that Christ is the truth of every man ; therefore the human and the Divine first reached a predestined goal in His Person.   Humanity, being ever imperfect, reached its completeness only in the Christ.   Deity, as in its Essence Love, being ever self-giving and self-sacrificing, found its fullest expression in that act of humiliation and self-sacrifice which reached its climax at Calvary.

The result of the Incarnation and work of Christ is shown to be the opening up of a new channel of communication between God and man, whereby Deity can ever continue to impart Himself to humanity, and ever strive to express Himself yet again in human form in and through Christ's Body.

Thus is perpetuated the truth of God as ever self-imparting, and the truth of man as ever God-receiving. We are thus enabled from our Christology to offer a theory of the Atonement, which is in harmony with some of the best lines of thought in ancient and modern times on this subject. It accords with that view of the Incarnation which was so strongly held by Irenæus, who put forward the doctrine of the Recapitulatio (ἀνακεφαλαίωσις, Eph. i. 10)—the summing up of all men in Christ—as the fulfilment of God's purpose in Creation (Westcott), and also, because of the Fall, the restoration of (a) the image of God in Man, and (b) the knowledge of God in Christ. We remember that it was this line of thought which Athanasius fully developed in his great work, the *De Incarnatione*, and which became the characteristic type of Greek thought upon the subject. It is definitely opposed to all those tendencies in modern Pelagianism, which lay stress upon man's self-sufficiency and capacity by his own unaided efforts to reach the goal of his destiny. Our Christology is for ever a refutation of this belief, and a challenge to the modern gospel of self-realisation. It demonstrates decisively man's incompleteness, and the fact that human nature can never be truly such without the Christ Who is its truth. It secures, further, a transcendent and all-powerful Divine Christ, Who thus can be for man, not only an Ethical Teacher, or even an Ideal Man, but that which man feels in moments of intensest penitence he most sorely needs, a Divine Saviour. The cruciality of the Cross is only secured by the Divinity of Him Who hung upon it, and the eternal significance of Calvary can rest upon no other foundation. Thus the doctrine of the

Enhypostasia enables us to deduce from our Christology a true Anthropology and a sound doctrine of Redemption.

Herein, if anywhere, lies the value of such an attempt at Christological reconstruction as we have endeavoured to make. Its abstruse and technical character necessarily makes it appear at first sight remote from the common needs of everyday life. It may seem a mere academic treatise of interest only to the few to whom such studies appeal. But if it results in a Gospel, our task has not been in vain ; nor shall we regard our labour as wholly outside that Service to which we have humbly dedicated our life. If our ministry has taught us nothing else, it finds us with each succeeding year grounded more firmly than ever in the conviction that the Church's power to win the world for Christ to-day lies only in the degree of faithfulness with which she continues to go forth in *His* Might to preach *His* Gospel to men. And what is *His* Gospel ? Not simply the teaching He gave during His earthly ministry, nor even the example He left of a perfect life, but something more crucial than this. *His* Gospel is Himself in the completion and consummation of His Work as the Crucified Saviour, the Lord of Glory and the Giver of Life. And His Gospel, thus interpreted by His followers under the inspiration of His Spirit, cuts clean across the subtle and persuasive forms in which modern Pelagianism is hourly luring man into the easy but ruinous paths of self-reliance, self-complacency, and blindness to the real character of sin and its soul-destroying consequences. The danger is not one happily to which the Church is blind. It is a commonplace to assert that the greatest need of our time is a real sense of sin, and a real comprehension of the meaning of true penitence. There can be no Gospel of Salvation for those who do not feel their need of it. Granted, however, that the Church to-day succeeds in touching the conscience of men, and brings home afresh to individuals the fact of sin, and man's utter powerlessness to atone for it, how will she minister to the need thus created ? What Christ shall she preach ? What Christology shall she teach ? Shall she offer for men's acceptance Jesus, the supreme Ethical Teacher, or even Jesus, the soul's ideal aspiration ? Men will accept Him as such, but still remain hungry and helpless. They will call out for a Saviour. They will demand One Who can offer the assurance of Salvation, complete and final. There can be no security for such a Salvation unto the uttermost, except it be that which an Eternal and Divine Lord alone can give. Hence the Church's Christology must be great enough to cover such a Gospel. Her Christ must be the Eternal Saviour-Judge. If the Christ we preach be less than God Himself in the act of putting away the sin of man, we have still to reckon with the Omnipotent and All-Holy God in the matter of our trespasses. Unless the Christ mediates a forgiveness and effects a salvation, which is God's forgiveness and God's salvation, we have no assurance of finality in the work He has done for us. Unless, moreover, in His creative activity in the regeneration and sanctification of our lives, He is God at work within us, our Christian experience in Him is less than the soul's perfect consummation and bliss in Communion with God, the All-Holy and the All-Loving. Hence our Christology must be great enough to secure the absolute character and finality of the Soteriology we preach. The absolute nature of the Salvation offered to man is bound up with the absolute nature of Him Who offers it. The only Gospel which can save the world is one which finds its centre in a Crucified Redeemer, and leads men to worship the King as He reigns from the Tree and saves through His Precious Blood.

Hence if our Christology can induce men to believe that Jesus Christ was the Absolute, Transcendent, Unlimited, Omnipotent, All-Holy God stooping down to meet sinful man, and by His work revealing Himself the deathless Conqueror of death and death's sting, we shall be offering for their acceptance One Who, because He was what He was, can be still to-day adequate for the work He must do for the salvation of men. He Whose sacrifice for sin has given His Church the only Gospel worth preaching, is One Whose work rests upon the truth of what He knew Himself to be—our only Saviour and Redeemer—God Incarnate.

For men whose sense of sin is blurred and deadened, the proof of this may be a matter for academic discussion and profitless exercise in metaphysical speculation. For those of us who are what we are only because we are His and who aspire to become better than the best in us only in virtue of what He can give, the proof of His Saviourhood, Omnipotent Divine Power, and Redeeming Love is a vital fact, something we know in our inmost spiritual experience, something also worth a life's labour to demonstrate. If spiritually discerned, it is none the less capable of being so set forth as to commend it to the intellect also. And if a study such as this which we now bring to a close can add but the smallest contribution to the task of commending Christology to the consideration of men for whom intellectual difficulties are a stumbling-block, preventing their whole-hearted acceptance of the Truth as it is revealed in Christ Jesus, the labour involved will have been worth the while, and this thesis, however imperfect, worth the effort.

INDEX

275

INDEX

INDEX

277

INDEX

AT THE BALLANTYNE PRESS
PRINTED BY SPOTTISWOODE, BALLANTYNE AND CO. LTD.
COLCHESTER, LONDON AND ETON

The Ancient Creeds in Modern Life.

A Lecture given by the Rev. H. B. SWETE, D.D., F.B.A.
6d. net.

The Chalcedonian Doctrine of the Incarnation.

By the Rev. Canon A. J. MASON, D.D. 6d. net.

The Athanasian Creed, Some Thoughts on.

By Professor F. C. BURKITT, D.D., F.B.A. 2d. net.

Early Church Classics.

[*Additions to the Series of small books, containing translations into English of the earliest Christian Writers either in whole or in part.*]

The Treatise of Irenæus of Lugdunum against the Heresies.

A translation of the principal passages, with notes and arguments by the Rev. F. R. MONTGOMERY HITCHCOCK, M.A., D.D. In two volumes. Small post 8vo, cloth boards, 2s. net each vol.

St. Gregory of Nyssa: The Catechetical Oration.

By the Ven. J. H. SRAWLEY, D.D., Archdeacon of Wisbech. Small post 8vo, cloth boards, 2s. net.

SOCIETY FOR PROMOTING CHRISTIAN KNOWLEDGE

LONDON: 68 HAYMARKET, S.W.